Routledge Questions & Answers Series

Torts
2013–2014

Routledge Q&A series

Each Routledge Q&A contains approximately 50 questions on topics commonly found on exam papers, with comprehensive suggested answers. The titles are written by lecturers who are also examiners, so the student gains an important insight into exactly what examiners are looking for in an answer. This makes them excellent revision and practice guides. With over 500,000 copies of the Routledge Q&As sold to date, accept no other substitute.

New editions publishing in 2013:

Civil Liberties & Human Rights
Company Law
Commercial Law
Constitutional & Administrative Law
Contract Law
Criminal Law
Employment Law
English Legal System
Equity & Trusts
European Union Law

Evidence
Family Law
Jurisprudence
Land Law
Medical Law
Torts

Published in 2012:

Business Law 2012–2013
Intellectual Property Law 2012–2013

For a full listing, visit http://cw.routledge.com/textbooks/revision

Routledge Questions & Answers Series

Torts

2013–2014

Janice Elliott Montague

Associate Senior Lecturer in Law, Coventry University

Routledge
Taylor & Francis Group

LONDON AND NEW YORK

Tenth edition published 2013
by Routledge
2 Park Square, Milton Park, Abingdon, Oxon OX14 4RN

Simultaneously published in the USA and Canada
by Routledge
711 Third Avenue, New York, NY 10017

Routledge is an imprint of the Taylor & Francis Group, an informa business

© 2013 Janice Elliott Montague

Based on material authored by Jason Lowther and published between 1994–2011

The right of Janice Elliott Montague to be identified as author of this work has been asserted by her in accordance with sections 77 and 78 of the Copyright, Design and Patents Act 1988.

First edition published by Cavendish Publishing 1993
Ninth edition published by Routledge 2011

British Library Cataloguing in Publication Data
A catalogue record for this book is available from the British Library

Library of Congress Cataloging in Publication Data
Montague, J. Elliott (Janice Elliott).
    Torts / Janice Montague. — Tenth edition.
        pages cm.—(Q&A)
    ISBN 978-0-415-52461-2 (pbk)—ISBN 978-0-203-08378-9 (ebk)
    1. Torts—England—Examinations, questions, etc.   I. Title.
    KD1949.6.L69 2013
    346.4203076—dc23

                                                                                    2012020331

ISBN: 978-0-415-52461-2 (pbk)
ISBN: 978-0-203-08378-9 (ebk)

Typeset in TheSans
by RefineCatch Limited, Bungay, Suffolk

Printed and bound in Great Britain by the MPG Books Group

Contents

Preface

The law of tort does not stand still. New cases concerning negligent misstatement, defamation and the ever increasing influence of the Human Rights Act on the law of tort, among others, have been incorporated into the answers in this book, as well as new questions relating to topical issues such as the compensation society, and a new take on the seminal case of *Donoghue v Stevenson*. However, as ever with this series, the emphasis is as much on how to tackle legal examination questions, especially problem questions, as the law itself. To this end, in the Introduction there are 10 general tips on answering exam questions, both essays and problems, based on decades of experience in marking law exam papers. Also, additional features have been added in this edition, such as comments and tips interspersed through the text and, especially, new diagrams to help with applying the law and using information that has been learnt to its best advantage. It is thereby hoped that this book, and the techniques and hints that are given throughout, will enable students to achieve their potential and obtain the level of marks in examinations that reflect the hard work they have done during the year.

The author has attempted to state the law as at May 2012.

Janice Elliott Montague
Coventry University
May 2012

Table of Cases

Table of Legislation

STATUTORY INSTRUMENTS

EU LEGISLATION

Directives

Treaties and Conventions

Guide to the Companion Website

http://cw.routledge.com/textbooks/revision

Visit the Routledge Q&A website to discover even more study tips and advice on getting those top marks.

On the Routledge revision website you will find the following resources designed to enhance your revision on all areas of undergraduate law.

The Good, The Fair, & The Ugly

Good essays are the gateway to top marks. This interactive tutorial provides sample essays together with voice-over commentary and tips for successful exam essays, written by our Q&A authors themselves.

Multiple Choice Questions

Knowledge is the foundation of every good essay. Focusing on key examination themes, these MCQs have been written to test your knowledge and understanding of each subject in the book.

Bonus Q&As

Having studied our exam advice, put your revision into practice and test your essay writing skills with our additional online questions and answers.

Don't forget to check out even more revision guides and exam tools from Routledge!

Lawcards

Lawcards are your complete, pocket-sized guides to key examinable areas of the undergraduate law.

Routledge Student Statutes

Comprehensive selections; clear, easy-to-use layout; alphabetical, chronological, and thematic indexes; and a competitive price make *Routledge Student Statutes* the statute book of choice for the serious law student.

Introduction to the Features of the Book

The principal purpose of this book is to provide a means of consolidating your knowledge of tort law and enabling you to marshal that knowledge more effectively when it comes to answering exam questions – or even, in some limited circumstances, written assignments. It is not intended to teach you the subject from scratch and therefore cannot do so. Answering legal questions, particularly problem questions, is a skill you will acquire and hone throughout the course of your undergraduate studies. It is not an innate skill we all possess and is something that is a unique feature of the study of law, which requires both logical and methodical application of rules to facts, so the more assistance you can give yourself, the quicker you will develop a useful and rewarding style.

The book sets out a series of 'typical' examination questions and provides structured suggested solutions to them. Used in conjunction with your textbooks, and perhaps also some of the specialist texts on learning the law, it is hoped that you will improve your skills and develop a greater confidence with your answers, which will ultimately lead to better grades. The book is arranged in a series of chapters which cover the range of subjects learnt on the majority of undergraduate tort courses, and provide some typical questions. Not every aspect of every course is set out here, but care has been taken to focus on areas of particular interest to examiners because, for example, they are important areas of knowledge that you should be able to demonstrate familiarity with, or because they introduce areas of controversy and debate.

PROBLEM AND ESSAY QUESTIONS

A different skillset and thus approach is required for answering essay and problem questions. In the case of the former, you will be presented with a specific question and asked for your criticism or analysis (etc) of the law. In a problem question you will be required not only to state the applicable law, but to apply it within the context of the factual scenario you are presented with. Most tort subjects, as this book will demonstrate, are able to be assessed by either method, although some are more generally seen as lending themselves to a specific format more readily. Usually, new developments in an area of law or in situations, for example, where there has been a legislative or, say, a Law Commission response to a particular issue, may be more amenable to a discursive, essay-based approach rather than a problem question. Often you will have been introduced to these areas of controversy and development through tutorial sessions or reading recommended by your lecturers. It is always worth your while gaining a thorough understanding of the competing views. By the very nature of the subject, however, your knowledge of the law of tort is best assessed by your ability to sensibly apply it. Different examiners will have different approaches, of course, and it is very important to you, the person to be examined, that you have a grasp of the current debates and critical opinion within the subject areas, as well as specific knowledge relating to the mechanics of the law itself.

Some students are wary of tackling problem questions, especially longer ones such as Question 28 on nuisance, as they appear complex and more difficult than an apparently straightforward essay question, e.g. Question 29. However, it should be borne in mind that for most essay questions, a whole book, or at least a chapter of a book, could be written on the answer; Question 29 is a good example of this. Thus, in an exam, it is unlikely that someone will be able to cover everything that is relevant, and indeed many students will 'waffle' a great deal without saying much that is relevant. Addressing the question in an essay is crucial to achieving a good mark (see below). On the other hand, in a problem question, the information you are given is 'leading you through' and 'pointing you in the direction' of your answer, so it is feasible to cover all the relevant law. By applying it well, as demonstrated in this book, it is thus possible to achieve a much higher percentage mark than for a rambling essay. The key is PLANNING your answer, whether an essay or a problem (see further below). No doubt sometimes it will be a better choice to do an essay, but do not dismiss problem questions (because at first glance they look more difficult) without due consideration, if you are given the choice.

Crucially, do not be rushed into beginning to write your answers before you have read the questions through carefully and planned your answers thoroughly: everyone around you may be scribbling away but they are unlikely to produce the high standard you can achieve if you follow this advice!

LENGTH OF ANSWERS

The answers contained in this book are roughly about the length of an essay that a well-informed and competent student would expect to write in an exam. There are also some longer examples, which could be informative when attempting other forms of assessment, or as a guide for the sort of structure and approach that might be adopted when answering essay-type questions. There is no hard and fast rule on length however. The content is all important and, sometimes, being succinct and concise is better than labouring a point to no end. So as far as the legal content and use of authorities is concerned however, 'more' is most definitely 'more'.

The amount that is able to be written is, subject knowledge and individual characteristics aside, dependent on the time you have available and the number of questions you are required to answer. Some of the answers here, especially those of greater length, may not

be feasibly achieved in an exam, but give an indication of the breadth of the
subject matter.

EXAM PAPERS

The typical tort paper will usually include questions on each of the principal areas of
liability and it would be a unique paper that did not contain at least one question relating
to negligence. The main interests protected are the person, property and reputation, so
that might include negligence, trespass to land/person, nuisance and/or *Rylands* and
defamation, at a minimum. More specialist application of negligence, in say the context
of psychiatric injury, product liability, pure economic loss and occupiers' liability are all
favourites with examiners, and developing areas such as privacy and breach of statutory
duty will always be possibilities. Ultimately it will depend on the syllabus you study. The
building blocks or basic requirements of particular torts are key to their explanation: such
as, for example, the requirement that there is a duty, a breach of that duty, and legally
and factually caused damage for a negligence claim. You will notice, therefore, that in the
suggested answers given in this book there is some repetition of this key material in
response to different questions. Certain principles such as defences, vicarious liability and
rules relating to limitation period and available remedies will apply to most areas,
although there will be more specialist application in different torts as well.

SUGGESTIONS FOR EXAM TECHNIQUE

Below are ten tips that might improve your exam technique; some failings that are very
commonly found on exam scripts are also pointed out. The two types of question are
dealt with separately because as noted above there are different issues with them, but
there are also some points which apply to both and these are included at the end.

Dealing with Problem Questions

Firstly do not be deterred by a seemingly long and complicated problem question. For
reasons outlined above, the information in the problem will be giving you clues and hints
about what to write about, and can therefore allow you to produce a far more focused,
and thus better, answer than a rambling and unstructured essay.

1. When tackling a problem question, do not write out the facts in the answer. It is a
    waste of your time, and the examiner already knows the question: (s)he wrote it.
    Answer the question logically and deal with the issues as they arise. Try not to jump
    between ideas, as it is very easy to miss aspects of the question or to repeat yourself.
    Make sure that you identify the area of law and say so in an introductory paragraph,
    particularly where this has not been given in the question. Always define your terms
    and ensure that you explain the legal principles that you are then going to go on to
    discuss. These are basic marks that you can earn very easily, but are often omitted,
    possibly because students think they are self evident.
2. Having clarified the RELEVANT law, apply the facts. This means showing how the law
    you have stated relates to the factual scenario you have been given. Both aspects of

the answer are crucial – but for good marks you need to do the latter well. NEVER write 'all you know' about a topic when answering a problem question – the skill you should be displaying is the ability to identify which aspects of the law you have learnt are relevant. For example, in a case involving personal injury in negligence the examiner does not need to know about the development and ultimate rejection of the two stage *Anns* test; it simply isn't relevant, looks like padding and will gain you no marks for your efforts. It may help to think about how you would explain the legal position to clients – they are only going to be interested in the aspects of the law that affect their situation, and the strengths and weaknesses of it; not, for example, the history of the law. It is for this reason that time spent PLANNING a problem question answer is never wasted, so that your answer is focused and logically structured; but do remember to check back with your plan when actually writing the answer. Examiners are often disappointed to see that crucial aspects of a plan have not been included in the relevant answer, and little(if any) credit for this can be given.

3. Don't begin with the answer e.g. *X will win because* . . . You may well be wrong, and you will not fully consider any alternative arguments if you start from such a definite position. It is also likely that you will rarely be able to be this definite, even at the end of your analysis, with the limited information you have been provided within the question. If you needed to know something more precisely e.g. the age of a child claimant, then raise this (with an explanation) because this will show that you have realised this is an important factor. (In real life, of course, you would ask your client these sort of questions, but that is not possible with a paper-based, academic exercise.) Conversely, try to use all the information you have been given when *applying* the law to the problem, as it is quite likely to be given to you for a reason and have an impact on your answer.

4. Treat your examiner as an intelligent lay person. You are, after all, being asked more often than not to provide 'advice' to someone (in the question) who is not a lawyer, while at the same time demonstrating (to the examiner) that you know the law. In that respect it is useful for you to have in mind what point you are trying to make. Ask yourself, for example, why could a person be liable? For what? How can that be made to happen? What steps do you need to go through to establish that liability? The process of getting to the answer, just as in a maths question, is almost as important as the answer itself.

Do not feel that you have to have a definite answer, but you can indicate in your conclusion what you think is the *most likely* outcome based on the strength of your arguments in your answer. The point is to get you to demonstrate the ability to sustain a legal argument based on a reasoned application of the law.

Dealing with Essay Questions

Almost all Law students will have written essay questions in exam conditions before, unlike problem questions which are less familiar. Therefore the specific advice here is more limited.

5.   Essay questions will ask you to do something specific, such as to criticise a proposition, to analyse developments within an area of liability, or to balance competing imperatives (such as privacy and freedom of expression). Make sure you do. It is a common frustration of examiners when the candidate answers their 'own' question rather than the one set. It is not advisable to try to 'question spot' in advance and then produce your rehearsed piece for whichever question is actually asked . . .

   You should try to ensure that you integrate the analysis of leading thinkers or commentators, including, of course, the judges where appropriate. An impersonal style is the preferred approach in both problem and essay answers. Avoid use of the word 'I' and do not explain concepts by writing things like 'in order to claim in nuisance *you* must have an interest in the land affected'. A more detached style enables you to appear to be more objective, and will prompt you into using the opinions of more learned commentators. As alternatives you might want to write 'it is submitted that' or 'it is arguable that' or 'a claimant would need to prove the following'.

6.   As with problem questions, writing 'all you know' about a topic is not a good technique and the time spent thinking about what the question is actually asking you, and then organising the information you have to fit this question, will be crucial to the mark you receive.[1] A plan is very helpful, and you should aim to end with a conclusion that refers back to, and answers, the question set.

General Advice

7.   It is important to back all your assertions and statements of law with authority (i.e. a case or a statute), if possible, in both essay and problem answers. In this book, a full case name and date is given, but your memory may not be able to retain all of this information, and trying to do so may make you spend less time on the more important aspect of your revision, namely understanding the legal concepts. The whole case name, and perhaps the date (especially if it is a recent, or very old case) and the court where the decision was made is obviously best; but if not, one name (preferably the first) will be better than nothing, or, if you cannot remember any part of the name, a BRIEF outline of the facts will identify it. Otherwise, the facts of cases are usually relatively unimportant and you can waste a lot of valuable time writing them out, UNLESS the facts are very similar to your scenario *or* different in an important aspect, which means that there is room for *distinguishing* the existing case law. It is the *ratio*, or legal reasoning, from the case that is important to include. However, you will need to know the facts of the cases to identify similarities etc, and

---

1   Look at the problem and essay questions in the chapters in this book, which demonstrate how basically the same information can be used differently when answering a problem or an essay. A good example of this can be found by comparing the essay and problem questions on product liability in Chapter 6, Questions 17 and 19.

in some essays, particularly in a developing area of law such as privacy, the facts of the cases will need to be included.

When citing statutes, the full name and year should be given (abbreviations are acceptable thereafter if you have explained them initially, e.g. **Occupiers' Liability Act 1957 (OLA 1957)**. If you are provided with statutory material, or allowed to take it in with you to the exam, it will be even more important to cite the section/subsection etc accurately, so ALWAYS CHECK, even if you think you remember it. This is where your familiarity with the statute from your preparation for and participation in workshops and seminars will pay off.

You are wasting your time if you copy out large segments of the statutory material, but you may want to include a short 'quote', e.g. referring to an independent contractor undertaking work on the premises as someone 'in the exercise of his calling', who will therefore 'appreciate and guard against any special risks ordinarily incident to it' (**OLA 1957 s 2(3)(b)**). Do not make the common mistake of referring to this as s 3(b).[2]

8.   Manage your time effectively so that you always provide the required number of answers. So if, for example, the examination requires four answers, make sure you *at least attempt* four answers. Failing to do so will greatly diminish your chances of success. For example, answering only three questions if you were required to answer four will immediately lose you 25 per cent of the marks for the paper, and it is unlikely that you will be able to compensate for that loss within the other answers. It is better to provide a limited answer than none at all, as the first, basic marks, are often the easiest to earn. Including them as bullet points if you have run out of time is better than nothing, but make sure that you have shown that this is your answer, and not just a plan, which probably will not be marked.

9.   Never leave an exam early, however tempting it may be to get out of the exam room. In fact, always allow enough time to go back over your answers when you finish, as there will almost always be small additions or amendments you can make. This will also give you the opportunity to rectify careless mistakes such as muddling up the names of the parties (rendering your advice incorrect), or missing out section numbers etc, which can cost you crucial marks. Examiners have to mark what is written, not what you may have intended to write, so ensure you have expressed yourself clearly and accurately (and preferably, legibly!)

10.   Practice. Use past examination papers and time yourself. Try to simulate exam conditions by not referring to your notes or texts. It is anticipated that the *Aim Higher*, *Common Pitfalls* and annotated prompts in this text will be useful in preparing for this.

---

2   For questions on the **Occupiers' Liability Acts**, see Chapter 7. These statutes demonstrate exactly why you need to include the dates of statutes and take care to indicate which one you are referring to, as they both have the same name but cover completely separate aspects of the law.

Common Pitfalls ✖

The most common mistake made when using Questions & Answers books for revision is to memorise the model answers provided and try to reproduce them in exams. This approach is a sure-fire pitfall, likely to result in a poor overall mark because your answer will not be specific enough to the particular question on your exam paper, and there is also a danger that reproducing an answer in this way would be treated as plagiarism. You must instead be sure to read the question carefully, to identify the issues and problems it is asking you to address and to answer it directly in your exam. If you take our examiners' advice and use your Q&A to focus on your question-answering skills and understanding of the law applied, you will be ready for whatever your exam paper has to offer!

General Introduction

The law of tort is a fundamental area of English law and, in addition to being a 'core' subject for the legal profession, a clear understanding of its principles is required for other areas as diverse as environmental law, employment law, media law and company law. It illustrates, moreover, another characteristic of English law, in that it is primarily a common law area – that is, its rules have been developed through the decisions of the courts rather than being laid down by statute. As a result of this, the student of the law of tort is faced with a bewildering array of cases and rules, and often finds difficulty in deciding what information is relevant to a problem.

This book attempts to help such students. It is not intended as a substitute for lectures or for reading standard textbooks or law reports or articles; it is rather aimed at students whose problem is not that they feel that the legal input they have received is insufficient, but rather that it is too great, and that they have difficulty in ascertaining what material is essential and what is of lesser importance. A careful study of the answers to the questions contained in this book should reveal those essential areas and the student will see how basic concepts reappear not only in questions designed to test that topic in depth, but in other questions that, at first sight, appear to be testing unrelated areas.

Another function of this book is to illustrate how to set about answering questions in the law of tort. These answers are not intended to be perfect solutions, if such a thing exists, and thus should not be used as blueprints or templates; rather, they are intended to illustrate the sort of well-structured answer that would attract high marks using the knowledge that a well-prepared student should possess. All the cases and principles cited should be familiar to the student – the book is attempting to show how, with the knowledge that the student has, he or she can present it in such a way as to gain the best possible grades. In particular, emphasis has been placed on the way in which the fundamental legal principles relevant to a question should be stated; it is often a habit of students to hunt through law reports or their minds to find a long-forgotten case that is on 'all fours' with the facts of a question and triumphantly present it as the 'right' answer. As any examination question should be designed to test the student's grasp of legal principles and ability to apply those principles to a factual situation, a moment's reflection will show that although such an approach may point to the correct answer as regards (say) liability, it will not attract the best possible grades. Thus, this book cites cases with which the student should be familiar, although the dynamic nature of the subject will always require the student to keep abreast of new developments. An ideal reaction by the reader to the suggested solutions in this book should be 'I can do that', not, 'I could never write an answer like that'.

The questions used in this book are typical LLB examination questions, as regards both style and complexity.

This book is not intended to replace lectures or standard textbooks. It is, however, intended to fill a need that, on the basis of much experience in teaching law, has been found to exist – namely, to enable the student to gain the best possible examination grades from whatever knowledge he or she possesses. The more reading a student does of lecture notes, textbooks, learned articles, cases and statutes, the more he or she should benefit from a study of this book. If one thing only can be recommended, it is that students practise writing examination-style responses in timed conditions. It is a skill that can definitely be honed and improved.

Negligence – Duty Generally and Economic Loss

INTRODUCTION

Questions on the imposition of a duty of care usually take the form of an essay, typically on the development of a test for imposing a duty of care. It is also vital to be thoroughly familiar with situations in which limits are placed on the duty of care – that is, in particular, with the areas of negligent misstatement and economic loss, and psychiatric injury or 'nervous shock'. These topics will be dealt with in the first two chapters.

Checklist ✔

Students must be familiar with the following areas:

(a) the development of a test for ascertaining the existence of a duty of care;

(b) negligent misstatement:

- statements made to a known recipient and the special relationship;

- statements put into general circulation;

(c) economic loss:

liability for negligent acts or statements

- the decision in *Junior Books v Veitchi* (1983);

the decision in *Hedley Byrne v Heller* (1964);

- the judicial retreat from *Junior Books*;

- the current position regarding economic loss.

QUESTION 1

'Although the decision of the House of Lords in *Anns v Merton London Borough Council* (1978) was welcomed as a rationalisation of the law, it is now regarded as too simplistic and the so-called "incremental" approach is now universally used to determine the existence of a duty of care.'

▶ Discuss this statement.

How to Answer this Question

This is a typical essay question on the development of the modern test for imposing a duty of care.

The following points need to be discussed:

- ❖ a brief background to *Anns v Merton London Borough Council* (1978);
- ❖ the *Anns* test;
- ❖ the judicial retreat from *Anns*; and
- ❖ the current approach of the courts – that is, the incremental approach.

Answer Structure

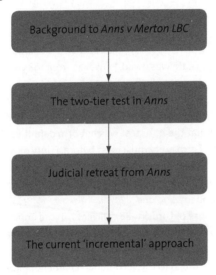

Background to *Anns v Merton LBC*

The two-tier test in *Anns*

Judicial retreat from *Anns*

The current 'incremental' approach

ANSWER

Although an attempt to formulate a general test or principle to decide whether, in any particular circumstances, a duty of care arose was made in *Heaven v Pender* (1883), it was not until 1932 and the judgment of Lord Atkin in *Donoghue v Stevenson* that a general principle was firmly established. There were, of course, many situations in which the courts had recognised the existence of a duty of care, but no general principle existed to decide, in any new situations, whether a duty existed. The courts were for some time a little hesitant in applying the neighbour test as a general principle, but in *Home Office v Dorset Yacht* (1970), Lord Reid stated that the neighbour test was a statement of principle and should be applied unless there was some reason for excluding it. Proceeding from this, Lord Wilberforce, in *Anns v Merton London Borough Council* (1978), stated that in order to establish whether a duty of care exists, the question is to be approached in two stages (the two-tier test). Firstly, is there a sufficient relationship of proximity of neighbourhood between the wrongdoer and the person who has suffered damage such that, in the reasonable contemplation of the former, carelessness on his part may cause damage to the latter, in which case a *prima facie* duty of care arises? Secondly, are there any considerations that ought to negate or reduce or limit the scope of the duty or the class of persons to whom it is owed or the damage to which a breach of it may give rise? Thus, *Anns* neatly rationalised the law regarding the imposition of a duty of care by essentially stating that *Donoghue* applied unless there was a legal reason to disapply or modify *Donoghue*.[1]

However, the courts have gradually come to realise that the imposition of a duty of care involves more complex considerations as *Anns* was used by the courts to expand the area of duty of care. Thus, in *Junior Books v Veitchi* (1983), the House of Lords held that liability could arise in respect of economic loss; in *McLoughlin v O'Brian* (1983), the House considered the scope of psychiatric injury. Also, in *Emeh v Kensington, Chelsea and Westminster Area Health Authority* (1985), the court was prepared to extend the range of persons to whom a duty of care was owed. However, from 1985 onwards, the courts retreated from the broad general principle of *Anns*.[2]

The starting point of this approach was *Peabody Donation Fund v Sir Lindsay Parkinson* (1985). Lord Keith stated that the *Anns* test was not of 'a definitive character' and that, although a relationship of proximity must exist before a duty of care can arise, the existence of duty must depend on all of the circumstances of the case and the court must consider whether it is just and reasonable to impose a duty. Further criticism of the two-tier test is to be found in *Leigh and Sillavan v Aliakmon Shipping*, both in the Court of Appeal (1985) and the House of Lords (1988). Oliver LJ, in the Court of Appeal, stated that *Anns* did not establish a new test of duty of care applicable in all cases, nor did it enable the court to determine policy in each case. The fear is that the first tier is so easily satisfied that it leaves too much to the second tier – namely, policy. In the House of Lords, Lord Brandon adopted a similar approach and claimed that *Anns* had been decided in a novel fact situation and not in a factual situation in which no duty had previously been held to exist. In the latter situation, *Anns* was not applicable and no duty of care was owed, which seems to be a pre-*Donoghue* approach, let alone pre-*Anns*. This attack was continued in *Curran v Northern Ireland Co-Ownership Housing Association* (1987) by Lord Bridge, who stated that *Anns* obscured both the distinction between misfeasance and non-feasance and between contract and tort. Lord Bridge also approved the judgment of Brennan J in the High Court of Australia in *Sutherland Shire Council v Heyman* (1985), in which the judge analysed the two-tier test and rejected it, holding that the test for the existence of a duty of care was more complex. Brennan J also commented that it was

---

1   This introductory paragraph puts **Anns** in its historical context.
2   It is important to explain why the courts began to retreat or move away from the two-tier test in **Anns**, as there was a fear of unrestrained expansion.

preferable to develop novel categories of negligence incrementally and by analogy with established categories, rather than by a massive extension of a *prima facie* duty of care restrained only by indefinable considerations that ought to negate, reduce or limit the scope of the duty or the class of persons to whom it is owed. Lord Justice Toulson expressly referred to this approach of incrementalism in the case of *Glaister v Appleby-in-Westmorland Town Council* (2008) and noted that determination on proximity and the 'fair, just and reasonable' aspects to a case should be determined by reference to reasonably analogous categories where a duty has been found.

The two-tier test was again criticised in *Yuen Kun-Yeu v AG of Hong Kong* (1988) by the Privy Council and by the House of Lords in *Hill v Chief Constable of West Yorkshire* (1989), *Caparo Industries plc v Dickman* (1990) and *Murphy v Brentwood District Council* (1990). Also, the House of Lords again expressed its preference for the incremental approach of Brennan J. Indeed, in *Ravenscroft v Rederiaktiebolaget Transatlantic* (1991), Ward J held at first instance that the two-tier test in *Anns* had been overruled by *Murphy*. In strict legal terms, this appears incorrect, but as the House of Lords has twice expressed its preference for the incremental approach over the two-tier test in *Anns*, it seems highly unlikely that the *Anns* test will be applied in the future. The incremental approach as expounded by the House of Lords in *Caparo* involves the consideration of three factors: the loss must be reasonably foreseeable; there must be a relationship of proximity between the claimant and the defendant; it must be fair, just and reasonable to impose a duty of care. Recently, however, the House of Lords warned against too literal an application of the test in *Customs & Excise v Barclays Bank* (2006).[3]

The first factor merely states that harm must be reasonably foreseeable, the test being the foresight of a reasonable person in the position of the defendant. The second factor, the relationship of proximity, is not expressed in a way that is immediately clear. The phrase was used in the *Anns* test and was considered in *Yuen Kun-Yeu*, in which Lord Keith stated that proximity was a composite test describing 'the whole concept of necessary relationship between plaintiff and defendant'. This factor of proximity would seem, in many circumstances, to be the policy tier of *Anns* expressed in another way. The third factor, that it must be fair, just and reasonable to impose a duty of care, also seems very similar to the policy test in *Anns*. Indeed, in *Marc Rich and Co AG v Bishop Rock Marine* (1995), Balcombe LJ doubted whether the words 'fair, just and reasonable' imposed any additional test to that of 'proximity' – a statement that was not disapproved of when the case was heard in the House of Lords. In *Caparo*, Lord Oliver stated that the above three factors overlap and are really three facets of the same thing; in *Marc Rich*, the Court of Appeal stated that the three factors were not to be treated as wholly separate and distinct requirements, but rather as convenient and helpful approaches to the pragmatic question as to whether a duty should be imposed in any given case. The Court of Appeal

3 An explanation here of the development of case law which lead to the current situation.

went on to state that to take this approach would resolve all, or virtually all, of the conflicts among the authorities and again this statement was not criticised when the case was heard in the House of Lords.[4]

Thus, the simple two-stage test in *Anns* has been replaced with a more complex three-stage (or possibly one-stage, according to *Marc Rich*) test in which the policy aspect of the court's decision has been restated in terms of proximity and fair, just and reasonable. However, despite the replacement of the wide test in *Anns* by the narrower incremental test in *Caparo*, the courts are willing, where appropriate, to impose a duty of care in novel fact situations. Thus, a referee in a rugby match owes a duty of care to players to ensure that no dangerous play occurs, whether in a colts' rugby match (*Smoldon v Whitworth* (1997)) or in an adults' match, and whether that match is amateur or professional (*Vowles v Evans* (2003)). In *Pearson v Lightning* (1998), a golfer was held to owe a duty of care to golfers playing at another hole on the same course. Furthermore, the police have been found to owe a duty of care to persons with suicidal tendencies, whether that person is of sound mind (*Reeves v Commissioner of Police of the Metropolis* (1998)) or of unsound mind (*Kirkham v Chief Constable of Greater Manchester* (1990)). In *Evertt v Comojo (UK) Ltd* (2011), the Court of Appeal held that a nightclub could owe a duty of care to a customer for harm caused to him by a fellow customer, i.e. a third party who the nightclub was not directly responsible for, even though in that case there was no breach of the duty.

QUESTION 2

Martin was on a train, reading a copy of the *Financial Times*. Norman, who was sitting next to him, asked Martin what his job was and Martin replied that he was a stockbroker. Norman then asked Martin for some advice on investment and Martin jokingly replied that publishing seemed to be a good area. As a result of this discussion, Norman invested his life savings in publishing shares. A few months later, the value of these shares fell dramatically and Norman lost all of his money. Depressed at being penniless, Norman then committed suicide.

▶ **Advise Norman's widow, Olivia, of any remedy she might have against Martin.**

How to Answer this Question

This is a typical 'one to one' negligent misstatement question that requires a discussion of *Hedley Byrne v Heller* (1964) and later relevant decisions.

The following points need to be discussed:

- ❖   the duty of care between Martin and Norman;
- ❖   social occasions and *Chaudry v Prabhakar* (1989);
- ❖   Martin's liability for loss of money and Norman's death.

4   Being able to identify and attribute arguments to individual judges adds quality to the answer.

Applying the Law

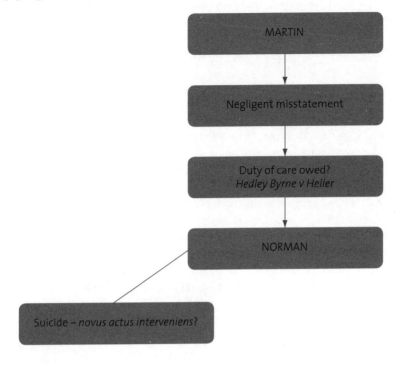

MARTIN

Negligent misstatement

Duty of care owed?
Hedley Byrne v Heller

NORMAN

Suicide – *novus actus interveniens?*

ANSWER

In order to advise Olivia, we must first decide whether or not Martin owed Norman a duty of care. The traditional approach to this question is to see whether a special relationship exists between Martin and Norman, as laid down in *Hedley Byrne v Heller* (1964). In *Hedley Byrne*, there were held to be three elements to special relationships.[5]

Firstly, the representor must possess a special skill. In *Mutual Life and Citizens Assurance v Evatt* (1971), the Privy Council held that liability would only arise when the statement was made in the course of a business. However, as *Evatt* is a decision of the Privy Council, it is only of persuasive authority and the dissenting minority held that *prima facie* a duty was owed by anyone who took it upon himself to make representations knowing that another person will reasonably rely on those representations. This view has been followed by the Court of Appeal in *Esso Petroleum v Mardon* (1976) and *Howard Marine v Ogden* (1976). More recently, in *Gran Gelato v Richcliffe* (1992), it was held as unarguable that a vendor of premises did not owe a duty of care to a purchaser to take reasonable care when

5   Here there is a potentially negligent misstatement, rather than action, and it is thus necessary to establish liability depending on the line of cases from *Hedley Byrne*. For further discussion of recovery for economic loss, as here, see Question 3.

answering inquiries regarding the property. In *Spring v Guardian Assurance plc* (1994), Lord Goff, with whose analysis Lord Lowry concurred, stated that the reference to 'special skill' in *Hedley Byrne* should be understood in the broad sense and that it would include special knowledge. It is suggested that this is the approach that would be followed today and thus Martin would satisfy this element of the test.

Secondly, the representee must reasonably rely on the representations. In *Smith v Eric Bush* (1990), it was held to be reasonable for the purchaser of a modest house to rely on the survey carried out by the lender's surveyor, but not reasonble for a buyer with a 'buy to let' mortgage to do so, as they are deemed to have more business acumen (*Scullion v Bank of Scotland* (2011)). In *Edwards v Lee* (1991), it was held that it was reasonable for the recipient of a reference provided by a solicitor concerning a client to rely on that reference. In *Royal Bank Trust (Trinidad) v Pampellonne* (1987), the Privy Council held that there was a difference between the giving of advice and the passing on of information, and that it may be more reasonable to rely on the former than the latter. Thus, the question here is whether it was reasonable for Norman to rely on Martin's statement. Here it does not seem reasonable for Norman to rely on Martin's reply to his question as to how to invest his life savings. In *Chaudry v Prabhakar* (1989), May LJ, dissenting, stated that a duty of care would not be imposed regarding statements made on social occasions, although in that case this point was conceded by the defendant. It seems that the meeting between Martin and Norman could be described as social, and therefore, overall, it seems that Martin does not satisfy this requirement.

Thirdly, the representor must have some knowledge of the type of transaction envisaged by the representee, and although this does seem to be so from the facts of the problem, Martin owes no duty of care to Norman, because the essential ingredient of reasonable reliance is absent.

In *Caparo Industries plc v Dickman* (1990), Lord Oliver analysed *Hedley Byrne* and held that the required relationship between the representor and the representee may typically be held to exist if:

(a)   the advice is required for a purpose, whether particularly specified or generally described, which is made known, either actually or inferentially, to the representor when the advice is given;

(b)   the representor knows, either actually or inferentially, that his advice will be communicated to the representee, either specifically or as a member of an ascertainable class, in order that it should be used by the representee for that purpose;

(c)   it is known, either actually or inferentially, that the advice so communicated is likely to be acted upon by the representee for that purpose without independent inquiry; and

(d)   it is so acted upon by the representee to his detriment.[6]

....

6   Being able to attribute aspects of a leading case to the appropriate judge will add quality to your answer.

Lord Oliver emphasised that these conditions were neither conclusive nor exclusive, but merely that the decision in *Hedley Byrne* did not warrant any broader propositions (see also Lord Bingham in *Customs & Excise v Barclays Bank* (2006)). Considering these conditions, it seems that Martin satisfies (a), (b) and (d), but that condition (c) is not satisfied and so again we conclude that Martin owes Norman no duty of care as regards the statement concerning shares. In *Hedley Byrne*, it was stated that a duty of care will arise where the representor voluntarily assumed a responsibility to the representee and it seems from the facts that Martin has not done this, as we are told he 'jokingly' recommended publishing shares. Despite the criticism of the assumption of responsibility concept by the House of Lords in *Caparo* and *Smith v Eric Bush*, more recent decisions of their Lordships have emphasised the importance of it: *Spring*; *Henderson v Merrett Syndicates* (1994); *White v Jones* (1995) (see especially the speeches of Lord Goff); *Williams v Natural Life Health Foods Ltd* (1998); the decision of the Court of Appeal in *Lennon v Metropolitan Police Commissioner* (2004). This is another factor that mitigates against the imposition of a duty of care on Martin. Thus, Olivia[7] cannot sue Martin in respect of the loss in value of the shares purchased by Norman, nor can she sue in respect of Norman's subsequent suicide. Even if Martin owed Norman a duty of care as regards the statement and was in breach of that duty, he would not be liable for Norman's subsequent suicide, as this is not a reasonably foreseeable consequence of the breach as is required by *The Wagon Mound (No 1)* (1961).

Norman's suicide could also be regarded as a *novus actus interveniens* that broke the chain of causation between the earlier negligence (if any) of Martin and the damage suffered by Norman. The criterion used by the courts seems to be whether the latter conduct by the claimant is reasonable or not. Thus, in *McKew v Holland and Hannen and Cubitts* (1969), the plaintiff was injured due to the negligence of the defendants and as a result suffered a residual intermittent loss of control of one leg. Despite this, the plaintiff went down a flight of steep stairs that had no handrail, and while doing so his leg gave way and he was injured. It was held by the House of Lords that his action in going down a steep flight of stairs without a handrail was so unreasonable that it broke the chain of causation. Lord Reid stated that 'if the injured man acts unreasonably, he cannot hold the defendant liable for injury caused by his own unreasonable conduct'. In contrast, in *Wieland v Cyril Lord Carpets* (1969), the plaintiff, due to the original negligence of the defendants, experienced difficulty in using her bifocal spectacles. She nevertheless continued to use them and as a result she too fell down a flight of stairs. It was held that the defendants were liable for this injury as the plaintiff had not been unreasonable in continuing to wear bifocals (see also *Spencer v Wincanton Holdings* (2009)). As by its nature suicide is unreasonable conduct, it is submitted that even if Martin were held to owe a duty of care in respect of his advice and to be in breach of that duty, he would not

7   Note that you are advising Norman's *widow*, who would be suing as his personal representative and/or as a dependant under the **Fatal Accidents Act 1976**. See further on this Questions 44 and 45.

be liable for Norman's suicide, as that act may be considered to have broken the chain of causation. This is fortunate for Martin, because Norman's suicide would not allow the defence of *ex turpi causa non oritur actio* (*Kirkham v Chief Constable of Greater Manchester* (1990)), nor would it allow the *volenti* defence, as presumably Norman was of unsound mind when he committed suicide (*Kirkham*).

QUESTION 3

Discuss the view that the current law relating to the existence of a duty of care in negligence for pure economic loss is so full of fine distinctions as to lack coherence and legal certainty.

How to Answer this Question

The question requires that you examine the basic exception to the rule against recovery for pure economic loss in negligence. The proposition that the law is somehow 'difficult' should be addressed by explanation of the development of the law.

The following points should be discussed:

- ❖ the general exclusionary rule in negligence concerning claims for pure economic loss;
- ❖ the principal exception in *Hedley Byrne*;
- ❖ the development and extension of the *Hedley Byrne* tests;
- ❖ the stretching of certain concepts, such as 'assumption of responsibility'.

Answer Structure

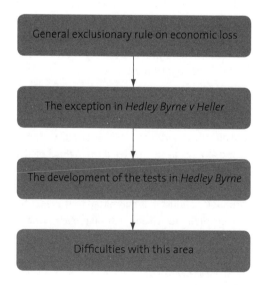

General exclusionary rule on economic loss

↓

The exception in *Hedley Byrne v Heller*

↓

The development of the tests in *Hedley Byrne*

↓

Difficulties with this area

ANSWER

Negligence operates as a means to compensate a claimant for foreseeable losses caused by a defendant's breach of a duty of care (*Donoghue v Stevenson* (1932)). Considerations of policy have defined some extensions and contractions in the application of the duty of care, but there would appear to be some certainties, such as the rule against the recovery of pure economic loss. Loss said to be purely economic, that is, loss that was not the foreseeable consequence of physical injury to the claimant or the claimant's property,[8] is not recoverable in negligence for acts or omissions according to the prevailing orthodoxy (*Weller & Co Ltd v Foot and Mouth Institute* (1966)). In *Spartan Steel & Alloys v Martin & Co* (1973) Lord Denning observed that the issue of recovery for economic loss was a question of policy; and Lord Fraser stated that in cases of pure economic loss some limit or control mechanism had to be imposed on the liability of a wrongdoer (*The Mineral Transporter* (1985)). Later cases have confirmed that approach, some involving complex issues as in *Leigh & Sillivan Ltd v Aliakmon Shipping (The Aliakmon)* (1986), where a non-owning third-party claimant was unable to claim for economic losses caused as a result of damage to certain goods. However, although it would have seemed that English law was clear on this point, a recent examination took place in *Shell UK v Total UK* (2010), where a *beneficial* ownership of an oil pipeline damaged in the Buncefield Refinery explosion was held by the Court of Appeal to be sufficient to permit an action for loss of profits on the oil that would otherwise have flowed through it. It can be submitted that this is a slight extension of the law as was seen in the Canadian case *Canadian National Railway Co v Norsk Pacific Steamship Co* (1992).

Before this there had been a degree of expansion in the duty of care in negligence to embrace the potential for claims for pure economic loss. The general expansion of means of establishing a duty of care that had taken place in *Anns v Merton LBC* (1978) led inexorably to the boundaries being pushed further, until, in the case of *Junior Books v Veitchi* (1983) a 'high point' was reached in claims for pure economic loss, where it was argued that the distinction between tort and contract liability was being blurred. *Junior Books* was never followed, and so is not considered further. Since *Murphy v Brentwood DC* (1990) overruled the decision in *Anns*, it would appear that a degree of stability and certainty has been reintroduced into the law in the case of pure economic loss caused by acts or omissions.

Otherwise, and relatively early on, the courts had developed an exception to the general rule. This arises in circumstances that involve what might loosely be called negligent misstatements, originating in the case of *Hedley Byrne v Heller and Partners Ltd* (1964). The case was important because the House of Lords accepted that in certain circumstances a duty of care could arise where a person gave advice to another. It was

---

8   There is sometimes confusion about what is meant by (pure) economic loss, but it should be remembered that loss of earnings as a result of being injured, or damage to property, though they are <u>monetary</u> losses, are *not* regarded as economic loss as they are as a result of physical injury.

acknowledged that cases of pure economic loss based on words were significantly different in terms of their potential 'reach' than claims involving physical damage, the potential claimant base being much larger. This is evidenced by the following components to establishing a duty of care: first, that the claimant relied on a 'special relationship' with the defendant to give correct advice; second, that the defendant voluntarily assumed the risk of the provision of the advice; third, that the defendant knew or ought to have known that the claimant was in reliance; and fourth, that it was reasonable in the circumstances for the claimant to rely on the defendant.[9]

Each of these tests has been the subject of considerable qualification and evolution over time, which has greatly expanded the complexity of the area and, arguably, affected certainty within the law. Each will be examined in detail below.

Regarding the special relationship aspect, it is envisaged that the claimant will rely on the skill of the defendant in relation to the advice (*Mutual Life & Citizens' Assurance Co v Evatt* (1971); *Esso v Mardon* (1976)). This seems to indicate that the advice should be given in a business context, although the case of *Chaudry v Prabhaker* (1989) adds a degree of doubt as advice given on a social occasion was held to be sufficient, although the case is understood as being exceptional on this point. The issue of voluntary assumption of risk ties in with the special relationship. If a person, as in *Hedley Byrne*, gives qualified or conditional advice, it is clear that they have not accepted responsibility; they could also choose not to give the advice. If they do give advice they will be held to have given that voluntarily. The leading contemporary case on this issue is *Henderson v Merrett Syndicates Ltd* (1994), where Lord Goff stated that if those accepting responsibility are assumed to provide a certain service and they do so negligently, they could be liable for economic losses stemming from this (see also *Lennon v Metropolitan Police Commissioner* (2004); and *Customs & Excise Commissioner v Barclays Bank* (2006)).

Reliance and the question of whether it was reasonable for the claimant to have relied on the information or advice given may be considered together. Due to the nature of the claimed relationship, it is, on its face at least, straightforward to assume that a claimant relied on what they had been told. It is important that it is reasonable for the claimant to have relied on the information and this will depend on the context and the nature of the advice given. The case of *Caparo Industries plc v Dickman* (1990) provides a simple illustration of this concept. The claimant attempted to argue that the defendant auditors were liable when it lost money having bought a company for which the defendant auditors had prepared accounts. The accounts, which were prepared under a statutory duty and not specifically for the claimant, were inaccurate and the company was actually worthless. The House of Lords held that it was not reasonable for the claimant to have

---

9   The two preceding paragraphs make the crucial distinction between economic loss for negligent acts (development of which appears to have halted) and economic loss as the result of negligent statements, where there continues to be developments.

relied on the accounts in this situation; when information is given for one purpose, it is not reasonable for a third party to rely on the information for another purpose (see also *James McNaughton Papers Group Ltd v Hicks Anderson & Co.* (1991) and *Reeman v Department of Transport* (1997)).

In contrast to this decision was the case of *Law Society v KPMG Peat Marwick* (2000), where the Law Society claimed for losses suffered by claims made to a compensation fund due to the defendant's failure to spot financial irregularities in the accounts it had prepared for a particular law firm. The Court of Appeal held it was fair, just and reasonable to impose a duty of care; it was foreseeable that incorrectly prepared accounts would lead to the fund being claimed upon, and because the law society was supposed to see the accounts annually, there was sufficient proximity between the defendants and the law society. It would seem that the degree of connection between the maker and receiver of the statement is important. This reasoning was also adopted in the cases of *Smith v Eric Bush and Harris v Wyre Forest DC* (1990), where the claimant was able to recover on the basis of a negligent mortgage survey, which was actually prepared for valuation purposes for the lender, not her. However, in *Scullion v Bank of Scotland* (2011), a buy to let purchaser was not owed a duty in these circumstances.

These developments suggest a degree of extension to the original principles. Other evidence of expanding liabilities can be seen in relation to the so-called 'wills cases' and also in relation to the provision of employment references (*Spring v Guardian Assurance Ltd* (1994)). The wills cases have permitted claimants to recover in situations of pure economic loss, but in situations that do not easily fit within the general *Hedley Byrne* principles. The first of these to note was *Ross v Caunters* (1980), which involved loss to a claimant who was unable to recover under a will because the defendant solicitor had negligently prepared the will for his client. Clearly, the claimant had suffered pure economic loss and was in no 'special relationship' with the solicitor. There was no information or advice passed by one party to another. In fact what had occurred was the negligent performance of a service.

Many commentators have noted that this was quite unremarkable at the time, following on from the landmark decision in *Anns v Merton LBC* (1978), and thus took place within a period of expansion of the duty of care concept. The real interest comes when the reasoning was adopted much later, after *Anns* had been overruled by *Murphy*, in the case of *White v Jones* (1995). That case involved a family dispute that meant that two daughters were cut out of their father's will. He later requested that they were reinstated as beneficiaries, but three months later he died, with the defendant having failed to make the amendment. Lord Goff referred to an 'impulse to do practical justice' in the case.[10] It

....

10 Being able to include a short quote from a leading case, and attribute it correctly, will add to the quality of your answer.

could be argued however that this laudable aim did nothing to promote legal certainty for claims in pure economic loss, particularly when seen in light of the further extension in *Carr-Glynn v Frearsons* (1999). The principles also apply beyond solicitors to other will-writing services (*Esterhuizen v Allied Dunbar Assurance plc* (1998)), and in *Gorham v British Telecom plc* (2000), negligent pension advice, which subsequently affected the level of benefits paid to the deceased's family, was also held to be recoverable.

The extension into reference writing in *Spring* is also notable. It is clear that a reference is a 'statement' at least; the difference lies in the fact that the person who suffered the loss was not the person to whom the statement was made. The House of Lords held that a 'special relationship' existed between the defendant, who provided an inaccurate and bad employment reference, and the claimant. In *McKie v Swindon College* (2011), the High Court allowed an ex-employee to recover compensation when his employer from six years previously made a false statement in an email to his present employer which lead to the claimant's dismissal. There was sufficient proximity between ex-employer and ex-employee, even at that distance in time and though the statement was not a reference.

The above discussion has demonstrated that there has been considerable development in the ability to recover for pure economic loss in negligence. Considerations of 'practical justice' have often seemed apparent, even if not always overtly expressed, in the judgments made, and while this is undoubtedly welcome for the claimant, the ability to predict which direction the law may take next is perhaps compromised. It could be concluded that the general incremental approach to the development of the duty concept in negligence has certainly found a receptive audience in relation to claims for pure economic loss.[11]

QUESTION 4

'Due to some of the difficulties of bringing an action in negligence, the tort of misfeasance in public office has recently become a popular alternative cause of action.'

▶ **Discuss the above statement, with particular reference to the scope of the tort of misfeasance in public office.**

How to Answer this Question

This is a question on misfeasance in public office and its relation to negligence. This question should only be attempted by candidates who have a good, detailed grasp of the principles of misfeasance in public office.

---

11   The question here was about the lack of coherence and legal certainty, so it was important not just to write 'all you know' about economic loss without the focus of the question.

The following points need to be discussed:

❖ an outline of circumstances in which misfeasance in public office offers advantages over negligence; and

❖ a discussion of the principles of misfeasance in public office with particular reference to *Three Rivers v Bank of England* (2000) and subsequent cases.

Answer Structure

Problems with negligence

Principles of misfeasance in public office

Three Rivers v Bank of England and other cases

Advantages of misfeasance in public office

ANSWER

Claimants seeking to rely on the tort of negligence to recover for any loss they have suffered may find several difficulties in establishing their cause of action.

In particular, they may find it difficult to establish the required degree of proximity between themselves and the defendant, which means that the claimant may be unable to establish the existence of a duty of care. Another problem might arise if the loss suffered is pure economic loss. Although recovery for pure economic loss was allowed in the House of Lords in *Junior Books v Veitchi* (1983), *Junior Books* has been so heavily criticised in later cases that it seems highly unlikely that the case will found any future actions involving pure economic loss. In such situations, the tort of misfeasance in public office may provide an alternative cause of action and this tort may be appropriate where policy reasons restrict a duty of care in negligence.

Although the tort of misfeasance in public office can be found in law reports of the seventeenth and eighteenth centuries, it was a comparatively unknown cause of action until 1985 and the case of *Bourgion SA v Ministry of Agriculture*. Here, the plaintiffs, who were French turkey producers, had been banned by the defendants from exporting turkeys to England. The defendants admitted that the true purpose of this ban was the protection of British turkey products and that this constituted a breach of **Art 30** of the **Treaty of Rome**. Nevertheless, the defendants claimed that they were not liable for misfeasance in public office, as they had no intent to injure the plaintiffs, but rather had the intent to protect British interests. The Court of Appeal found that malice is not an essential ingredient of the tort: it was sufficient that the defendant knew that he had acted unlawfully and that his acts would injure the plaintiff. As in this case the plaintiff had suffered only pure economic loss, an action in negligence was almost certain to fail.

The next example of this tort concerned a local authority. In *Jones v Swansea City Council* (1990), the House of Lords held that the plaintiff could sue the council for misfeasance in public office if she could prove that the majority of councillors who had voted for a resolution had done so with the aim of damaging the plaintiff with knowledge of the unlawful nature of this act. Again, in this case, the plaintiff had suffered only pure economic loss.

The House of Lords was called upon to undertake a comprehensive review of the tort in *Three Rivers District Council v Bank of England (No 3)* (2000).[12] Their Lordships held that the tort has the following ingredients:

(a)   The defendant must be a public officer. This clearly covers government departments and local authorities. If a local authority exercises private law functions as, for example, a landlord, this would satisfy this ingredient.
(b)   The exercise of power must be as a public officer.
(c)   The state of mind of the defendants. A study of the case law shows two different forms of liability for the tort exist:
   ❖   cases in which a public power is exercised for an improper purpose with the specific intention of injuring a person or persons (the 'targeted malice' limb); and
   ❖   cases in which a public officer acts in the knowledge that he had no power to do the act complained of and that it would probably injure the claimant (the 'illegality' limb).
   Both limbs involve bad faith. In the targeted malice limb, the bad faith is the exercise of public power for an improper purpose; in the illegality limb, the bad faith is the lack of honest belief on the part of the public officer that the act is lawful. The House of Lords made it clear that for the illegality limb, reckless indifference as to the illegality and its probable consequences is sufficient to establish the required mental

---

12   As the leading case in this area, it is important to give details of the judgment.

element. The recklessness must be subjective, so that the claimant must prove that the defendant lacked an honest belief in lawfulness of his actions, or wilfully disregarded the risk of unlawfulness.

(d) Duty to the claimant. Although the Court of Appeal in *Three Rivers DC* held that proximity between the claimant and the defendant was required, this finding was expressly overturned by the House of Lords. Their Lordships held that the required mental element will keep the tort within reasonable bounds and that there was no need to introduce proximity as a control mechanism.

(e) Causation is an essential ingredient of the tort.

(f) Damage covered includes pure economic loss, but the plaintiff must suffer special damage – that is, loss that is specific to the plaintiff and not suffered in common with the general public. In *Watkins v Secretary of State for the Home Department* (2006), the House of Lords overruled the Court of Appeal and held that the tort was actionable only where the claimant had suffered loss or damage due to the defendant's tortious conduct. Lord Bingham noted that the rationale of the tort was to compensate the claimant rather than to punish the public officer, as other means would be better suited. The case concerned a prisoner's complaints that his mail had been withheld and that there was no actual damage to speak of.

(g) The test for remoteness for this tort is not reasonable foreseeability, but knowledge by the defendant that the decision would probably damage the claimant. The *Three Rivers DC* case arose out of the collapse of a bank (BCCI). Many of the bank's depositors brought misfeasance proceedings against the Bank of England. The plaintiffs alleged senior officials at the Bank of England licensed BCCI when they knew that doing so was unlawful, had shut their eyes to activities at BCCI once the licence was granted and had failed to close down BCCI when they ought to have done so. Had this case been brought on negligence, the problem of pure economic loss would have caused insurmountable difficulties, and in addition the claimants could have faced problems in establishing the necessary degree of proximity to found a duty of care.

Some short time after *Three Rivers DC* was heard, the Court of Appeal was faced with a misfeasance case involving for the first time personal injury or death: *Akenzua v Secretary of State for the Home Department* (2003). Here, an immigration officer attached to a special police unit allowed a gangster with a record of violent crime in Jamaica to remain in the UK illegally in return for information concerning criminal activity in the UK. The gangster sexually assaulted and killed a friend of the woman with whom he lived. The personal representatives of the deceased sued the Home Secretary and the police in misfeasance in public office. It is highly likely that an action in negligence would have failed for insufficient proximity and possibly on public policy grounds: see *Hill v Chief Constable of West Yorkshire* (1989). The case was brought under the illegality limb of the tort and the defendant claimed that the deceased was not a member of a closely defined class at risk from the gangster's presence in the UK. Essentially, the Court had to decide whether the claimant had to prove (i) that the probable harm was to the claimant or a class of which the claimant was a member or (ii) only that the probable harm was to someone and that someone turned out to be the claimant. The Court held that the second requirement was the correct one and that the first requirement amounted to an attempt to introduce proximity into the tort.

From the above discussion, it can be seen that the tort of misfeasance in public office is particularly apposite where the claimant may face problems of proximity, pure economic loss or public policy considerations should the action be brought in negligence. However, it is of only limited application, as has been shown, and thus is unlikely to be 'popular' in the sense of a large number of cases.[13]

QUESTION 5

Zena and Yang have just begun a relationship. Two years ago, Yang, who had been married before, had a vasectomy operation. He tells Zena that the surgeon, Dr Ahmed, told him that the operation was 100 per cent successful and he would not be able to have more children. Zena, who does not want a family, is keen not to have to use contraception as she has had problems with some methods in the past. She therefore checks on the internet, on a site called Health-E-U, which states that this type of operation is wholly dependable. She notices a small box which states that the website does not accept liability in negligence for the information it contains. She therefore also checks with her GP, Dr Snow, who confirms that Yang's sterilisation operation renders contraception unnecessary.

Six months later, Zena finds out that she is pregnant. She subsequently discovers that recent scientific research has shown that such operations can 'spontaneously reverse'. She decides to go ahead with the birth.

◗ Advise her if she is entitled to any compensation from Drs Ahmed and Snow, and Health-E-U.

◗ Would it make any difference if you knew that the baby was born disabled?

How to Answer this Question

This question involves considering potential liability for wrongful advice, i.e. a negligent misstatement, giving rise to economic loss in the form of bringing up a baby. As such, it also covers an area known as 'wrongful birth', which courts were initially willing to give compensation for, but for policy reasons discontinued. It thus gives an opportunity to demonstrate understanding of the difference between liability for actions and words, and for physical and economic loss, plus an appreciation of the role of policy in some court decisions.

13 In an essay question, it is important to return in the conclusion to attempt to answer the question set.

You will have to consider:

* ❖ duty of care for economic loss;
* ❖ the standard of care for professionals;
* ❖ liability for 'wrongful birth';
* ❖ causation.

Applying the Law

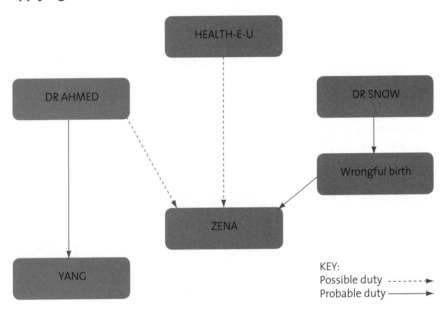

KEY:
Possible duty - - - - - ▸
Probable duty ——————▸

ANSWER

In order to obtain compensation, Zena will have to prove that she was owed a duty of care by one or more of the defendants, that the duty was breached because the defendant(s) fell below the standard of reasonable care, and that the breach caused her loss.

Her claim will be based on the various statements that were made to her, which subsequently turn out to be incorrect. As her claim is based on a statement rather than actions, she will be arguing that the duty was owed based on the line of cases starting with *Hedley Byrne v Heller* (1964). In that case it was held that where there is a special relationship between the parties, and one negligently (without sufficient care) gives wrong information to the other expecting it to be acted on and which the other acts on to their detriment, then the information giver will be liable for the economic losses that flow from that. However, the courts have been concerned to restrict the boundaries of this duty because of the large number of people who could potentially be harmed by wrong information. Subsequent cases such as *Caparo Industries v Dickman* (1990) have built on this and referred to an 'assumption of responsibility' which the defendant must have undertaken.[14]

The standard of care required by professionals is not that of a reasonable layperson, but 'that of the standard of the ordinary skilled man exercising and professing to have that special skill' (*Bolam v Friern Hospital Management Committee* (1957)). Thus if 'a responsible body of medical men' can be found who accept the procedure as 'proper', then it will be regarded as reasonable. It does not matter if the professional is a trainee, or junior, as it is an objective standard (*Wilsher v Essex Area Health Authority* (1987)). This may seem as though the courts are allowing the professionals to set their own standards, but in the case of doctors, the House of Lords in *Bolitho v City and Hackney Health Authority* (1997) held that, exceptionally, if the professional opinion could not be logically sustained, then the judges could substitute their own standard.

Causation normally falls to be decided using the 'but for' test (*Barnett v Chelsea and Kensington Hospital* (1968)).

In *Goodwill v British Pregnancy Advisory Service* (1996) it was held that a hospital did not owe a duty of care to the subsequent partners of a man who had a vasectomy; there was insufficient proximity between them. The situation may have been different if it had been Yang's wife who had become pregnant (*Thake v Maurice* (1986)). This would seem to rule out any liability for Dr Ahmed, and as the information was given a couple of years before, it is likely that in any case, he could argue that a reasonable doctor at that time would not have had the newly available research information, and thus there would have been no lack of reasonable care. He would be judged against the standard of care prevailing at the time – the 'state of the art' defence (*Roe v Minister of Health* (1954)).

Health-E-U is likely to argue that it has excluded liability for negligence anyway, but notwithstanding this, it could not be said to owe a duty of care to everyone who read its contents. There is no special relationship or proximity. The success of this latter argument might depend on how the site was 'got-up': did it, for instance include highly visible commendations and recommendations from esteemed medical establishments, which might demonstrate that it was assuming responsibility to its browsers? It is however highly unlikely. Health-E-U should be informed that any attempt to exclude liability for death or personal injury will be ineffective under s 2(1) of the **Unfair Contract Terms Act 1977**, unless it does not qualify as acting in the course of a business, which might be the case if it were a small charity for instance. It would do better to make it clear on its site

---

14 Do not get confused between the importance of *Caparo* in setting out the three-part test for the existence of a duty of care generally, and the important role it also plays in the development of liability for pure economic loss.

that individuals should not rely on its advice, but check with their own doctors, to ensure the failure of any argument of assumption of responsibility.[15]

In the case of Dr Snow, it is well established that a doctor owes a duty of care to his/her patients, as shown in *Bolam* and *Bolitho*. The standard would be that of the reasonably competent GP, who is not of course an expert in sterilisation procedures but would be expected to know more than a layman. Thus the fact that Dr Snow was unaware of the latest research would suggest that she is in breach of duty, but if she can find a body of medical opinion which would have advised similarly, she may be able to satisfy the *Bolam* test.

Zena would still need to prove causation, that 'but for' the doctor's advice she would not have got pregnant. This might be difficult to establish, as she has made it clear that she is wary of using contraceptives, and anyway no contraceptive method is 100 per cent guaranteed. However, she may be able to demonstrate that on the balance of probabilities (*Hotson v East Berkshire Area Health Authority* (1987)) she would not have become pregnant.

Dr Snow might argue that the fact Zena chose to continue with the pregnancy, rather than have an abortion, might amount to a *novus actus interveniens* by the claimant themselves (*McKew v Holland and Hannen and Cubbitts* (1969)) or possible contributory negligence. In *Emeh v Kensington Area Health Authority* (1985) it was held that the claimant's failure to have an abortion was not so unreasonable as to 'eclipse the defendant's wrongdoing'.[16]

In *McFarlane v Tayside Health Authority* (2000), the House of Lords held that the costs of raising an unwanted but healthy child were not recoverable in a negligence action, as this economic loss was not part of the duty that the hospital took on. The damages in that case were limited to the discomfort of pregnancy and the pain of giving birth, i.e. personal injury. In *Rees v Darlington Memorial Hospital NHS Trust* (2003), the House of Lords said that there were policy reasons for not allowing the recovery of the costs of caring for a child because there was 'an unwillingness to regard a child (even if unwanted) as a financial liability and nothing else, a recognition that the rewards which parenthood (even if involuntary) may or may not bring cannot be quantified'.[17] However, their Lordships felt that there should be a 'conventional award' in cases of wrongful birth

---

15 Note that in the **Hedley Byrne** case, the disclaimer was effective to defeat liability. However, this was before the introduction of the **1977 Act**, and this demonstrates the importance of being aware of the chronology of the leading cases.

16 For further information on these defences, see Chapter 15.

17 This quote from Lord Bingham in **Rees** clearly adds to the authority and quality of your answer. If in exam conditions it is not possible to remember quite all of it, even the first part of the phrase (up to 'nothing else') would be worthwhile including.

to recognise that a harm had been done, over and above pain and suffering, and awarded £15,000.

If the child was born disabled, the case of *Parkinson v St James Hospital* (2001) allowed for the extra costs of caring for a disabled child to be claimed (although the hospital's negligence was not the cause of the disability). Whether this Court of Appeal decision stands after the later Lords decision in *Rees* (where the disabled mother was denied the extra costs of bringing up her unwanted child) is arguable, as now the courts may simply award the 'conventional award'.[18]

Thus Zena will, at most, be able to recover damages from Dr Snow for the pain and discomfort associated with birth and a 'conventional award' to mark that a wrong has occurred. She may want to balance this relatively small sum against the stress of pursuing a legal claim, and the possible future psychological harm the awareness of the label of a 'wrongful birth' may cause to the child. Only if the baby is disabled will she have the possibility of claiming towards the cost of raising her child.[19]

18 This demonstrates the importance of knowing and being able to comment on the standing of a decision and the date when it was decided.
19 Although it is not wise, of course, to base the entire answer on practical or other advice, rather than the legal position, it will demonstrate understanding of the issues to point out such considerations if there is time.

Negligence – Duty of Care 2

2

INTRODUCTION

In relation to psychiatric injury and the imposition of a duty of care on the emergency services, it is well to bear in mind that there may be policy reasons for restricting the scope of the duty of care.

Checklist ✔

Students need to be familiar with:

psychiatric injury/nervous shock

- the criteria for recovery:
    - the restrictions on recovery;
    - the possible extensions of persons owed a duty of care;

emergency services

- duty owed to police, fire and ambulance services;
- limitations on the duty.

QUESTION 6

Clive has a part-time job in a petrol station. He was working one evening when three rockets, part of an organised firework display, crashed into the garage forecourt. It was later discovered that the rocket's launch mechanisms had not been properly assembled by the event organiser.

Alex was filling his car with petrol when the rockets landed, causing a violent explosion. Miraculously Alex was not badly hurt but was powerless to get to his wife Katie who was trapped in the burning car. Unable to save her, he collapsed with shock.

Dave, the station manager, watched the chaos unfold on CCTV in the office behind the petrol station. Concerned for his own safety, and that of his lovingly restored vintage

Bentley, which was parked on the garage forecourt, he told Clive to 'take the fire extinguisher, get outside and save my car'. He then bolted the fire door and dialled the emergency services. Clive attended to Alex, and also Jodie, who was walking her dog when the explosion happened. Jodie was otherwise unhurt, but the Bentley was completely destroyed.

▶ Advise all of the parties to their likely success in claiming damages for the psychiatric harm each claims to have suffered.

How to Answer this Question

This is a fairly involved question relating to potential recovery for psychiatric harm. It picks up on a number of issues and should help to crystallise the sort of structure that it is useful to adopt for these sorts of questions.

The following points need to be discussed:

❖   the basis of the duty for psychiatric harm;
❖   primary and secondary victims;
❖   damage to property;
❖   rescuers.

Applying the Law

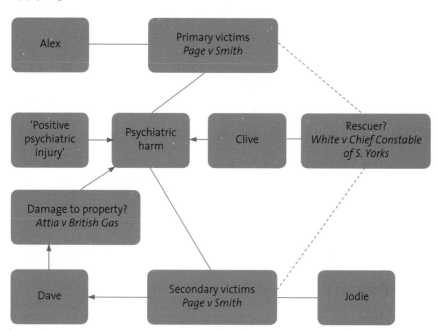

This diagram considers each victim's claims for psychiatric injury.

ANSWER

The scenario requires an evaluation of the law relating to the recovery of damages for psychiatric harm (PH)[1] caused by negligence. The law is complex and has evolved a number of key principles and tests, which must be applied to the parties seeking advice. In this scenario four parties would be seeking to make a claim against the event organiser whose negligence in relation to the assembly of the launching mechanism caused the explosion at the petrol station. Given the facts as expressed we can assume negligence on the part of the defendant.[2]

The law on PH has developed from a situation where recovery was completely denied (*Victorian Railway Commissioners v Coultas* (1888)) to a relatively clear, but involved, position governed generally by the decision of the House of Lords in *Alcock v Chief Constable of South Yorkshire* (1991), which was one of the cases that arose as a result of the Hillsborough football stadium disaster. In the early years, issues around the ability to prove the illnesses that a claimant may have suffered hampered any development of liability and there was a judicial fear of fraudulent claims and recourse to the 'floodgates' policy argument of proliferating claims. Initially, when it was finally accepted, claims were limited solely to those situations where a claimant was put in fear of their own safety (*Dulieu v White* (1901)).[3]

In the modern law, liability is limited to instances of recognised mental injury. This means that temporary grief or fear is insufficient to ground a claim (*Alcock*; *Brice v Brown* (1984); *Vernon v Bosley* (1997)). Medical science has improved to the extent that there are a number of recognised conditions, such as clinical depression and post-traumatic stress disorder, which would enable a claim for PH. The current law states that the PH caused by the defendant's negligence must either result in physical injury (*Bourhill v Young* (1943)), or create a 'positive psychiatric illness' (*per* Lord Bridge in *McLoughlin v O'Brian* (1983)), and, following the decision of the House of Lords in *Grieves v F.T. Everard & Sons and others* (2007) a claim must be based on a real, rather than imagined, injury. The burden of proving PH would fall on the four claimants who would have to show that they had such injuries.[4]

---

1 An abbreviation such as this can be a good idea in exam situations where there is limited time; however, ensure that it is written out in full and then the chosen abbreviation put in brackets when using it for the first time.

2 It should be remembered that psychiatric harm, or injury, is not a separate tort in its own right, and if a duty to avoid causing PH was established, it is still necessary to demonstrate breach of that duty, as here, and causation.

3 In an exam situation, and particularly in a problem question, do not waste too much time on historical background, and be sure to focus on the leading modern case, here *Alcock*.

4 Students often fail to give sufficient emphasis to the need for a genuine psychiatric illness, such as post-traumatic stress disorder, to be proved by the claimant.

As above, the current leading case to use in establishing a duty is *Alcock*. Lord Oliver distinguished primary and secondary victims, the former being those who could be identified as being involved directly or indirectly as a participant, and the latter whereby the claimant was (no more than) a passive and unwilling witness of the damage that had been caused to other people. Primary victims are much more likely to be able to claim successfully, although there has been some further refining of the liability basis. In *Page v Smith* (1996), it was restricted to people in foreseeable physical danger, although in *W v Essex CC* (2000) the position was not understood to be quite so defined. A more recent examination of the classification in the case of *Corr v IBC Vehicles Ltd* (2008), where the suicide of the claimant's husband was held to be a manifestation of the depression he suffered, concluded that is was foreseeable injury consequent upon a physical injury. Nuances apart, it is clear in this situation that Alex is a primary victim: he was directly involved in a horrific incident and, subject to proving PH, he would be likely to succeed in a claim. Dave may wish to claim that he was a primary victim, 'in the zone of danger' but it is unlikely, following the decision in *McFarlane v EE Caledonia* (1994), that he would be considered such. He was safely out of harm's way.

The position is less clear when advising secondary victims. According to the decision in *Alcock* there are three considerations to satisfy. These were based on the reasoning in the decision in *McLoughlin v O'Brian* (1983) which set clear limits on the ability to make a claim. In order to recover, a claimant now needs to prove, first, their relationship with a primary victim was sufficiently close that it was reasonably foreseeable that the claimant might suffer PH; second, the claimant's proximity to the incident or its immediate aftermath (that concept being explained in *McLoughlin* and refined in *Ravenscroft v Rederiaktiebolaget* (1991)) in time and space (see *Bourhill v Young* (1943)); and third, that the claimant suffered PH through seeing or hearing the accident or its immediate aftermath. The final aspect was further refined to the extent that a claimant must be witness to the incident or aftermath with their own unaided senses. The Lords in *Alcock* also were at pains to state that a claimant did not have to be in a particular class of relationship to make a claim (preferring the use of the term 'a close tie of love and affection'), and indeed even suggested that a mere bystander could claim if the event was particularly horrific. This has so far not transpired, and cases such as *McFarlane v EE Caledonia Ltd* (1994) in relation to the Piper Alpha oil rig disaster, and *Robertson v Forth Road Bridge Joint Board* (1995) have not seen compensation forthcoming for those considered bystanders by the courts. There has been some judicial consideration in relation to the duration of the event that has led to the PH. The preferred interpretation is that it is a sudden event that precipitates the PH (*Sion v Hampstead Health Authority* (1994)), which this undoubtedly is, although the decision in that case has been reviewed (see *North Glamorgan NHS Trust v Walters* (2002)).[5] Dave and Jodie both fall within the

---

5   It is essential to distinguish clearly between primary and secondary victims and clarify the case law.

category of secondary victims and would thus need to satisfy the above tests to stand any chance of claiming for their PH. On the facts presented it would appear, initially, that both would be unable to succeed. This is because, although both were proximate in time and space to the incident, neither apparently had a sufficiently close relationship with any of those involved. Should that be proved, Jodie may have a claim as she did see and hear the incident with her own unaided senses. Dave probably heard it, but viewed the rest on CCTV cameras and opted to stay in a 'safe' environment. On balance, it is unlikely that either would be successful.[6]

Clive might be in a different position altogether. He might initially be classed as being a primary victim, along with Alex. It could be that he was directly involved in the incident, and despite not actually being harmed was in reasonable fear of his own safety. A more likely outcome could be that he is considered to be a rescuer. A rescuer had, until relatively recently, occupied a privileged position in relation to negligence claims. On the basis that the person involved was mitigating the harm caused by a defendant to a claimant it was understood as being good policy to permit claims for injuries suffered, including psychiatric injuries. The basis for recovery as a rescuer in PH cases is the decision in *Chadwick v British Transport Commission* (1967), where a claim was permitted on behalf of the actions of a rescuer who had no connection to the people he was helping following a rail disaster, and who suffered severe PH as a result of his experience.

The issue was blurred slightly by the decision of the House of Lords in *White v Chief Constable of South Yorkshire Police* (1998), which involved a claim by police officers involved in the Hillsborough stadium disaster. The decision in *Alcock* had restricted the claims of secondary victims, and thus the police officers fell outside of that category of claimants. They thus attempted to claim as rescuers. It was held that they were not entitled to do so. Linking the concept of 'rescue' to something analogous to being a primary victim, the House of Lords, by a majority, held that only a rescuer who either was or believed themselves to be in danger could claim, unless they fulfilled the *Alcock* criteria. This view has been subject to a degree of criticism and there has been a view expressed that the 'danger' requirement should apply solely to those who may be termed 'professional' rescuers (see for example *Greatorex v Greatorex* (2000)). That said, a rescuer must actually be involved in a rescue, and not as in *McFarlane*, some distance away from the actual disaster and merely handing out blankets and support to 'walking wounded'. Fortunately for Clive the situation would more than likely not be so complex. He would appear to have placed himself in a certain amount of danger when he tended to both Alex and Jodie, who were injured and traumatised respectively. It is submitted that Clive would be likely to be

---

6   As no information is given about the possible relationship between Jodie and Dave (as secondary victims) and Katie (which might suggest that none exists), it is not possible to be more definite as to whether they would succeed. However, the issue must be raised, as it is a crucial factor in determining liability to secondary victims.

able to sustain an action, and if so, the case of *Tolley v Carr* (2010) suggests that he would not have any damages deducted for contributory negligence.[7]

One final consideration would be the novel approach to PH adopted by the courts in the case of *Attia v British Gas* (1988), where the claimant successfully sued for PH on the basis of property damage, having witnessed her house being destroyed by fire. Dave may wish to attempt to claim in this regard for the destruction of his car, but post-*Alcock* the tests may prove hard to satisfy, making his chances of success unlikely. This would be, not least, because he watched the event unfold on the CCTV cameras, and thus not with his 'unaided senses'. There would be no obvious reason why, on grounds of normal negligence principles, he would not be able to claim for the damage to the car, however, as damage to property would be a foreseeable consequence of a breach of a duty of care to ensure the safety of a firework display.[8]

In conclusion, it would appear that the claimants most likely to succeed in an action for PH would be Alex, as a primary victim, and Clive as a rescuer. The remaining claims would not be likely to satisfy the current test for secondary victims.

Aim Higher

Maintain an effective structure. Deal with primary and secondary victims in order. Having a keen sense of the status of 'rescuers' following the decision in *White* will often help as many examiners will use this as a layer of complexity.

Common Pitfalls

The chronology and status of the cases often trips candidates up – make sure you know which case informed which subsequent decision. Applying the cases for secondary victims to primary victims is a waste of your time and will not gain you any marks.

QUESTION 7

'The House of Lords has stated in the clearest possible terms in *White v Chief Constable of South Yorkshire Police* (1999) that the law on nervous shock or psychiatric injury is so illogical that only Parliament can come up with a solution.'

▶ Discuss the above statement.

---

7 For more on contributory negligence, see Chapter 15.
8 The question was confined to psychiatric injury, but it could be relevant to briefly mention the damage to property point.

How to Answer this Question

This essay on psychiatric injury requires the candidate not only to recite the current state of the law, but also to highlight any inconsistencies that exist and to discuss how a statute might improve the situation.

The following points need to be discussed:

❖ the criteria for liability in psychiatric injury, per *Alcock v Chief Constable of South Yorkshire* (1991);
❖ the uncertainties as regards possible claimants – rescuers, intervention of third parties, lapse of time;
❖ the extent to which a statute might improve the current situation;
❖ the possible problems that a statute might bring.

Answer Structure

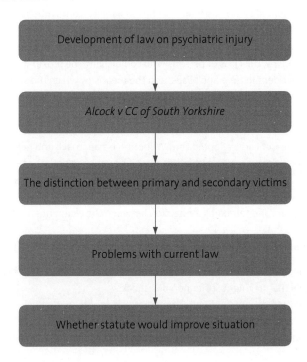

Development of law on psychiatric injury

Alcock v CC of South Yorkshire

The distinction between primary and secondary victims

Problems with current law

Whether statute would improve situation

ANSWER

The law on 'nervous shock', or 'psychiatric injury' as it is usually now called, has developed considerably since the original refusal to impose liability in *Victorian Railway Commissioners v Coulthas* (1888). Initially the courts were wary of imposing liability for something that could not be seen, unlike physical injuries such as broken bones, because of the fears of fraud and the 'floodgates' argument. But as the knowledge of psychiatry has developed the judiciary has been more ready to accept the existence of mental trauma as a result of witnessing or being involved in a tort. It has progressed from allowing recovery where the claimant was reasonably put in fear of his own safety (*Dulieu v White* (1901)) to allowing recovery for a wide range of persons, albeit within constraints. With the exception of rescuers (*Chadwick v British Transport Commission* (1967)), these persons have usually been close family members of the victim (see the speech of Lord Wilberforce in *McLoughlin v O'Brian* (1983)). However, all liability for psychiatric injury must now be considered in the light of the decision of the House of Lords in *Alcock v Chief Constable of South Yorkshire* (1991).9

In *McLoughlin*, the House of Lords considered the area of psychiatric injury and held that the test to be applied was whether it was reasonably foreseeable that the claimant would suffer from psychiatric injury as a result of the defendant's negligence. However, the House of Lords adopted two distinct approaches to liability. Lord Wilberforce held that, as it was capable of affecting such a wide range of persons, there was a need for the law to place some limitation on claims. He considered that there were three elements inherent in any claim – namely, the class of persons who could claim, the proximity of such persons to the accident in time and space, and the means by which the shock was caused. Lord Bridge held that this approach would place arbitrary limits on recovery and preferred the test of reasonable foreseeability *simpliciter*.10

In *Alcock*, the House of Lords adopted Lord Wilberforce's approach and held that a claimant could only recover for psychiatric injury if he satisfied both the test of reasonable foreseeability (that he would be so affected because of the close relationship of love and affection with the primary victim), and the test of proximity to the tortfeasor (in terms of physical and temporal connection between the claimant and the accident).

Hence, a claimant regarded as a secondary victim could only recover if:

(a) his relationship to the primary victim was sufficiently close that it was reasonably foreseeable that he might suffer nervous shock;

(b) his proximity to the accident or its immediate aftermath was sufficiently close in both time and space; and

(c) he suffered shock through seeing or hearing the accident or its immediate aftermath.

Thus, a claimant does not satisfy the tests of reasonable foreseeability or proximity unless the psychiatric illness was caused by sudden shock through seeing or hearing the

---

9 This introductory paragraph sets the scene and introduces the main aspects of the coming discussion.

10 Being able to distinguish between the opinions of two different judges adds to the quality of the answer.

accident and its immediate aftermath. Also, a claimant who suffered psychiatric injury caused by being informed of the accident by a third party does not satisfy these tests.

Thus, given the television broadcasting guidelines which forbade the transmission of pictures of any identifiable individuals involved, persons who witnessed the disaster live on television had not suffered psychiatric injury induced by the sight and sound of the event, as they were not in proximity to the event and did not suffer shock in the sense of a sudden assault on the nervous system. The House of Lords also held that the class of persons who may claim for psychiatric injury was not limited to particular relationships such as husband and wife or parent and child, and went on to suggest that a bystander who witnessed a particularly horrific catastrophe might be able to recover and that, in certain circumstances, a claimant might recover on witnessing an event on contemporaneous television (for example, where the claimant knew that the primary victim could be injured in a live televised event, even though the primary victim was not identified in the televised pictures). However, in *McFarlane v EE Caledonia Ltd* (1994), the Court of Appeal held that despite the *dicta* of three Law Lords in *Alcock*, a mere bystander or witness of horrific events could not recover unless there was both sufficient proximity in time and space to the accident, and a close relationship of love and affection with the primary victim. To hold otherwise, held the Court, would reduce the test for recovery to pure reasonable foreseeability, which goes against the whole judgment in *Alcock*.

We should note here that by 'psychiatric injury' the courts mean actual mental injury or a recognisable psychiatric illness, and that mere grief and sorrow are insufficient (*Brice v Brown* (1984); *Grieves & ors v Everard & ors* (2007)). In *Re The Herald of Free Enterprise* (1989), it was held that post-traumatic stress disorder and pathological grief in excess of normal grief are recognised psychiatric illnesses, for which compensation can be awarded. However, In *Reilly v Merseyside RHA* (1996) it was held that fear, apprehension, discomfort and shortnesss of breath owing to being trapped in a lift did not amount to a psychiatric illness. The courts have also allowed recovery where property damage has occurred. Thus, in *Attia v British Gas* (1988), a plaintiff was allowed to recover when she saw her house being burnt to the ground. Presumably, since *Alcock*, a claimant will have to show that the property was of such a nature that if a claimant witnessed its destruction, it was reasonably foreseeable that psychiatric injury would follow, as well as satisfying the criteria of proximity and of seeing the accident through his own senses.

At first glance, in *Alcock*, the House of Lords seemed to have widened considerably the range of potential claimants, although a close reading of the judgments might suggest that this range has been narrowed in some circumstances. Thus, their Lordships rejected the concept of limiting the class of persons who can claim to specified relationships with the primary victim such as spouses or parents and children in favour of the close relationship test. This is both logical and just in that, *per* Lord Keith, it is the existence of the close tie of love and affection that leads to psychological injury. Thus, the spouse or parent will be presumed to have such close ties of love and affection, and siblings and other relatives will have to prove such ties. Presumably, it would be open to the defendant in the cases of spouses to rebut the presumption by proving (say) that the partners have separated and have not been living together for some years. This wide approach, however, is not free from difficulties. It seems that *Alcock* would allow recovery by a particularly close friend who can satisfy the criteria of love and affection, but how is a defendant to reasonably foresee the existence of such a close friend? While it is foreseeable that the primary victim of an accident may have a spouse or children or a brother or sister, is the existence of such a friend reasonably foreseeable? Given the readiness of some judges to foresee a great deal and others to take a narrower view, can this approach be said to bring certainty or logic to the law? It may be just from the point of view of the secondary victim, but is it just as regards the defendant to impose such wide liability?[11]

Another area that gives rise to problems of justice and uncertainty arises from the second requirement that the claimant's proximity to the accident or its immediate aftermath is close in both time and space. The necessity for such a requirement is obvious, in that the claimant should not be allowed to claim a long time after the accident, but just what is meant by being close in both time and place? In *Alcock*, Lord Ackner was not prepared to allow recovery to a plaintiff who saw the body of a brother-in-law at the mortuary some eight hours after the accident, and Lord Wilberforce stated in *McLoughlin* that a two-hour delay period was at the margin of the time span for recovery. This seems to be an arbitrary timescale that would appear to suggest that a claimant who is contacted by mobile telephone and told to attend at a hospital, and has access to a fast car, may be able to recover, whereas a claimant who has to depend on public transport may not. Is a claimant who is away on business and, on return, identifies a dead spouse affected any differently from a person who is called from work to identify a dead spouse? In *Galli-Atkinson v Seghal* (2003), a mother who was told of the death of her daughter, visited the accident site and then later saw the body in the mortuary was allowed to recover compensation.

The problem as to just what is meant by the claimant's proximity to the event or its immediate aftermath has been rendered even more confusing by the decision of the House of Lords in *W v Essex County Council* (2000). Here, the claimant parents fostered a youth placed with them by the defendant local authority. The youth committed severe acts of sexual abuse on the claimants' children and, when the parents discovered what had happened, they suffered psychiatric illness. The defendant authority sought to strike out the claim, but this was refused by the House of Lords. Lord Slynn, with whom all the other Law Lords agreed, stated that it was by no means certain that the parents would fail to satisfy the required proximity to the event or its immediate aftermath in both time

---

11   This paragraph tackles head on the central issue of the question set, about the current illogical state of the law as developed by the judges.

and space. Lord Slynn stated that he was not certain that, in this case, the parents would have to come across the abused or abuser immediately after the sexual event. Given the statements regarding time in *Alcock* and *McLoughlin* above, this seems a very strange proposition of law. In addition, the parents were not witnesses to the abuse – they found out about it some time later. Their position is analogous to that of parents who are told of their offspring's involvement in an accident after the event and, in *Ravenscroft v Rederiaktiebolaget Transatlantic* (1992), such a person was denied recovery for nervous shock. Hence, there would appear to be considerable uncertainty in deciding in any particular case whether or not there was sufficient proximity to the accident or its immediate aftermath in time and space.[12]

The word 'shock' is also not without its problems. In *Walters v North Glamorgan NHS Trust* (2003), the Court of Appeal had to decide whether an event that lasted for 36 hours could constitute 'shock', or whether it was a gradual assault of the mind over a period of time. On the facts, the Court held that this 36-hour period constituted an event and stated that the present law permits a realistic view to be taken in each individual case. As in similar cases – for example, *Taylorson v Shieldness Produce Ltd* (1994), in which it has been held that there was a dawning realisation rather than a sudden shock over such a period of time – it is clear that the facts and medical reports regarding just how the psychiatric damage eventuated are of the utmost importance.

Finally, *Alcock* retained the rule that the shock must be caused through seeing or hearing the accident or its immediate aftermath. Thus, if a mother attends a hospital to be told that her children have been burnt to death and feels unable to see the bodies, but still suffers psychiatric injury, she cannot recover. Presumably, if she did see the bodies, it would be open to the defendant to argue that it was the news of the death of her children, related to her by a nurse or doctor, that caused the shock, rather than the sight of the bodies, in other words, a *novus actus interveniens*.[13] This seems to be a most illogical and unjust result, but it follows from *Alcock*.

Two decisions of the House of Lords have attempted to introduce some logic into the area of psychiatric injury. In *Page v Smith* (1995), their Lordships held that once it can be established that a defendant is under a duty of care to avoid causing personal injury to a claimant, it is immaterial whether the injury caused is physical or psychiatric. Thus, provided that it is reasonably foreseeable that the claimant might suffer personal injury, that will suffice in a psychiatric injury claim. The House went on to state that, in such cases, it is vital to distinguish between primary and secondary victims, as only secondary victims are subject to the restrictions in *Alcock*. Thus, for primary victims, the illogical distinction between physical and psychiatric injury has been abolished. This has been

---

12 Being able to refer to a specific judge's views will add to the quality of the answer.
13 For more on this, see Question 12.

highlighted further in the case of *Corr v IBC Vehicles Ltd* (2008). The claimant was able to recover for the suicide of her husband. The suicide was held to be a manifestation of depression he suffered consequent upon a head injury sustained as a result of the defendant's negligence. *Page* was recently evaluated by the House of Lords in *Grieves & ors v Everard & Sons & ors* (2007) and Lord Hoffmann stated that psychiatric illness created by an apprehended risk of contracting cancer was not actionable, whereas psychiatric harm occasioned upon *actually* contracting it would.

In *White v Chief Constable of South Yorkshire Police* (1999), the House of Lords removed what most commentators had recognised was an illogical and unjust distinction between claimants that had been brought about by the decision of the Court of Appeal in this case (reported as *Frost v Chief Constable of South Yorkshire Police* (1997)). The case concerned the Hillsborough stadium disaster and while in *Alcock* the claims of the deceased's families were not allowed, in *Frost*, the claims of the police officers who were present were (mostly) allowed. The Court of Appeal reached this decision by holding that as the plaintiff police officers were in an employee/employer relationship with the defendant chief constable, a duty of care was owed to them where injury was caused by the negligence of the chief constable. Thus, the distinction between primary and secondary victims was irrelevant in the employment situation. The Court of Appeal also held that the police officers were rescuers and could recover relying on that status, which also did not involve the application of the *Alcock* criteria. This decision was overturned by the House of Lords, which held that an employee who suffered psychiatric injury in the course of employment had to prove liability under the general rules of negligence – that is, employers' liability is not a separate tort with its own rules, but merely an aspect of the law of negligence. Their Lordships also went on to deal with the rescuer argument and held that a rescuer had to show that he had exposed himself to danger or reasonably believed he was so doing. Thus, rescuers are not to be treated as primary victims merely because they are rescuers. Consequently, in *Greatorex v Greatorex* (2000), the High Court, following *White*, refused to allow recovery to a rescuer *qua* rescuer as he had not been exposed to danger in the course of the rescue, nor had he been in reasonable fear of such danger.

While *White* brings some logic to the area of psychiatric injury, in that employees are treated in an identical manner to other claimants, it has weakened the position of rescuers. Furthermore, because of the rule in *Ogwo v Taylor* (1987), professional rescuers are treated in exactly the same way as pure volunteer rescuers, which might seem illogical.

In *Hunter v British Coal Corp* (1998), the Court of Appeal attempted to formulate some logical guidelines to help distinguish between a participant and a bystander, the *Alcock* criteria being applicable only to the latter. The Court of Appeal held that a claimant is a participant if he reasonably believes he is in physical danger as a result of the accident, or if he is an unwitting instrument of another person's negligence and therefore feels responsible for the accident. The claimant in *Hunter* was 30 metres away when the accident occurred and never returned to the scene of the accident. Thus, he was not a participant in the accident and his claim failed because he could not satisfy the *Alcock* criteria. A similar decision was reached by the Court of Appeal in *Duncan v British Coal Corp* (1997), in which the plaintiff was 300 metres away from the accident.

A further degree of uncertainty arises in this area as regards those statements of the Law Lords in *Alcock* that may be regarded as *obiter*, rather than forming part of the *ratio decidendi*. In *Alcock*, three Law Lords recognised the possibility of a mere bystander recovering after witnessing a particularly horrific accident but, in *McFarlane v EE Caledonia Ltd* (1994), the Court of Appeal held that such a bystander could not recover unless a close relationship of love and affection existed between him and the primary victim. To allow recovery in such a case would be to reduce the criteria to pure reasonable foreseeability, which runs counter to the whole of the judgment in *Alcock*.

It should also be borne in mind that in recent years the courts have been prepared to award compensation to employees who have suffered from stress, another category of psychiatric harm, as a result of their employers' failure to deal with over-heavy workloads etc, as in *Walker v Northumberland CC* (1995) and more recently in *Connor v Surrey CC* (2010), and this is another area where there is some uncertainty and lack of clarity.

Finally, it should be noted that when the High Court had to consider an extension to the law of psychiatric injury in *Greatorex*, in which the rescuer was the father and the personal injury to the primary victim was self-inflicted due to the primary victim's own negligence, the court relied almost entirely on policy considerations in denying recovery to the rescuer. As decisions that involve matters of policy are notoriously difficult to predict and are subject to a wide amount of judicial variation, this adds to the uncertainty prevalent in the area of psychiatric injury.

Thus, it can be seen that the current state of the law on psychiatric injury is illogical and uncertain in some respects. The enactment of a statute could remove some of the uncertainty, but whether this would be at the expense of justice and flexibility is a problem.[14] Should the law specify categories of relationship into which a claimant must fit to recover? Should the criteria for proximity in time and space be defined? Surely, the only limits that could be so defined are 'reasonable' proximity in time and space, which are hardly certain. A statute could remove the necessity for direct sight or sound of the accident or its immediate aftermath, and allow recovery where the claimant is informed by a third person, subject to the claimant proving that it was the accident that caused the injury, rather than his mind imagining what the accident and its effects were. A

....

14 The concluding paragraph of an essay question should refer back to the question and attempt to answer it directly; avoid writing 'all you know' about a topic without focusing on the question.

statute would not at a stroke solve all of the problems associated with nervous shock, but it could introduce a welcome degree of certainty and logic into this area of the law. Guidance in putting together such a statute could be taken from the draft bills which the English and Scottish Law Commissions appended to their reports on psychiatric injury, in 1998 and 2004 respectively.[15] However, the length of time since these reports were published suggests that there is little parliamentary appetite for such legislation.

QUESTION 8 ---

A group of young people, aged between 13 and 15, were hanging around outside a parade of shops. During some light-hearted jostling, one youth, Raymond, picked up an empty plastic bottle and threw it. The bottle hit Dirk in the face and his eye began to bleed. In the general angry confusion which followed, a waste bin was set on fire. Sam, a passerby who had some first aid training, decided not to try to help Dirk as he did not want to get involved, but he did phone for an ambulance and the fire brigade on his mobile.

When the fire brigade arrived it hosed down the bin and the surrounding area vigorously to ensure the fire was out. A stream of water from the hoses flooded into a nearby cellar, where Bilbo kept his collection of rare books, ruining many of them. On the way back to the fire station, a piece of equipment that had been insecurely attached to the fire engine fell off and injured a passing cyclist.

The ambulance took some time to arrive, and when Dirk was eventually examined in hospital, the doctor said that he would lose the sight of one eye, but if he had been treated earlier there would have been a 50/50 chance of his sight being saved.

Local residents subsequently told Dirk's mother that they had repeatedly asked the police to move the young people away because of their anti-social behaviour, but no action had been taken. She and Bilbo believe that if there had been more police patrolling the area the damage would not have occurred.

▶ Advise Dirk, Bilbo and the cyclist as to the legal position in tort.

How to Answer this Question

This case centres on aspects of duty, especially of the emergency services, and causation, two of the three central features in a negligence action. This is one of the situations where establishing duty is not straightforward, largely for policy reasons, and gives an opportunity for you to display awareness of this issue. However, it is not an essay on policy, and as there are other aspects to cover as well, your discussion of this should be kept relatively brief.

....

15 Demonstrating awareness of official reports on the topic under consideration will add quality to the answer.

You will need to look at:

- ❖ liability in negligence and trespass to the person of young people /children;
- ❖ liability for omissions;
- ❖ duty of care owed by emergency services;
- ❖ standard of care required in an emergency;
- ❖ causation in fact and law.

Applying the Law

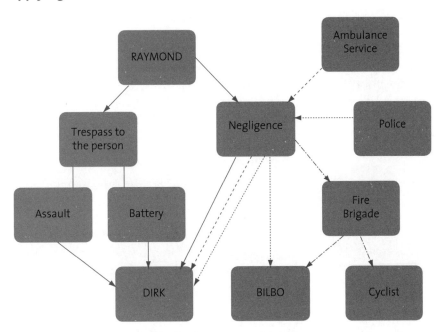

This diagram demonstrates potential liability to Dirk, Bilbo and the cyclist.

ANSWER

This question concerns aspects of duty, breach and causation.[16]

In relation to the possible liability of Raymond, it could be argued that he owed a duty of care to his neighbour, Dirk, who a reasonable person would foresee could be harmed if he did not take sufficient care, on straightforward *Donoghue* neighbour principles. However, as we are told that Raymond is at most 15 years old, it may be that he is considered too

16 This problem question covers a wide range of potential liability, and will need careful planning (see diagram). Time spent planning a problem question answer will not be wasted, especially when it is complex.

young to foresee the consequences of his actions, as in *Mullin v Richards* (1998). In that case, the court decided that an 'ordinarily prudent and reasonable' 15-year-old would not foresee the risk of a plastic ruler breaking during the 'play fight' and was thus not liable. Although there is no set age at which a child or young person can be said to have tortious liability, in contrast to the criminal law, the court will ask whether a reasonable child of the age of the defendant would foresee the risk. In *Orchard v Lee* (2009), it was held that a child would have to act with a 'very high degree of carelessness' to be found liable in negligence.[17]

Alternatively, Dirk could claim against Raymond in trespass to the person. This would involve establishing that the bottle was intended to hit someone, but it is not necessary to show that Raymond intended to apply force to Dirk specifically, if he had 'transferred intent' as in *Livingstone v Ministry of Defence* (1984). There is doubt as to whether it has to be done with a 'hostile' intent (*Wilson v Pringle* (1986)). In *Re F*, Lord Goff suggested that a 'prank that got out of hand' could be a battery, as could be said to be the case here. We are not told whether Dirk saw the bottle coming towards him, when it would be an assault and battery, rather than only a battery if he was not looking, as he would not be in fear.

No claim for contributory negligence would be available for an intentional tort such as trespass (*Pritchard v Co-Op Group* (2011)).

Sam cannot be liable for failure to act, or his omission, as he was under no obligation to do so; as expressed by Lord Keith in *Yuen Kun-Yeu v Attorney General for Hong Kong* (1988) there is no liability in English law if someone 'sees another about to walk over a cliff with his head in the air, and forbears to shout a warning'.[18]

The courts have been reluctant to impose a duty of care on the emergency services, although one can exist in limited circumstances. This is due in large part to policy considerations, which were well rehearsed in the House of Lords in *Hill v Chief Constable of W. Yorks* (1989) and the Court of Appeal in *Capital and Counties v Hampshire Fire Brigade* (1997), as it is argued that the emergency services would act defensively and divert resources from the public generally if they had to be concerned about individual actions against them. It is highly unlikely, following the reasoning in *Hill* and subsequent cases involving the police, that it would be held that there was sufficient proximity between Dirk and the police to create a duty (*Van Colle v Chief Constable of Herts* (2006) and *Smith v Chief Constable of Sussex* (2008)). The situation might have been different if the police had been aware of previous threats made by Raymond to Dirk, and had placed Dirk under some sort of special protection, but this is unlikely given the known facts and

---

17   Short phrases quoted from the cases that are cited will add to the quality of the answer.
18   Being able to quote from a named judge will add to the quality of the answer.

the decision of the House of Lords in *Van Colle* and *Smith*.[19] Given this, it is even less likely that Bilbo could maintain a successful claim against the police. Even if a duty was owed which was breached, the police would no doubt rely on the *novus actus interveniens* of the fire brigade (see below).

In the case of the fire brigade, the position is that the fire brigade is not obliged to attend and will only be liable to an individual if the position is made worse by their actions (*Capital and Counties* (1997)). This means that Bilbo may find it difficult to demonstrate that a duty was owed, but the facts seem to indicate that the firemen did not take reasonable care and thus breach, at least, could be established. The normal rule as to whether a type of loss that is somewhat unexpected, like the valuable books here, is the 'eggshell skull' rule, which means that the defendant must take the claimant as s/he finds him/her as far as their physical characteristics are concerned (*Smith v Leech Brain* (1962)). Here there is property damage about which the courts take a more restrictive view and so it may be held to be too remote. It is fair to say therefore that Bilbo has little chance of recovering his loss from either the police or the fire service, and will have to rely on his own personal insurance, if any.[20]

The cyclist could sue the fire service in negligence as it is well established that one road user owes a duty to another (*Nettleship v Weston* (1977)). The fire service would no doubt argue that the standard of care required in an emergency is lower than normal (*Watt v Hertfordshire County Council* (1954)). However, it should be noted that the accident occurred on the way <u>back</u> from attending the emergency, so this argument may not be successful.

In the case of the ambulance, the courts have said that the position is closer to the NHS which owes a duty to individual patients once a specific call has been accepted (*Kent v Griffiths* (2000)). We would thus have to discover exactly what Sam said when he phoned for help – if he just gave a general request for assistance the court may hold no duty existed. If the duty was established, it would still be necessary to establish that the reason for the delay was lack of reasonable care by the ambulance driver, and not for example a justifiable reason such as, maybe, traffic congestion.

Whether Raymond and/or the ambulance service could be liable for the loss of sight is a question of causation. The normal position is the application of the 'but for' test (*Barnett v Chelsea and Kensington Hospital Management Committee* (1969)), and anything less than a 50 per cent chance would fail (*Hotson v East Berkshire Health Authority* (1987)). Therefore here, Dirk would need to establish not only that a duty was owed which was

....

19 Some speculation is allowable if it can be demonstrated that it is clear how the law applies to the facts given.

20 Commenting on the insurance position demonstrates an awareness of this issue.

breached, but that considered medical evidence can be provided to show that it was more likely than not that had he been examined earlier he would not have lost his sight, i.e. more than a 50 per cent chance. In *Rahman v Arearose Ltd* (2001), which involved a hospital's negligence on top of an initial injury caused by another, there was an attempt to divide up liability between successive defendants, but Raymond could argue that the delay caused by the ambulance was a *novus actus interveniens* which broke the chain of causation (*Knightley v Johns* (1982)). As it is unlikely that Raymond will be in a position to fulfil any award of damages made against him, even if found liable, it would be preferable for Dirk to pursue the ambulance service (depending on the evidence of what was said and proof that the delay was due to lack of care) which would be in a position to pay him compensation.[21]

QUESTION 9

To what extent has the **Compensation Act 2006** been successful in dealing with the problems associated with the 'compensation culture'?

How to Answer this Question

This essay requires an explanation of what the compensation culture is, what problems are associated with it and how far the Act has been successful in tackling them.

Answer Structure

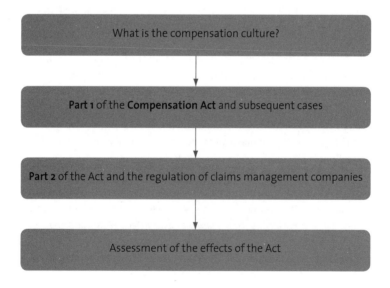

What is the compensation culture?

Part 1 of the **Compensation Act** and subsequent cases

Part 2 of the Act and the regulation of claims management companies

Assessment of the effects of the Act

---

21   Including a practical consideration like this at the end of your answer will demonstrate that the realities of the situation are appreciated.

ANSWER

The **Compensation Act 2006** was introduced largely to counter the perceived problems created by the compensation culture. This phenomenon has been described by the government as one where 'people believe that they can seek compensation for any misfortune that befalls them, even if no one else is to blame'. It has the pejorative meaning that many of the claims made are at best frivolous or at worst fraudulent. Evidence of the problems caused by the compensation culture was produced by the government's Better Regulation Task Force report *Better Routes to Redress* (2004).[22] Although the report found that the huge increase in successful claims was largely illusionary, it concluded that the perception that this was the case had lead to 'risk averse' behaviour ranging from a decrease in school trips and activities to a failure of businesses to invest in new products or move away from well-tested procedures.

The Act itself is in two parts, the majority of which is directly aimed at the compensation culture, while **section 3** gave the government the opportunity to reverse a decision of the House of Lords in relation to asbestos-related diseases.

Section 1 of the Act is targeted towards both the torts of negligence and breach of statutory duty. It is aiming to deal with the perception that people, and particularly organisations, are becoming risk-averse. In other words, there is a fear of litigation, the result of which could prevent certain activities from happening. This issue has been considered by the media in relation to issues such as schools no longer taking pupils on educational trips and the social utility in determining a duty of care. The section is supposed to reflect the fact that there is a basic standard of care, that of the reasonable person (*Blyth v Birmingham Waterworks* (1856)), the breach of which can lead to an action in negligence. What will amount to 'reasonable care' in any given circumstance may vary due to a multitude of factors: for example, what might be required to prevent harm in one circumstance may be too much of an imposition on the defendant (*Latimer v AEC Ltd* (1952)) and the law is stated to be intended to 'remind' people and organisations about this fact. It is clear that it does not alter the standard of care or the situations in which a duty of care may actually be owed. It does, however, present some uncertainty. The Act refers to so-called 'desirable activities' to which the courts should have regard when considering the standard of care, but is silent on the meaning of the term.

There has been very little litigation directly on **section 1** of the Act, the first reported case being *Hopps v Mott MacDonald & the Ministry of Defence* (2009), where it was used in a case concerning a civilian injured in Iraq. The Act was said to have retrospective effect as it simply restated existing law, and interestingly, the 'desirable activities' in **section 1** were not to be restricted to social or leisure activities but could include the reconstruction of a

---

22 Being able to refer by name and date to government reports will add to the quality of the answer.

war damaged country. In the case of *Cole v Davis Gilbert* (2007), Mrs Cole injured her spine by tripping over on a village green, apparently after having caught her foot in a hole left from where the maypole had been erected. It was held by the Court of Appeal that there was no breach of duty by any of the defendants because as Lord Justice Scott Baker concluded: 'If the law courts were to set a higher standard of care than what is reasonable, the consequences would quickly be felt. There would be no fetes, no maypole dancing and no activities that have come to be a part of the English village green for fear of what might go wrong.'[23] This case illustrates the point, which was made by the government at the time, that the Act did not represent a change in the law, but was just a statutory statement of it, which perhaps had the effect of bringing the consequences of their decisions to the forefront of the judges' minds. Some commentators have argued that it was unnecessary to do so and that this was 'legislation as PR', especially in the light of the decision of the House of Lords in *Tomlinson v Congleton BC* (2003) where the House of Lords dealt robustly in denying compensation to a trespassing swimmer, and roundly condemned the compensation culture.

The case of *Perry v Harris* (2008), where a child was injured accidentally by another child on a bouncy castle, is another case which can perhaps be used to demonstrate that, without specifically mentioning the **2006 Act**, the approach of the courts has changed. The Court of Appeal found that there was no liability on the parents who had hired the bouncy castle for their children's party, as it was 'a tragic accident' that happened 'without fault'. But the difficulties of dispelling the myth of the compensation culture can be demonstrated by the fact that there was far more press coverage of the first instance decision, where the parents *were* held liable, than the reversal by the Court of Appeal. A more recent example of the trend can be seen in *Bowen v National Trust* (2011), where the Trust were not liable for the death and injuries caused when a branch fell on child visitors, and *XVW & YZA v Gravesend Grammar Schools for Girls* (2012), where a school was not liable for the rape of pupils during an overseas trip, although again the Act was not specifically referred to in these judgments.[24]

Section 2 of the Act has been referred to as a 'rather bizarre clarification of an existing point', as it simply restates the position that giving an apology does not amount to admitting liability. The idea behind this section was to encourage people to give apologies, in situations where, for example, an operation has not turned out successfully, rather than saying nothing for fear of subsequent civil action. Research has shown that many people state that if they had at least been offered an apology, and maybe some explanation, in those circumstances they would not be driven to pursue litigation. However it is difficult to see how it can be measured whether this section has been a success.

---

23 Use of an appropriate quote will strengthen your argument.
24 Knowledge of up to date case law will add quality to the answer.

Section 3 of the Act directly addresses the decision in the case of *Barker v Corus* (2006). The case concerned a series of claimants who had (or who were married to people who had) contracted mesothelioma, a cancer caused by exposure to asbestos fibres, through their employment with the defendants. The allegation was that they had been negligently exposed to the asbestos. There had been a decision of the House of Lords some four years previously (*Fairchild v Glenhaven Funeral Services Ltd & ors* (2002)).

The House of Lords in *Barker* made a decision in relation to the apportionment of damages. The essence of that decision was that, provided that the claimant had actually contracted mesothelioma, all of the defendants could be held liable for the negligent exposure to the asbestos dust. However, unlike the decision in *Fairchild*, all of the defendants could only be held to be liable according to the relative contribution they had made to the chance of the claimant actually having contracted the disease. Essentially, that meant that the liability would be classed a several liability, whereas in *Fairchild*, the presumption, if not the decision itself, was that liability would be joint and several. It meant that a claimant would run the risk of an employer being insolvent, and therefore losing a proportion of the damages, and that the claimant would be faced with the burden of tracing all of the potential defendants. Considering that the disease is crippling and almost inevitably fatal, this would cause great hardship to either the claimant or their descendants. There was considerable outcry against this decision, and the government took the opportunity of the fact that the Compensation Bill was going through Parliament to take action. **Section 3** therefore reversed the effect of the *Barker* judgment and, as a result, a claimant can claim the full damages from any liable defendant. Cases in relation to this dreadful disease continue to reach the courts, as with *Sienkiewicz v Greif (UK) Ltd* (2011), where again a causation issue had to be dealt with by the Supreme Court.[25]

Part II of the Act lead to the establishment of the Claims Management Regulation Unit under the auspices of (now) the Ministry of Justice in 2007, involving registration and regulation of claims management services (or so called 'claims farmers'), which are defined as 'advice or other services in relation to the making of a claim' **s 4(1)**. This part of the Act may be said to have been more obviously successful, as it has lead to a disappearance of the worst forms of marketing for 'no win-no fee' services. It was clearly targeted towards the perceived mischief of claims proliferation, particularly where the claims are lacking merit, and nearly 900 companies had been registered by 2012. However, the situation is not entirely resolved, as witness the recently expressed concerns about the way these companies have dealt with compensation for mis-sold PPI insurance. It was felt that many consumers were paying out a significant proportion of their winnings to these companies when they could have gone directly to the banks

---

25 Although this does not specifically touch on the compensation culture, some mention should be made of this section for the sake of a thorough review of the Act.

themselves, having been subjected to aggressive marketing techniques such as constant texting and cold calling. There have been calls for even tighter controls of these companies.

Apart from the above, there is other recent evidence to suggest that the **2006 Act** has not yet been successful in dealing with the problems associated with the compensation culture. For example, Lord Young's report, entitled 'Common Sense Common Safety' (2010) called for a reduction on restrictions preventing beneficial activities; the private members' bill the Compensation Act 2006 (Amendment) Bill 2010 unsuccessfully attempted to deter the fear of litigation by changing the burden to ensure that courts considering a claim of negligence apply a *presumption* that defendants undertaking a desirable activity have satisfied the relevant standard of care; and in 2012, the Prime Minister pledged to deal with the issue again in relation to whiplash injuries. The media regularly decry its existence, and are likely to continue to do so whenever a large settlement becomes public, such as a £10.8 million 'payout' to a brain damaged child in May 2012.[26] In any assessment of the Act and its effect on the compensation culture, it should also be borne in mind that a willingness to engage in litigation and the relative ease of access to justice that a 'compensation culture' encourages is not necessarily a wholly bad thing.

26 Again, recent and topical material will improve the authority of your answer.

Negligence – Breach, Causation and Remoteness of Damage

3

INTRODUCTION

Questions involving breach, causation and remoteness of damage are popular with examiners, either as questions in their own right or as part of a question. Thus, the rule that a tortfeasor takes his victim as he finds him often features as part of a negligence question.

Checklist ✔

Students must be familiar with the following areas:

(a) breach:

- standards and guidelines used to assess whether the defendant's actions are in breach of a duty of care;
- *res ipsa loquitur*;

(b) causation:

- the 'but for' test and the decision in *Fairchild v Glenhaven Funeral Services Ltd* (2002);

(c) remoteness:

- reasonable foreseeability and the eggshell skull rule;
- *novus actus interveniens*.

QUESTION 10

One day, while walking home, William trips and falls, damaging his knee. Several days later, while driving to work, he sees Victor crossing the road and brakes to avoid running into him. Unfortunately, due to the pain in his knee, he cannot fully press his brake pedal and, as a result, he runs into Victor. The collision occurs at a fairly slow speed and a normal person would only have suffered bruising as a result, but Victor has brittle bones and suffers two broken legs and a number of broken ribs. He is taken to the local hospital where, due to an administrative mistake, his right arm is amputated.

▶ Advise Victor.

How to Answer this Question

This is a straightforward question on breach and causation, together with remoteness of damage, the eggshell skull rule and *novus actus interveniens*. As it is relatively simple, care must be taken to discuss the relevant legal principles in depth.

The following points need to be discussed:

- ❖ breach of duty by William;
- ❖ William takes Victor as he finds him;
- ❖ amputation of the arm – *novus actus interveniens* by the hospital.

Applying the Law

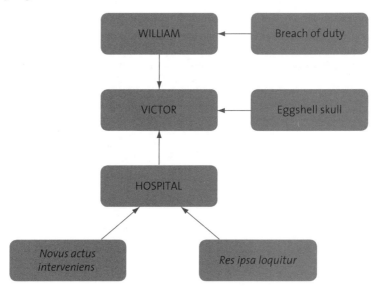

ANSWER

It is well-established law that a road user owes a duty of care to other road users, including pedestrians (*Donoghue v Stevenson* (1932); *Roberts v Ramsbottom* (1980)). Where a duty of care has previously been found to exist, there is no need to apply the modern incremental formulation preferred by the House of Lords in *Caparo Industries plc v Dickman* (1990) or *Murphy v Brentwood District Council* (1990). One could also note the statement of Potts J at first instance in *B v Islington Health Authority* (1991), in which he stated that, in personal injury cases, the duty of care remains as it was pre-*Caparo* – namely, the foresight of a reasonable person (as in *Donoghue*), a finding that does not appear to have been disturbed on appeal (1992).[1]

---

1   In negligence answers, it may be that you have prepared a set response in relation to establishing 'duty' in most unexceptional situations, as here. However, do not overlook including it, as it is a crucial element of the answer.

As William owes Victor a duty of care, we must consider whether he is in breach of this duty of care. The standard of care required is the objective one of a reasonable person. Thus, in *Blyth v Birmingham Water Works* (1856), Alderson B stated that 'negligence is the omission to do something which a reasonable man, guided upon those conditions which ordinarily regulate the conduct of human affairs, would do, or the doing of something which a prudent and reasonable man would not do'. It is important that the correct question is addressed – the question is not 'did William act reasonably?', but 'what would a reasonable person, placed in his position, have done, and did William meet that standard?'. Applying this objective standard to car drivers, it can be seen that the correct standard to adopt is that of the reasonable, competent driver. Thus, it is irrelevant that a particular driver is a learner (*Nettleship v Weston* (1971)) or, through no fault of his own, he cannot fully control the car for medical reasons and he is otherwise not at fault (*Roberts*). To hold otherwise, as Megaw LJ pointed out in *Nettleship*, would mean adopting a variable standard that could not logically be confined to car drivers and would have to be a universal principle, giving great uncertainty and making it impossible to arrive at consistent decisions. Thus, William must be judged by the standard of the reasonable, competent driver, and he clearly does not meet this standard. The fact that this is due to a medical reason that is outside his control is irrelevant (*Roberts*), although in *Mansfield v Weetabix* (1998), the Court of Appeal held that where a medical reason that was not, and could not reasonably have been, known to the defendant brought his performance below that objective standard of care, it was a factor that could be considered in deciding the defendant's negligence. William's knowledge in this situation would ensure his breach.

Having decided that William is in breach of his duty, we must determine whether his breach caused Victor's injuries. Turning first to Victor's broken legs and ribs, it is clear, applying the 'but for' test proposed by Lord Denning in *Cork v Kirby MacLean* (1952) and illustrated further in *Barnett v Chelsea and Kensington Hospital Management Committee* (1969), that this damage would not have happened but for his breach of duty. Hence William will be liable for Victor's broken legs, provided that the damage is not too remote. The test for remoteness of damage is that the damage must have been reasonably foreseeable (*The Wagon Mound* (1961)). Therefore, the important question is just what damage has to be foreseeable to render that damage not too remote. Also for harm to the person, as long as some personal injury is foreseeable, it does not matter that the exact consequences were unforeseeable (see, for example, *Dulieu v White* (1901); *Smith v Leech Brain* (1962)). Thus, William must take his victim as he finds him – that is, with brittle bones.

We must also consider whether William is responsible for Victor's amputated arm by applying the 'but for' test. As a matter of pure logic, but for William's negligence Victor would not have been at the hospital and the amputation would not have taken place. But we need to consider whether there has been a break in the chain of causation – that is, whether the negligence of the hospital constitutes a *novus actus interveniens*. The new act is that of a third party over which William has no control. To break the chain of causation, it must be something unwarrantable, a new cause that disturbs the sequence of events and something that can be described as either unreasonable or extraneous or extrinsic (*per* Lord Wright in *The Oropesa* (1943)). Thus, the defendant will remain liable if the act of the third party is not truly independent of the defendant's negligence. It seems in William's case that the act of the hospital does satisfy this criterion. In *Knightley v Johns* (1982), a third party acted negligently. The court held that negligent conduct was more likely to break the chain of causation than non-negligent conduct and that, in *Knightley*, there were so many errors and departures from common-sense procedures that the chain of causation had been broken. Looking at the facts of Victor's case, it seems that the hospital has been negligent, and there must have been some errors and departures from common-sense procedures. Hence, the chain of causation has been broken. Thus William is not liable for the amputated arm; liability for this damage will rest with the hospital.

As Victor was presumably under anaesthetic when his arm was amputated, he may have problems in proving the hospital's lack of care. However, in such a situation, he can rely on the maxim *res ipsa loquitur* – that is, the thing speaks for itself. Where the maxim applies, the court may be prepared to find a breach of duty in the absence of specific evidence of the defendant's actions (see, for example, *Scott v London and St Katherine's Docks* (1865)).

For the maxim to be applicable, it must be shown:

(a) that the defendant is in control of the thing that caused injury to the claimant;
(b) that the accident would not have occurred in the ordinary course of events without negligence; and
(c) that there is no other explanation for the accident.

An example of the maxim in action is *Mahon v Osborne* (1939), in which a surgeon left a swab in a patient's body. A more recent example in a medical context can be seen in *Lillywhite v University College London Hospitals NHS Trust* (2005), in which it was observed that there would be strong evidence of negligence if an unexplained accident were to occur in relation to something under the defendant's control and if medical evidence were to show that this would not have occurred had proper care been taken. The application of the maxim will not shift the burden of proof, which will remain on Victor throughout (*Ng Chun Pui v Lee Chuen Tat* (1988)), but it will allow the court to draw an inference of negligence (*Ng Chun Pui*, *per* Lord Griffiths).

Thus, Victor is advised to sue William in respect of his broken legs and ribs, and the hospital in respect of the amputated arm.[2]

---

2   You should try to make time in an exam to sum up your answer at the end, as, apart from providing a conclusion, it gives you the opportunity to check that you have not made careless errors in relation to the names of the claimants/defendants.

QUESTION 11 ---

Last winter Stacey was driving in excess of the speed limit in a heavy snow storm when she skidded and crashed her car, injuring herself, killing Ahmet (the driver of a car coming in the opposite direction), and resulting in significant back and neck injuries to Leona (her passenger).

Stacey was airlifted to hospital, where she was treated for facial injuries by Jackie, a junior doctor who was nearing the end of a double shift. Stacey's skin became infected, with the result that she had to have skin grafts. Jackie unfortunately prescribed the wrong anti-infection drug, and subsequent tests indicated that this error might have deprived Stacey of a 30 per cent chance of a complete recovery from her injuries without the need for skin grafts, although it is not clear at all whether she would have made a full recovery.

A few weeks after the accident Leona began to suffer from severe cramps in her back. It is known that the injury she suffered in the accident could cause this cramping, although it could also be caused by sciatica from which she had suffered in the past. Returning from a party, she climbed over a low wall to take a short-cut, which she had regularly done in the past. As she did so her back cramped and she fell to the ground, breaking her leg.

▶ Advise the parties of their potential claims and liabilities in the tort of negligence.

How to Answer this Question

The question is a relatively straightforward negligence scenario, which adds a couple of layers of complexity in terms of the causation aspects.

The following points need to be discussed:

- ❖ (briefly) the establishment of a duty of care and breach of it;
- ❖ the issue of a loss of a chance;
- ❖ supervening causes;
- ❖ intervening acts.

Applying the Law

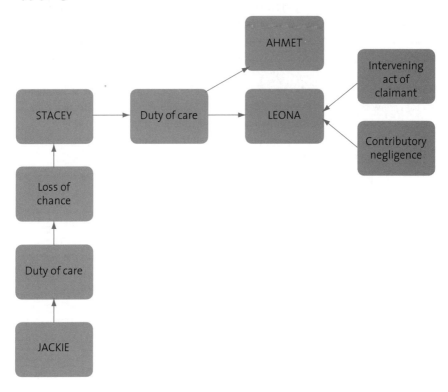

ANSWER ---

This question requires an examination of the tort of negligence, specifically in relation to establishing the necessary causative links to permit recovery. A successful claim in the tort of negligence requires that a claimant prove that they were owed a duty of care by the defendant, who subsequently breached the duty, and that foreseeable damage was caused as a result of that breach. It is clear enough that Stacey would owe a duty of care to both Ahmet and Leona. This duty would arise on the basis of the neighbour principle outlined by Lord Atkin in *Donoghue v Stevenson* (1932), as they are persons who Stacey could reasonably and foreseeably be likely to affect as a result of any negligent act on her part; and a duty to take care not to cause personal injury does not require that a full *Caparo* assessment be undertaken (*B v Islington Health Authority* (1991) *per* Potts J). Whether she breached that duty would depend on ascertaining if her conduct fell below the standard expected of a reasonable person (*Blythe v Birmingham Waterworks* (1856); *Glasgow Corporation v Muir* (1943)).[3] As she was driving she would be assessed by the

....

3   In negligence answers, it may be that you have prepared a set response in relation to establishing 'duty' in most situations, as here. However, do not overlook including it, as it is a crucial element of the answer.

standard of the reasonable driver (*Nettleship v Weston* (1971)), and driving at excessive speed in poor weather conditions would, it is submitted, fall well short of that standard. Ahmet would clearly not have died and Leona would not have suffered injury to her neck and back 'but for' Stacey's breach of duty (*Barnett v Chelsea and Kensington Hospital Management Committee* (1969)). Both would thus easily satisfy the requirement of proving factual causation. The test for legal causation is reasonable foreseeability of the type of damage suffered (*The Wagon Mound (No 1)* (1961)). In this case, it is clear that personal injury would be a reasonably foreseeable harm 'type': the extent of that harm (*Hughes v Lord Advocate* (1963); *Page v Smith* (1996)) is not taken into account. So, at a basic level, Stacey is immediately liable in negligence for the initial damage suffered.

Stacey's own injuries were as a result of her negligence. However, when she presented at the hospital, she would be entitled to expect that she would be treated adequately. Jackie, as a healthcare professional, would owe a duty of care, by virtue of the tests above. She would be judged by reference to the skill level of the reasonable person with her skill (*Bolam v Friern Barnett Hospital Management Committee* (1957)); the fact that she was a junior doctor would have no bearing (*Wilsher v Essex AHA* (1988)) on establishing whether she fell below the standard of care expected of her. By prescribing the wrong drug she is clearly in breach of her duty of care. The crucial issue here, though, is the extent to which she has *caused* Stacey foreseeable damage or any damage at all.

The burden of proving the causal link between Jackie's misprescribing and Stacey's failure to recover is initially one of fact and falls on Stacey who is required to prove causation on a balance of probabilities. The facts indicate that this may be difficult for her. In recent years there has been consideration of the concept that a defendant's negligence deprived the claimant of the opportunity of avoiding a certain result – so called 'loss of a chance'. The issue was considered in *Hotson v East Berkshire AHA* (1987), where the loss of a 25 per cent chance of a complete recovery was held not to give rise to a cause of action. Here the original misdiagnosis was held, on a balance of probabilities, not to have caused the subsequent disability in that it was likely to have happened even without the negligence of the defendant. The issue was revisited in *Gregg v Scott* (2005) where Baroness Hale commented that the difficulties of trying to establish liability for loss of a chance mean that it would not be desirable to do so.[4] This was especially so, given that an action would lie for damage that was *actually* caused by a doctor's negligence. It would appear unlikely that Stacey would succeed, but were she to do so it would be Jackie's employer, ultimately, who would be liable, through the principle of vicarious liability, as Jackie would have been acting in the course of her employment (*Lister v Helsey Hall* (2001)).

Leona's claim for her broken leg should be examined next. The issue is one of causation and the extent to which Stacey can be held to be liable for her further injury. Leona has a

4   Referencing the view of a particular judge, as here, adds to the quality of the answer.

claim in negligence against Stacey for her damaged back, as established above. It may be that the further injury suffered as a result of the cramping was an aggravation of that negligence, enabling a claim for the leg. First it would need to be shown on a balance of probabilities that it was the accident injuries that caused the cramping and not a recurrence of the sciatica. Assuming this was able to be done, Leona may wish to claim against Stacey for her additional harm. She would then need to prove that the damage she had suffered was not too remote a consequence of Stacey's breach of duty.

At this stage Stacey could point to the fact that what had actually happened was a *novus actus interveniens*, or intervening act. The effect of such an act, if it is found to apply, is to break the chain of causation from the defendant's breach of duty to the harm suffered by the claimant. In this case, if an intervening act was established, it would mean that Stacey would be exonerated from liability. An intervening act may arise through the action of a third party (*The Oropesa* (1943); *Knightly v Johns* (1982)), through an act of nature (*Carslogie Steamship Co Ltd v Royal Norwegian Government* (1952)), or even an act of the claimant themselves (*McKew v Holland, Hannen and Cubitts* (1970); *Weiland v Cyril Lord Carpets* (1968)). Here it is Leona's action in climbing the wall that would be up for consideration. The authorities necessitate a consideration of whether her actions would be considered to be reasonable or not. If so, then according to *Weiland*, Stacey continues to be liable; if not, then as with the decision in *McKew*, where an injured defendant was held to have acted unreasonably, putting himself in a dangerous situation by descending stairs knowing his leg was prone to 'give way', Leona's actions would be said to have broken the chain. The issue has recently been revisited by the Court of Appeal in *Spencer v Wincanton Holdings Ltd* (2009) and a degree of guidance provided. The claimant in that case had suffered an injury, agreed to be the fault of the defendant, which resulted in him having a leg amputated. Sometime later, and before the case had been settled, the claimant slipped over at a petrol station and further injured himself with the result that he was permanently confined to a wheelchair. The slip occurred when the claimant did not have his prosthetic leg attached, nor was he using crutches. Instead he was balancing against his car. The question was whether or not the claimant's behaviour was reasonable. The Court of Appeal held that it was. It was not 'unfair' to maintain the chain of causation, and it was not the case that the claimant's behaviour had fallen within the type of recklessness that had been identified in *McKew*. A further question would relate to whether the person's behaviour was reasonably foreseeable. In that context the decision in *Corr v IBC* (2008) vehicles is illustrative. There it was held that the question as to whether a consequence was reasonably foreseeable needed to be judged at the time the breach took place. Thus, if Stacey could have foreseen personal injury, which she definitely could, and that injury could have then caused Leona's subsequent injury, then the subsequent injury would be foreseeable. The issue then must turn on the concept of unreasonableness: would it be unreasonable for Leona to have climbed the low wall as a short cut with the knowledge her back was injured? In *Spencer* the issue was decided for the claimant because it was not wholly unreasonable for him to have attempted the operation he did in the way that he did, and a court here would now probably proceed on that basis.

It may be that Stacey could claim that contributory negligence under the **Law Reform (Contributory Negligence) Act 1945** could apply in relation to Leona's actions. Such a finding would fall short of a break in the chain of causation, but would nonetheless limit her liability (*Sayers v Harlow UDC* (1958)). In *Spencer*, the issue was raised again and the claimant's damages award was reduced by one-third. Leona may, therefore, be subject to a reduction in any award she may get in relation to this additional damage, if it is determined that Stacey is liable at all.[5]

In conclusion, Stacey would be held liable for Ahmet's death, and most likely for the injuries suffered by Leona to her back and neck. The determination of liability in relation to Leona's subsequent injury is less straightforward, although, applying *Spencer*, it may be that the court would dispose of the issue by recourse to contributory negligence. It would seem unlikely that Jackie could be held to be liable to Stacey for her less than complete recovery.

Aim Higher

Focus on the real issues in the question and provide reasoned application. This is how you are able to demonstrate to the examiner you are fully engaged with the subject matter.

Common Pitfalls ✗

Often in a question on negligence, certain aspects are assumed (or 'a given') such as the fact that Stacey was negligent. In such cases do not waste your time addressing those points – keep the discussion to a minimum.

QUESTION 12

'[T]wo causes may both be necessary preconditions of a particular result ... yet the one may, if the facts justify that conclusion, be treated as the real, substantial, direct or effective cause and the other dismissed ... and ignored for the purposes of legal liability ...'

Per Lord Asquith in *Stapley v Gipsum Mines* (1953)

▶ **Does this statement accurately reflect the law and, if so, does it allow a judge to choose any previous act as the real cause of the claimant's damage?**

....

5   It is always worth considering whether there is an element of contributory negligence, particularly, as here, when you are told of the claimant's action.

How to Answer this Question

This question calls for a discussion of the 'but for' test of causation and some of the situations in which its application is not straightforward.

The following aspects of causation need to be discussed:

- ❖ the 'but for' test;
- ❖ pre-existing conditions;
- ❖ successive causes;
- ❖ *novus actus interveniens.*

Answer Structure

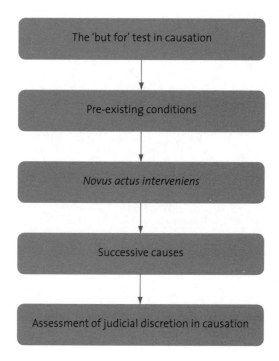

The 'but for' test in causation

Pre-existing conditions

Novus actus interveniens

Successive causes

Assessment of judicial discretion in causation

ANSWER

The test that the courts usually use in deciding whether or not a particular act was the cause of the claimant's injury is the 'but for' test. The test was elucidated by Lord Denning in *Cork v Kirby MacLean* (1952), in which he said that 'if the damage would not have happened but for a particular fault, then that fault is the cause of the damage; if it would have happened just the same, fault or no fault, the fault is not the cause of the damage'.[6]

---

6   A short quotation from a named judge will add to the quality of the answer.

A good example of this test is provided by *Barnett v Chelsea and Kensington Hospital Management Committee* (1969), in which a man went to the casualty department of a hospital complaining of vomiting. The doctor refused to examine him and sent him home. Some five hours later, he died from arsenic poisoning. It was held that the doctor was negligent in not examining the man, but that his negligence had not caused the man's death, as even if the doctor had examined and treated him, he still would have died because the poisoning could not have been detected and cured in time.

Although the 'but for' test works well in the vast majority of cases, it does give rise to problems in some situations, especially where there is more than one possible cause of the claimant's loss. Thus, where the claimant's loss is due to a pre-existing condition, rather than to the defendant's actions, the defendant may only be liable for part of the damage suffered by the claimant. In *Cutler v Vauxhall Motors* (1971), the plaintiff suffered a graze to his ankle due to the negligence of the defendants. The plaintiff had an existing varicose vein condition and, as a result of the graze, it was decided to operate immediately to cure this condition. It was held that the plaintiff could recover for the graze, but not for the operation, as the varicose vein condition would have required an operation at some time in the future in any event. *Performance Cars v Abraham* (1962) is an example of a pre-existing condition working in favour of the plaintiff, rather than against him as in *Cutler*. In both *Cutler* and *Performance Cars*, the pre-existing condition was treated as the effective cause of part of the plaintiff's loss.

Another area in which the 'but for' test can give rise to problems is where there is more than one cause of the claimant's injury: for example, where two persons both cause harm to the claimant, so that he still would have suffered harm but for the negligence of either of the defendants. In such a situation, the 'but for' test would mean that neither defendant was liable to the claimant, but a court would not reach such a conclusion in practice. This situation was considered by the Court of Appeal in *Holtby v Brigham and Cowan (Hull) Ltd* (2000). Here, the claimant suffered injury as a result of exposure to a noxious substance by two or more persons, but claimed against only one. The Court of Appeal held that the defendant was liable, but only to the extent that he had caused the claimant's injury. The courts tend to be rather proud of the fact that they approach causation as a matter of common sense, rather than from any academic or theoretical point of view. As Lord Wright stated in *Yorkshire Dale Steamship v Minister of War Transport* (1942): 'Causation is to be understood as the man in the street, and not as either the scientist or the metaphysician would understand it.'[7]

This common-sense approach to causation can be seen in those situations in which another act has occurred after the original negligent act of the defendant – that is, the *novus actus interveniens* situation. The judge must then decide which of the two acts is

7   See note 6, above.

the real, substantial, direct or effective cause. The *novus actus* may be an act of the claimant or of a third party or of nature. Taking these in turn, the latter act of the claimant that causes additional harm may be held to have broken the chain of causation between the original negligent act of the defendant and the additional harm suffered by the claimant. For example, this latter act of the claimant may be treated as the real or effective cause of the claimant's additional loss and the original negligent act of the defendant ignored for the purposes of the additional liability. However, a judge does not have a completely free choice in deciding whether or not this latter act is the effective cause of the additional harm: the decided cases lay down a rule that the latter act of the claimant will only be held to be the true cause if the additional harm is caused by an act that is unreasonable. An example is *McKew v Holland and Hannen and Cubitts* (1969), in which the plaintiff, as a result of the defendants' negligence, suffered an injury that occasionally caused him to lose control of his leg. Despite this injury, the plaintiff still went down a steep flight of stairs that had no handrail, and fell when his leg gave way. The House of Lords held that he could not recover for this injury. The House held that this act was so unreasonable that the original negligence of the defendants could be ignored for the purposes of legal liability. In contrast, consider *Wieland v Cyril Lord Carpets* (1969), in which the plaintiff, as a result of the defendants' negligence, was unable to use her bifocal spectacles in the normal manner. As a result of this, she fell down a flight of stairs. It was held that the defendants were liable for this additional harm to the plaintiff because she had not acted unreasonably in continuing to wear her bifocals. Thus, the court has a guideline in deciding whether to allow recovery for the latter damage suffered by a claimant. However, as the guideline involves a decision as to the reasonableness or otherwise of a claimant's (or other party's) conduct, it will often give the judge a certain amount of discretion. This discretion is highlighted in the case of *Spencer v Wincanton Holdings* (2009), where the Court of Appeal considered the point in favour of the claimant.

Where the latter act is that of a third party, this latter act will be treated as the real cause of the claimant's additional damage where it is something 'ultroneous, something unwarrantable, a new cause which disturbs the sequence of events, something which can be described as either unreasonable or extraneous or extrinsic' (*per* Lord Wright in *The Oropesa* (1943)). Thus, the latter act of the third party will not be treated as the true cause of the additional damage unless it is independent of the defendant's original negligence. If the act of the third party is itself negligent, the courts are usually willing to hold that this act is the true cause of the claimant's additional damage (*Knightley v Johns* (1982)). In the case of *Wright v Lodge* (1993), the Court of Appeal held that a driver who is involved in a collision partly due to his own negligence could be exonerated for responsibility for subsequent events that occurred because another driver drove recklessly if those events would not have occurred had that other reckless driver merely been negligent. Again, a guideline is available to a judge, but the decision as to whether the actual latter act is unreasonable or independent will involve a certain amount of discretion. It should perhaps be noted here that a defendant cannot rely on his own additional wrong action to break the chain of causation: *Normans Bay Ltd v Condert Brothers* (2004).

Finally, the latter act may be an act of nature, such as a violent storm, and if it is independent of the original negligence of the defendant, the defendant will not be liable for the additional consequences (*Carslogie Steamship v Royal Norwegian Government* (1952)). Again, a test is available to the judge and it will also involve a certain amount of discretion.

An additional restriction on a judge's freedom to choose which previous action was the real cause of the claimant's injury is the need for the claimant to prove causation. A claimant who has difficulties in this area will usually rely on the decision of the House of Lords in *McGhee v National Coal Board* (1973). This case is authority for the proposition that a claimant may recover if he can show that the actions of the defendant materially increased the risk of damage occurring. The House of Lords took a restrictive approach to *McGhee* in the later cases of *Kay v Ayrshire and Arran Health Board* (1987), *Hotson v East Berkshire Area Health Authority* (1987) and *Wilsher v Essex Area Health Authority* (1988). Indeed, in *Wilsher*, Lord Bridge stated that *McGhee* 'laid down no new principle of law whatsoever. On the contrary, it affirmed the principle that the onus of proving causation lies on the plaintiff.' However, in *Holtby v Brigham and Cowan Ltd* (2000) the Court of Appeal applied the traditional ratio of *McGhee*, and in *Fairchild v Glenhaven Funeral Services* (2002) the House of Lords emphatically reinstated *McGhee* and held that the statement of Lord Bridge in *Wilsher* did not accurately reflect the decision in *McGhee* and should no longer be treated as authoritative.

There are particular difficulties in relation to medical negligence problems such as *Hotson* and *Wilsher* because medical science may not be capable of identifying the exact cause of the injury. In *Bailey v Ministry of Defence* (2008), the principle of material contribution was applied to medical negligence cases.

Thus, a judge does have a certain amount of discretion in approaching causation and, indeed, in *Fairchild* the House of Lords recognised that in applying *McGhee* rather than requiring strict proof of causation they were making a policy decision to arrive at a fair result for the claimant. A similar policy decision regarding causation was reached by the House of Lords in *Chester v Afshar* (2004), a case involving the question of whether a claimant has the right to be told the risks associated with medical treatment.

Breach of Statutory Duty

INTRODUCTION

Questions on breach of statutory duty may appear in examinations and usually involve a consideration as to whether a breach of statutory duty gives rise to a cause of action in tort. Such questions can also contain issues such as causation, together with employer's liability and contributory negligence.

Checklist ✔

Students must be familiar with the following areas:

(a) whether breach gives rise to a tort:

- the presumption that enforcement provided by statute is exclusive;
- the exception to the presumption where the statute is enacted for the benefit of a class and where the claimant has suffered harm in excess of that suffered by the public at large;

(b) if breach does give rise to a tort, that the claimant must prove that:

- the action caused harm of a type regulated by statute;
- the claimant is a person whom the statute was intended to protect;
- the harm suffered is of the kind that the statute was intended to protect.

QUESTION 13

Regulations made under the (fictitious) Oil Products (Protection of Workers) Act 1997 provide, *inter alia*, that: 'Employers shall ensure that all workers engaged in the manufacture of oil products wear the protective clothing prescribed in these Regulations when they are at work or likely to come into contact with oil products, and shall ensure that such clothing is maintained in a good state of repair.' These Regulations apply to the premises of Refiners plc.

One day, Alan, who works directly with oil products, puts on a pair of protective overalls but, because he cannot be bothered to take his safety boots off, he rips them down the leg. He replaces these torn overalls on a hanger and puts on a fresh pair. Shortly afterwards, Brian, who works in the accounts section, goes into an area where it is necessary to wear overalls. He puts on the torn overalls without noticing the defect and, whilst in the oil product area, he trips over the torn leg of the overalls and falls, injuring his elbow.

▶ Advise Brian.

How to Answer this Question

This is a typical breach of statutory duty question and the following points need to be discussed:

- ❖ whether the breach gives rise to a tort;
- ❖ whether the harm is of a type intended to be prevented by statute;
- ❖ the employer's liability of Refiners;
- ❖ Alan's liability and Refiners' vicarious liability.

Applying the Law

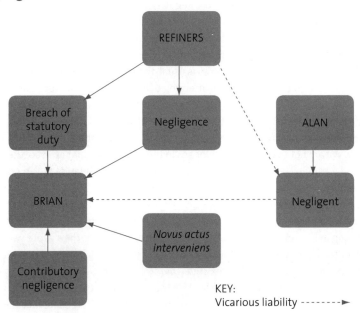

This diagram shows Refiners' primary and vicarious liability.

ANSWER

Brian has three possible causes of action against Refiners. The first is for breach of statutory duty, the second is for breach of its duty as employer and, thirdly, Refiners may be vicariously liable for Alan's negligence. We shall consider each possible action in turn.[1]

As regards possible liability for breach of statutory duty, the Regulations provide that the protective clothing worn by Brian 'must be maintained in a good state of repair'. The important question is just what standard of care the Regulations impose on Refiners. Typically, statutory obligations are either subject to a phrase such as 'so far as is reasonably practicable', when they usually add little to the common law of negligence, or are absolute, when the only question to be decided is whether the statutory regulations have been complied with or not. The reasons for not complying will be irrelevant to liability in the latter case. An example of absolute liability is the duty to fence dangerous machines imposed by s14 of the **Factories Act 1961** (*John Summers v Frost* (1955)). In the instant case, the requirement is that the employer shall ensure that such clothing is maintained in a good state of repair and, as there is no mention of reasonableness in the Regulations, the obligation is absolute and so Refiners is in breach of its statutory duty. The next question to be decided is whether or not this breach gives rise to an action in tort. The correct test is to see whether the Regulations on their true construction confer upon Brian a right of action in tort (*Cutler v Wandsworth Stadium* (1949); *X v Bedfordshire County Council* (1995)). If the Regulations address this point as, for example, s5(1) of the **Guard Dogs Act 1975**, which expressly excludes civil actions for breach of this Act, that disposes of the matter. Alternatively if, as is usual, the statute (or Regulations) is silent on the point, the court must ascertain the intention of Parliament. In the House of Lords in *Lonrho v Shell Petroleum* (1982), Lord Diplock stated that the initial presumption was that where the statute created an obligation, together with a means of enforcing that obligation (for example, by a criminal penalty), the obligation cannot be enforced in any other way. We are not told of any such means in the Regulations, but even so, the presence of a criminal penalty would not necessarily be fatal to Brian's case. In *Atkinson v Newcastle Waterworks* (1877), the imposition of a fine for breach of a statutory duty was held to be exclusive, whereas in *Groves v Lord Wimborne* (1898), the provision in the regulations of a fine for breach was held not to deny the plaintiff a cause of action. It is worth noting in this respect that, in *Groves*, as in the present case, the statute was enacted for the benefit of a class. The absence of any such provision would make it easier for Brian to claim that a right in tort existed (*Thornton v Kirklees Metropolitan Borough Council* (1979)). Lord Diplock continued to state that there were two exceptions to this general rule and one is relevant here – namely, when the statute is enacted for the benefit of a class of persons and the claimant is a member of that class. As employees are regarded as a class of persons for whose benefit industrial safety legislation is enacted, as in *Groves*, it would seem that *prima facie* Brian can sue in respect of Refiners' breach of statutory duty.

---

1   Breach of statutory duty will involve careful analysis of the words of the statute or regulations, which in an exam is probably fictitious and simplified.

However, Brian has only cleared the first hurdle here. The next matter that he must prove is that the act that caused the harm is regulated by statute, that he was one of the persons whom the statute was intended to protect and that the harm suffered was of a kind that the statute was intended to prevent.

Brian should have no problem with the first two requirements, but he will have a problem with the third. It seems from the Regulations that the requirement to provide protective clothing in good condition was to stop oil products from coming into contact with a person's body and not to prevent tripping or falling. In *Gorris v Scott* (1874), a shipowner was required by statute to provide pens on board his ship for cattle. He failed to do this and the plaintiff's cattle were swept overboard. It was held that the shipowner was not liable, because the harm that the statute was intended to prevent was the spread of contagious diseases and not the cattle being swept overboard. Similarly, in *Fytche v Wincanton Logistics plc* (2004), the House of Lords held that an employer who issued an employee with boots with steel toecaps for protection from impact injuries was not liable for an injury, frostbite, caused by a defect in the boots that had no effect on impact protection. By analogy with *Gorris* and *Fytche*, it would seem that Brian cannot bring himself under the ambit of the statute.[2]

We must next consider whether Brian can sue Refiners in negligence. As Brian's employer, Refiners owes Brian a duty of care to provide proper plant and equipment (*Smith v Baker* (1891)). Clothing comes under the definition of equipment (see, for example, s1(1) of the **Employers' Liability (Defective Equipment) Act 1969**). However, this duty is not an absolute one, but merely one to take reasonable care for employees' safety. In *Toronto Power v Paskwan* (1915), Sir Arthur Channell stated that 'if in the course of working plant becomes defective and the defect is not brought to the master's knowledge and could not by reasonable diligence have been discovered by him, the master is not liable'.[3] Interestingly, in *PRP Architects v Reid* (2007), a defective lift was held to be work equipment. The failure to maintain it led to liability under the **Provision and Use of Work Equipment Regulations 1998** for breach of statutory duty. As we are told that Brian put on the overalls 'shortly afterwards', it would seem that Refiners is not in breach of its duty regarding equipment, as it would not be reasonable to expect them to keep a constant check on the condition of the overalls. Brian could perhaps attempt to show that Refiners is in breach of its duty to provide a safe system of work, in that it has failed to provide a disposal system for torn overalls and a sufficient quantity of overalls in good condition. Refiners could reply that it does normally meet these two requirements of a safe system of work and that it was the action of Alan in replacing the overalls that was the cause of the harm. However, in *McDermid v Nash Dredging and Reclamation* (1987), the House of

---

2   Although the conclusion is that there has been no breach of statutory duty, the requirements have been thoroughly explored.

3   A quote from a named judge will add quality to your answer.

Lords held that the duty of the employer was not only to provide a safe system of work, but also to ensure that a safe system was actually operated. Such a duty is non-delegable and it would be no defence for Refiners to show that it delegated performance to an employee whom it reasonably believed to be competent to perform it (*per* Lord Brandon).

It is clear that Alan himself owes Brian a duty of care under normal *Donoghue v Stevenson* (1932) principles, in that he can reasonably foresee that any lack of care on his part may cause injury to Brian. There is no need to apply the modern incremental formulation preferred by the House of Lords in *Caparo Industries plc v Dickman* (1990) and *Murphy v Brentwood District Council* (1990). Indeed, in *B v Islington Health Authority* (1991), at first instance, Potts J stated that in personal injury cases, the duty of care remained as it was pre-*Caparo* – namely, the foresight of a reasonable person (as in *Donoghue*), a finding that does not appear to have been disturbed on appeal (1992). Alan will be in breach of this duty if a reasonable person, placed in his position, would not have acted in this way (*Blyth v Birmingham Waterworks* (1856)). It is submitted that a reasonable person would not have replaced the torn overalls on the hanger, but would have disposed of them in a safe manner. This breach must have caused Brian's injury and the 'but for' test in *Cork v Kirby MacLean* (1952) proves the required causal connection. Additionally, the injury suffered by Brian must not be too remote, in that it must be reasonably foreseeable (*The Wagon Mound (No 1)* (1961)). All that Alan need foresee is some personal injury; he need foresee neither the extent (*Smith v Leech Brain* (1962)) nor the exact manner in which the damage occurs (*Hughes v Lord Advocate* (1963)). All of these criteria are satisfied and so Alan has been negligent as regards his conduct to Brian. As Alan is an employee of Refiners and was acting in the course of his employment when this negligence took place, it follows that Refiners is vicariously liable for Alan's negligence.[4]

It could be argued that neither Refiners' breach of statutory duty nor Alan's breach of common law duty caused Brian's injury; rather, it was Brian's carelessness in failing to note the damaged overalls that caused the injury – that is, that this action by Brian constituted a *novus actus interveniens* that broke the chain of causation. A subsequent act of the claimant may amount to a *novus actus* where his conduct has been so careless that his injury can no longer be attributed to the negligence of the defendant. An examination of the two leading cases in this area, *McKew v Holland and Hannen and Cubitts* (1969) and *Wieland v Cyril Lord Carpets* (1969), shows that the test the courts apply is whether the claimant's conduct was reasonable or not and, if it is unreasonable, it will break the chain of causation, an approach considered in *Spencer v Wincanton Holdings* (2009). However, the claimant's damages in that case were reduced by one-third on the grounds of his contributory negligence. It does not seem unreasonable of Brian, who normally has no need to wear overalls, to assume that those provided by Refiners are in

----

4   See further on vicarious liability: Chapter 8.

good condition. Also, as regards Refiners' breach of statutory duty, in *Westwood v Post Office* (1974) it was held that the fact that the plaintiff was himself at fault did not allow the defendants to act in breach of their statutory duty, and that the plaintiff was entitled to assume that the defendants would comply with their statutory obligations. Thus, *Westwood* would dispose of this argument (if it were to be decided that this case fell outside of *Gorris*). It is more likely that a defence of contributory negligence might succeed in reducing Brian's damages if it could be shown that Brian had taken insufficient care for his own safety (*Jones v Livox Quarries* (1952)). As there seems to be no emergency as in *Jones v Boyce* (1816), contributory negligence cannot be ruled out.[5]

Aim Higher

Where possible bring some wider examples to the consideration to demonstrate that you are aware of the key tests, and note also that since the **Human Rights Act 1998** a claimant may wish to pursue a claim for compensation against a public body if they are the source of the harm. In this regard see *Secretary of State for Justice v Walker; Secretary of State for Justice v James* (2008) EWCA Civ 30.

Common Pitfalls ✗

Questions will often involve an employer's negligence, as there is a large body of statutory duties that is focused towards this issue. Do not fall into the trap of merely going on to discuss an employer's liability from the basis of, say, *Wilsons and Clyde Coal v English* (1938), for more on which see Chapter 5.

---

5   Consider whether Brian's actions amount to a *novus actus interveniens* or contributory negligence, even though these were not specifically asked for in the question.

Employers' Liability

INTRODUCTION

Questions on employers' liability often appear in examinations. As the topic is only a specialised branch of the law of negligence, it does not introduce any new legal concepts, but generally tests such areas as breach, causation, remoteness, contributory negligence and vicarious liability. The topic may be combined with breach of statutory duty. Students should refer to Chapters 4 and 8 for examples of questions that involve an element of employers' liability. The non-delegable nature of employers' duties should be noted, especially where independent contractors are involved.

Checklist ✔

Students must be familiar with all of the above topics and especially:

(a) the provision of competent fellow employees;

(b) the provision of safe plant and equipment;

(c) the provision of a safe place of work;

(d) the provision of a safe system of work.

QUESTION 14

Ken is employed by Lomad plc as an electrician. One day, he is asked to repair a ceiling fan located in Lomad's workplace, and is told to dismantle the fan and take it to the electrical workshop for repair. In order to save time, Ken attempts to repair the fan whilst standing on a stepladder. As he is doing so, he drops his pliers, which land on Martin's head. Because Martin is of a rather nervous disposition, he is off work for two months following this accident, rather than the two days that would be normal for such an injury. Following this incident, Ken decides to comply with his instructions and dismantles the fan but, while he is doing this, his screwdriver snaps and a piece of metal enters his eye.

▶ Advise Martin and Ken of any remedies available to them.

How to Answer this Question

This is a straightforward question on employers' liability, involving issues of both primary and secondary liability on the part of the employer.

The following points need to be discussed:

- ❖ vicarious liability for Ken's action;
- ❖ the eggshell skull rule;
- ❖ the duty to provide a safe place of work.

Applying the Law

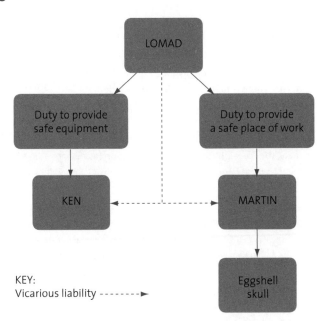

This diagram demonstrates the primary and vicarious liability of Lomad.

ANSWER

Martin will wish to sue Lomad for the harm that he has suffered, and he can sue it in respect of its primary liability to him as his employer, and its secondary liability as being vicariously liable for the negligence of Ken. As regards Lomad's primary liability, Lomad has a duty to provide Martin with a safe place of work. (This is not an absolute duty, but merely places on the employer the duty to take reasonable steps to provide a safe place of work: *Latimer v AEC* (1953); see also *Gitsham v Pearce* (1991) for a more recent example.) We must decide therefore whether Lomad has taken such reasonable steps. It has of course instructed Ken to take the fan to the electrical workshop to repair it, but the problem for Lomad is that the duty to provide a safe place of work is non-delegable. In other words, the employer may entrust the performance of this work to an employee, but he cannot thereby discharge his duty. In *McDermid v Nash Dredging and Reclamation* (1987), Lord Brandon said:

> 'The essential characteristic of the (non-delegable) duty is that, if it is not performed, it is no defence for the employer to show that he delegated its performance to a person, whether his servant or not his servant, whom he reasonably believed to be competent to perform it. Despite such delegation, the employer is liable for the non-performance of the duty.'[1]

Thus, following *McDermid*, we can see that Lomad is in breach of its duty to provide a safe place of work. Considering Lomad's secondary liability, as Ken is employed by Lomad, Lomad will be liable for any tort committed by Ken in the course of his employment. It is clear that Ken himself owes Martin a duty of care under normal *Donoghue v Stevenson* (1932) principles, in that he can reasonably foresee that any lack of care on his part may cause injury to Martin. There is no need to apply the modern incremental formulation preferred by the House of Lords in *Caparo Industries plc v Dickman* (1990) and *Murphy v Brentwood District Council* (1990). Indeed, in *B v Islington Health Authority* (1991), at first instance, Potts J stated that in personal injury cases the duty of care remained as it was pre-*Caparo* – namely, the foresight of a reasonable person (as in *Donoghue*), a finding that does not appear to have been disturbed on appeal (1992). Ken will be in breach of this duty if a reasonable person placed in his position would not have acted in this way (*Blyth v Birmingham Waterworks* (1856)) and it is submitted that a reasonable person would not have dropped a pair of pliers. This breach must have caused Martin's injury and the 'but for' test in *Cork v Kirby MacLean* (1952) proves the required causal connection. Additionally, the harm suffered by Martin must not be too remote, in that it must be reasonably foreseeable (*The Wagon Mound (No 1)* (1961)). All that Ken need foresee is some personal injury; he need foresee neither the extent (*Smith v Leech Brain* (1962)), nor the exact manner in which the damage occurs (*Hughes v Lord Advocate* (1963)). All of these criteria are satisfied and so Ken has been negligent as regards his conduct to Martin.

As Ken is an employee of Lomad and was acting in the course of his employment when this negligence took place, it follows that Lomad is vicariously liable for Ken's negligence. We are told that Ken is an electrician and, in repairing the fan, he is *prima facie* acting within the course of his employment. However, we need to consider the effect of the express prohibition that he should not repair the fan *in situ* and whether, by acting in contravention of this prohibition, he has stepped outside the course of his employment. The authorities show that acting in contravention of a prohibition will not automatically take the act outside the course of the employment: for example, *Rose v Plenty* (1976) and

1   Using a relevant quote from a judgment, properly attributed, will add to the quality of the answer. A shorter phrase, if well chosen, can also be effective.

Limpus v London General Omnibus (1862). What a prohibition can do is to limit those acts that lie within the course of the employment, but it cannot restrict the mode of carrying out an act that does lie within the course of the employment (see, for example, *Limpus*). Thus, the question that must be decided is whether Ken, in repairing the fan *in situ*, has done an unauthorised act or whether he was merely carrying out an authorised act in an unauthorised manner. The court would have to decide whether the authorised act was repairing the fan (that is, the wide approach to course of employment, as in *Rose v Plenty* and *Limpus*) or whether it was to repair the fan in the electrical workshop (that is, the narrow construction, as in *Conway v Wimpey* (1951)). It is submitted that a court would take the former approach and thus Lomad would be liable for Ken's negligence.[2]

While liability seems likely, it should be noted that, in recent years, the courts have distinguished between careless and deliberate acts, and have taken a very narrow view of the course of employment where deliberate acts are concerned (see *Heasmans v Clarity Cleaning Ltd* (1987); *Irving v Post Office* (1987)). Perhaps the most dramatic example of this approach is to be found in *General Engineering Services v Kingston and St Andrews Corp* (1989). Here, firemen who drove very slowly to the scene of a fire were held not to be within the course of their employment in so doing. They were employed to travel to the scene of the fire as quickly as reasonably possible and, in travelling as slowly as possible, they were not doing an authorised act in an unauthorised manner; rather, they were doing an unauthorised act. However, one of the grounds for the decision in *General Engineering Services* included the finding that 'this decision [that is, the slow driving] was not in furtherance of their employer's business' (*per* Lord Ackner). In Lomad's case, we are told that the reason for Ken's action was to save time – that is, it was in furtherance of the employers' business. It is thus submitted that Ken's situation is legally distinguishable from that in *General Engineering Services*.[3]

We should also consider the extent of the liability, as we are told that Martin is of a rather nervous disposition and that a normal person would not have suffered nearly as much harm. Fortunately for Martin, Ken and Lomad must take their victim as they find him.

The rule covering remoteness of damage for personal injury is that the defendant need only foresee some harm to the person (*The Wagon Mound (No 1)* (1961)). The extent of the injury is irrelevant, even if it was unforeseeable (*Dulieu v White* (1901); *Smith v Leech Brain* (1962)) – that is, Ken and Lomad must take their victim as they find him and are liable for his injuries. See, for example, *Brice v Brown* (1984), in which a plaintiff with a hysterical personality disorder recovered a substantial sum for the extremely bizarre behaviour that she suffered following her witnessing an accident to her daughter.

....

2   Take care to distinguish employers' primary liability (their own negligence) from vicarious liability (liability for their employees' negligence).

3   For more on vicarious liability, see Chapter 8.

Turning now to Ken's damage, Lomad, as his employer, is under a duty to provide Ken with safe equipment (*Smith v Baker* (1891)). It is no defence for Lomad to show that it purchased the screwdriver from a reputable supplier because, by s 1(1) of the **Employers' Liability (Defective Equipment) Act 1969**, where the defect is attributable to the fault of a third party, it is deemed to be attributable to negligence on the part of the employer. There is, of course, no problem in proving that a screwdriver is 'equipment' under the **Employers' Liability (Defective Equipment) Act 1969**, as the House of Lords has twice taken a wide approach to the meaning of this term (*Coltman v Bibby Tankers* (1988); *Knowles v Liverpool City Council* (1993)). Although this would appear to make life simple for Ken, it would have to be shown that the defect was attributable to the manufacturer. If the screwdriver was relatively new and it can be shown that nothing has happened since it left the manufacturers to cause the defect, the defect can be attributed to the manufacturer (*Mason v Williams and Williams Ltd* (1955)). Thus, by s 1(1), it will be attributed to negligence on the part of the employer. However, if the screwdriver had been in use for some time, it may be difficult to show that the defect was due to fault on the part of the manufacturer (see *Evans v Triplex Glass* (1936)). As the duty to provide safe appliances is not an absolute one, but merely one to take reasonable care (see *Toronto Power v Paskwan* (1915)), the **Employers' Liability (Defective Equipment) Act 1969** might not apply. If, for any reason, this is the case, then the situation is covered by *Davie v New Merton Board Mills* (1959) and Lomad will not be liable if it had not been negligent: for example, if it had purchased the screwdriver from a reputable supplier and the defect was not discoverable on reasonable examination, no liability will arise.[4]

QUESTION 15

Iambic plc owns some premises and decides to have the rather old-fashioned central heating system replaced with a modern, efficient system. It engages Lead Ltd to carry out this work and Lead Ltd sends two plumbers to Iambic's premises. While the plumbers are working, one of them carelessly leaves a blowlamp running and the partition to an office catches fire. Jenny, who is working in the office, is burnt. Peter, who is an employee of Iambic plc, carelessly leaves a screwdriver on the floor of another office, and Katherine trips over it and twists her leg. In the ensuing commotion caused by these two accidents, an unknown thief enters the premises and steals a sheepskin coat belonging to Richard, another employee of Iambic plc. Richard kept his coat in a cupboard that was not provided with a lock.

▶ Advise Jenny, Katherine and Richard.

How to Answer this Question

This is a typical employers' liability question in the sense that, while mostly involving employers' liability, it also requires a discussion of vicarious liability.

4   Take care to give the full name of the Act, and to consider the position if the Act does not apply.

The following points need to be discussed:

❖ the liability of Iambic plc for the negligence of Lead Ltd;
❖ the liability of Iambic plc for the negligence of its employees;
❖ the liability of Iambic plc for the negligence of Peter;
❖ employers' liability – the limits on the duty of care.

Applying the Law

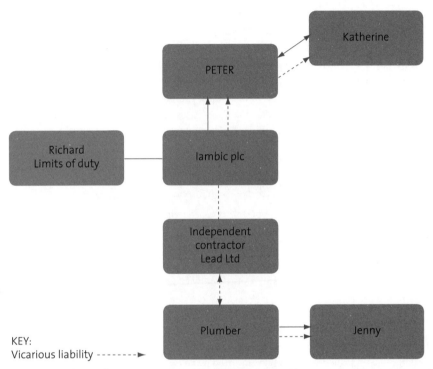

KEY:
Vicarious liability ------->

This diagram shows the primary and vicarious liability of Iambic.

ANSWER

JENNY

Considering Jenny first, we need to see against whom any cause of action might lie.[5]

It is clear that the plumber himself owes Jenny a duty of care under normal *Donoghue v Stevenson* (1932) principles, in that he can reasonably foresee that any lack of care on his

5 Dealing with the claimants individually avoids a confused answer. The time spent planning and structuring the answer to a problem question before starting to write it is never wasted.

part may cause injury to Jenny. There is no need to apply the modern incremental formulation preferred by the House of Lords in *Caparo Industries plc v Dickman* (1990) and *Murphy v Brentwood District Council* (1990) Indeed, in *B v Islington Health Authority* (1991), at first instance, Potts J stated that in personal injury cases the duty of care remained as it was pre-*Caparo* – namely, the foresight of a reasonable person (as in *Donoghue*), a finding that does not appear to have been disturbed on appeal (1992). The plumber will be in breach of this duty if a reasonable plumber placed in his position would not have acted in this way (*Blyth v Birmingham Waterworks* (1856)) and it is submitted that a reasonable plumber would not have carelessly left a blowlamp running. This breach must have caused Jenny's injury and the 'but for' test in *Cork v Kirby MacLean* (1952) proves the required causal connection. Additionally, the injury suffered by Jenny must not be too remote, in that it must be reasonably foreseeable (*The Wagon Mound (No 1)* (1961)). All that the plumber need foresee is some personal injury; he need foresee neither the extent (*Smith v Leech Brain* (1962)), nor the exact manner in which the harm occurs (*Hughes v Lord Advocate* (1963)). All of these criteria are satisfied and so the plumber has been negligent as regards his conduct to Jenny.

As the plumber is an employee of Lead Ltd, Lead Ltd will be vicariously liable for any tort committed by the plumber in the course of his employment. As we are told that 'while the plumbers are working, one of them carelessly . . .', it would seem that the plumber has been careless within the course of his employment. The fact that the carelessness is gross and its consequences are obvious will not take the action outside the course of employment (*Century Insurance v Northern Ireland Road Transport Board* (1942)). Hence, Jenny could sue Lead Ltd in respect of her injury.

From the facts of the problem, there seems to be no reason for assuming that Lead Ltd is anything other than an independent contractor. The normal rule is that an employer is not liable for the torts committed by an independent contractor during the course of the contractor's duties (*Morgan v Girls Friendly Society* (1936); *D and F Estates v Church Commissioners* (1989)). There are some situations in which liability will arise – namely, where the employer authorises the independent contractor to commit the tort (*Ellis v Sheffield Gas Consumers Co* (1853)), where he negligently chooses an incompetent contractor (*Pinn v Rew* (1916)) and where a non-delegable duty is imposed on him by common law (that is, a duty, the performance of which can be delegated but not the responsibility). The first two situations are not relevant here, but a non-delegable common law duty that may arise is that which exists where an independent contractor is employed to carry out work that is extra-hazardous (*Honeywill and Stein v Larkin Bros* (1934); *Alcock v Wraith* (1991)). In *Alcock*, the Court of Appeal held that a crucial question was: 'Did the work involve some special risk, or was it from its very nature likely to cause damage?' It is suggested that plumbing does not satisfy these criteria; the use of a blowlamp may carry some special risk, but Iambic plc could claim that the plumber's negligence was merely collateral to the performance of his work and that, as an employer, it is not liable for this collateral negligence (*Padbury v Holliday and Greenwood* (1912)). If Jenny were to sue Iambic under the **Occupiers' Liability Act 1957**, she would be met with the defence in **s 2(4)(b)** that Iambic plc acted reasonably in entrusting the work to an independent contractor, and took such steps as were reasonable to satisfy itself that the contractor was competent and that the work had been properly done. As the work in question is technical, there would be no requirement for Iambic plc to check that it had been properly done (*Haseldine v Daw* (1941)).[6]

If Jenny were to sue Iambic plc for breach of its common law duty as an employer to provide her with a safe place of work, she would be met with the defence that Iambic plc had taken reasonable steps to do so, as this duty is not absolute, but merely requires reasonable steps to be taken (*Latimer v AEC* (1953)). This situation should be distinguished from that in *McDermid v Nash Dredging and Reclamation* (1987), as in this case it was held to be no defence to breach of a non-delegable duty to show that the employer had delegated performance to a person, whether his employee or not, whom he reasonably believed to be competent to perform it (*per* Lord Brandon). In Iambic plc's case, it did not delegate the provision of a safe place of work to Lead Ltd or to the plumber.

Jenny is thus advised to sue Lead Ltd in respect of her injuries.[7]

KATHERINE

Turning now to Katherine and following the analysis we used with the plumber, we can see that Peter has been negligent as regards his conduct to Katherine, as the necessary ingredients of duty, breach and damage are all present. We are told that Peter is an employee of Iambic plc and, assuming that when he left the screwdriver on the floor he was acting within the course of his employment, Iambic plc will be vicariously liable for his negligence. In addition to this secondary liability, Iambic plc, as Katherine's employer, has a primary duty to provide Katherine with a safe place of work. This is not an absolute duty, but merely requires Iambic plc to take reasonable steps to provide a safe place of work (*Latimer v AEC* (1953); see also *Gitsham v Pearce* (1992)). We need to decide therefore whether Iambic plc has taken such steps. Iambic plc has presumably instructed Peter not to leave any obstructions on the floor, but the problem for Iambic plc is that the duty to provide a safe place of work is non-delegable. In other words, an employer may entrust

---

6   Be prepared to consider liability outside the main area of the question, as here with occupiers' liability. For more on this, see Chapter 7.

7   In reality, Jenny might find it easier (in the sense of being less personally difficult) to sue Lead Ltd rather than her own bosses.

the performance of this duty to an employee, but he cannot thereby discharge his duty. In *McDermid v Nash Dredging and Reclamation*, Lord Brandon said: 'The essential characteristic of the (non-delegable) duty is that, if it is not performed, it is no defence for the employer to show that he delegated its performance to a person, whether his servant or not his servant, whom he reasonably believed to be competent to perform it. Despite such delegation, the employer is liable for the non-performance of the duty.' Thus, following *McDermid*, we can see that Iambic plc is in breach of its duty to provide a safe place of work.

Thus, Katherine is advised to sue Iambic plc for breach of its primary duty to provide a safe place of work and as being vicariously liable for Peter's negligence.

RICHARD

Finally, we must consider Richard's situation. The courts have held consistently that the duty that an employer owes is a duty to safeguard the employee's physical safety (and this includes his mental state: *Walker v Northumberland County Council* (1994); *Daw v Intel Corporation (UK) Ltd* (2007)), but does not extend to protecting the economic welfare of the employee (*Crossley v Faithful & Gould Holdings Ltd* (2004)). This whole area was considered extensively in *Reid v Rush and Tomkins* (1990), in which this distinction was upheld. In *Deyoung v Stenburn* (1946), in a similar fact situation, it was held by the Court of Appeal that no duty arose to protect the employee's clothing from theft (see also *Edwards v West Hertfordshire General Hospital Management Committee* (1957)), hence Richard cannot sue Iambic plc for the loss of his coat. On the facts given, it seems most unlikely that he could sue either the plumber or Lead Ltd (as being vicariously liable) or Peter or Iambic plc (as being vicariously liable) for the loss of his coat, as such loss is not reasonably foreseeable and no duty of care would arise in respect of it.

This situation differs from that in *Stansbie v Troman* (1948), in which a contractor left a house unoccupied and the front door unlocked. The contractor was found liable for the subsequent theft of some property from the house, because, in that situation, it could be foreseen that a thief might enter and steal property from the house.

QUESTION 16 -

To what extent, if any, does an employer's vicarious liability for the torts of his employees and his liability for breach of statutory duty add anything at all to the liability resulting from the employer's personal duty of care?

How to Answer this Question

This is a question that requires careful thought. It would not be enough merely to list the main ingredients of vicarious liability, liability for breach of statutory duty and duty of care. What is required is a clear discussion of the limits of each of these doctrines and the extent to which any remedies that are not available through the duty of care route can be supplemented by the other two routes, and vice versa.

The following points need to be discussed:

- ❖ the elements of the employers' personal duty of care, including an employee's physical and mental condition;
- ❖ the vicarious liability of the employer, including limitations on vicarious liability;
- ❖ the statutory duties of the employer and rights of action in tort for breach.

Answer Structure

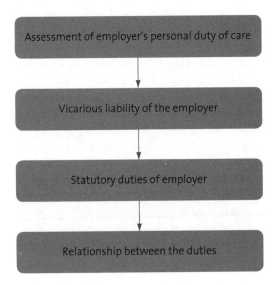

Assessment of employer's personal duty of care

Vicarious liability of the employer

Statutory duties of employer

Relationship between the duties

ANSWER

The personal duty of care that an employer owes to its employee is to take reasonable care in all of the circumstances for the employee's safety. Traditionally, this is formulated as the duty to provide competent fellow employees, properly maintained plant and equipment, and to provide a safe place and system of work (*Wilsons and Clyde Coal Co v English* (1938)). Two points should be noted immediately before these duties are considered in detail. Firstly, these duties are non-delegable, by which we mean that an employer can delegate performance of these duties, but by doing so, he cannot thereby discharge those duties. In *McDermid v Nash Dredging and Reclamation* (1987), Lord Brandon stated that the essential duty of a non-delegable duty is that: 'if it is not performed, it is no defence for the employer to show that he delegated performance to a person, whether his servant or not his servant, whom he reasonably believed to be competent to perform it. Despite such delegation, the employer is liable for the non-performance of the duty.'[8]

Secondly, the duty that an employer owes to an employee is owed to that employee personally, with all of his faults and idiosyncrasies, and is not a duty owed to his employees as an amorphous body (*Paris v Stepney Borough Council* (1951)).

Thus, in *Paris*, the employer was held to be in breach of its duty when it failed to provide with safety goggles an employee who had sight in only one eye. Although it was not usual practice to provide goggles for the work that the plaintiff carried out, the employer should have realised that, in his particular case, the consequences of an accident to his good eye would have been particularly disastrous. The criteria for breach were stated in some detail in *Stokes v Guest, Keen & Nettlefold* (1968) and these criteria were approved by the House of Lords in *Barber v Somerset County Council* (2004).

To consider these personal duties in turn, the first duty is to provide competent fellow employees. An example of this can be seen in *Hudson v Ridge Manufacturing* (1957), in which it was held that an employer was liable for the consequences of a practical joke played on one employee by a fellow employee who was known to perpetrate such jokes over a considerable period of time. In such a situation, the employer might not be vicariously liable for the actions of the practical joker, as they might well not lie within the course of his employment. Consequently, the personal duty of care of the employer goes further than his vicarious liability. This restriction on employers' vicarious liability has become particularly important in recent years, as the courts tend to take a much more restrictive approach to what constitutes the course of employment where the employee commits a deliberately wrongful act, as can be seen by the Court of Appeal decisions in *Heasmans v Clarity Cleaning* (1987) and *Irving v Post Office* (1987). In *Heasmans*, an employer was held not to be vicariously liable for the actions of an employee who was employed to clean telephones, but who made unauthorised telephone calls costing some £1,400. The Court noted that the employee was employed to clean the telephones and that, in using them, he had done an unauthorised act that had taken him outside the course of his employment. In *Irving*, the employee, who worked for the Post Office and was employed to sort mail, wrote some racial abuse concerning the plaintiff upon a letter addressed to the plaintiff. The employee was authorised to write upon letters, but only for the purposes of ensuring that the mail was properly dealt with. It was held that the employer was not vicariously liable for the actions of the employee, as in writing racial abuse, he was doing an unauthorised act and not an authorised act in an unauthorised manner. The Court stated, *per* Fox LJ, that limits had to be set to the doctrine of vicarious liability, particularly where it was sought to make employers liable

---

8   It adds to the quality of the question to be able to quote accurately from a relevant passage in a judgment.

for the 'wilful wrongdoing' of an employee.[9] Thus, in *General Engineering Services v Kingston and St Andrews Corp* (1989), the firemen who drove very slowly to a fire were held not to be in the course of their employment in so doing. They were employed to travel to the scene of fire as quickly as reasonably possible and, in travelling slowly, they were not doing an authorised act in an unauthorised manner, but were doing an unauthorised act.

In such situations, as the vicarious liability of the employer may be limited, the primary duty to take reasonable care for the employee's safety may provide the employee with a remedy.

The next personal duty of the employer is to provide properly maintained plant and equipment (*Smith v Baker* (1891)). This is a duty to do what is reasonably practicable (*Toronto Power Co v Paskwan* (1915)). However, by **s 1(1)** of the **Employers' Liability (Defective Equipment) Act 1969**, if an employee suffers personal injury in the course of his employment due to a defect in equipment provided by his employer and the defect is due wholly or partly to the fault of a third party (whether identified or not), the injury is deemed to be also due to negligence on the part of the employer. Hence, an employer cannot discharge its duty to provide safe equipment by simply purchasing equipment from a reputable supplier and its common law duty has been extended by statute from one that requires the exercise of reasonable care to what is, in effect, an absolute duty.

The employer is also under a duty to provide a safe place of work, again subject to taking steps that are reasonably practicable (*Latimer v AEC* (1953)). Similarly, the employer must not only provide such a system, but also ensure that it is operated safely (*McDermid v Nash Dredging and Reclamation* (1987)). The Supreme Court was given the opportunity to review this duty in relation to the level of noise at work in *Baker v Quantum Clothing Group Ltd* (2011), and the case provides clarity in regards to employers' liability and the standard of care expected from an employer to employees. The above duties extend not only to safeguarding the employee's physical condition, but also to safeguarding the employee's mental state (*Walker v Northumberland County Council* (1994); *Hatton v Sutherland* (2002); *Barber, Grieves & ors v Everard & Sons & ors* (2007)). In *Daw v Intel Corporation (UK) Ltd* (2007) it was held that even though an employer provided the opportunity, which was not taken up, of independent counselling, it was still liable where it should have realised that the increased workload would damage an employee's health. However, in *Reid v Rush and Tomkins Group* (1990), it was held by the Court of Appeal that an employer had no duty to protect an employee's economic well-being, although there was a duty to warn prospective employees of any physical risks inherent in a job (*White v Holbrook Precision Castings* (1985)).

....

9   It adds to the quality of the question to be able to quote accurately from a relevant passage in a judgment.

An employer is also vicariously liable for the torts committed by an employee in the course of his employment. Thus, where by his negligence an employee injures a fellow employee, the employer will also be liable, providing that the act was in the course of the employment. There will often be an overlap between this ground of liability and that which arises from employers' duty to provide competent fellow employees but, where a known practical joker causes damage to a fellow employee, as in *Hudson*, the joker may well be acting outside the course of his employment. *Majrowski v Guy's and St Thomas's NHS Trust* (2006) has confirmed that the concept is not limited to common law torts, Lord Nicholls observing, in the context of a claim under the **Protection from Harassment Act 1997**, that 'the principle of vicarious liability is applicable where an employee commits a breach of a statutory obligation sounding in damages while in the course of his employment'.[10] It has also been held that an employer can be liable where it is known or foreseen that psychiatric harm could be caused to a claimant by a co-worker (*Waters v Commissioner of Police of the Metropolis* (2000)).

Finally, an employer may be liable for breach of statutory duty. As with employers' personal duty of care, this is non-delegable and an employee who relies on this cause of action will have to show that the breach conferred a right of action in tort. This usually gives rise to few problems as the statute will have been enacted for the benefit of a particular class of person – namely, employees (*Groves v Lord Wimborne* (1898); see also *PRP Architects v Reid* (2007)). However, a problem may arise in that the harm suffered may not be of the type that the statute was intended to prevent – that is, the *Gorris v Scott* (1874) situation. Thus, when considering a possible breach of s 14 of the **Factories Act 1961**, it has been held that the duty to fence dangerous machinery exists to protect the worker and to prevent him being injured through having his clothing caught in the machinery, but that is not relevant where a tool that a worker is using is caught in the machinery and the worker is thereby injured (*Sparrow v Fairey Aviation* (1964)). In such a case, however, there would be a clear breach of the employer's personal duty of care and, indeed, in *Fairey*, the breach of this duty was admitted, and the case was only brought to the House of Lords to determine whether or not there had been a breach of s 14.

Statutory duties may be subject to the 'reasonably practicable' requirement when they may add little to the common law duty of care or they may be absolute requirements. In the latter case, a breach is constituted when those requirements are not met and the presence or absence of negligence is irrelevant.[11]

Thus, to return to the statement under discussion, it can be seen that liability arising out of employers' personal duty of care is often wider than vicarious liability or liability for

10   A short quotation from a named judge will add quality to the answer given.
11   For more on breach of statutory duty, see Question 13.

breach of statutory duty. However, the three duties are separate and should not be confused. Obviously, where a statutory obligation is absolute, it will add to employers' personal duty of care.[12]

Aim Higher ★

One of the more interesting aspects of late has been the growth in cases relating to employee 'stress'. Appreciating how the basic requirements fit this new challenge will help you understand the tests more fully.

Common Pitfalls ✗

Failing to take account of the basic range of employers' duties by just 'seeing' the issue at hand (equipment, for example) is a common mistake. A good answer will set out the basic landscape, and then may focus on the most salient aspect, but it is always useful to provide at least a summary of the overall picture in this area.

---

12 A conclusion to an essay should normally summarise the arguments in the body of the answer, and not introduce new material.

Product Liability

INTRODUCTION

Essay questions on the effect of the **Consumer Protection Act 1987** and the differences that it has made on product liability are a favoured mode of testing this area but, where problem questions are set, the student must take care to consider the common law that has not been affected by the **1987 Act**.

Checklist ✔

Students must be familiar with the following areas:

(a) the common law position:

- the *dictum* in *Donoghue v Stevenson* (1932);
- intermediate examination;
- the problems regarding defective product economic loss;

(b) the position under the **Consumer Protection Act 1987**:

- defects;
- persons liable;
- defences;
- loss caused;
- the invalidity of exclusion clauses.

QUESTION 17

'Although many manufacturers feared the introduction of the **Consumer Protection Act 1987**, they are in a no worse position since the Act than before.'

▶ **Critically discuss the above statement.**

How to Answer this Question

This question is typical of the essays that examiners may set. It requires a discussion of the main elements of Part 1 of the Act and a comparison of the statutory and common law regimes regarding product liability. The effect of the Act on manufacturers must be analysed, with particular reference to recent cases. Note, however, that the question requires candidates to discuss critically; it will not be sufficient merely to list the statutory requirements. These requirements must be compared with the still-valid common law rules and the effect of these changes from the manufacturers' point of view must be analysed.

In particular, the following points must be discussed:

* the position under the Consumer Protection Act 1987;
* persons liable – s 2;
* the definition of defect and guidelines for assessing safety – s 3;
* the defences, especially the state-of the-art defence – s 4;
* the limitations on property damage;
* the position at common law;
* the burden of proof;
* the requirement of causation and foreseeability,
* whether manufacturers are in a worse position after the introduction of the Act.

Answer Structure

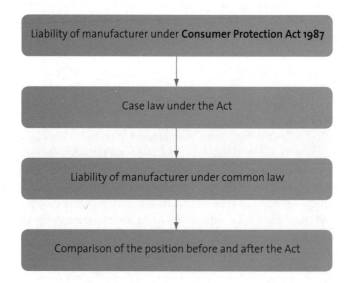

Liability of manufacturer under Consumer Protection Act 1987

Case law under the Act

Liability of manufacturer under common law

Comparison of the position before and after the Act

ANSWER

Part 1 of the **Consumer Protection Act 1987** was introduced into English law to implement the EC **Directive 85/734/EEC** relating to product liability. The main provision of the Act is to be found in **s 2(1)**, which states that where any damage is caused wholly or partly by a defect in a product, the persons detailed in **s 2(2)** shall be liable for the damage, regardless of any negligence on the producers' part. This change from 'fault' liability, as demonstrated by the leading negligence case of *Donoghue v Stevenson* (1932), to 'strict' liability was viewed with concern by manufacturers. They prophesised increased costs and a failure to introduce new products for fear of the level of litigation seen in the USA in regard to product liability. However, in reality there has been very little litigation in this area and many commentators have argued that the legal position was barely altered by the Act.[1] The position can be judged by contrasting the decision in the 'McDonalds' cases': in the UK a case brought after the introduction of the Act was thrown out at first instance, the judge declaring that hot coffee was not a defective product even though it had caused scalding to children (*Bogle v McDonalds* (2002)), whereas in the USA an adult claimant received thousands of dollars in compensation for a similar incident.

Section 2(2) lists the producer of the product, any person who holds himself out as the producer of the product, the importer of the product into the European Union and (by **s 2(3)** in certain circumstances) the supplier of the product. A product is defined by **s 1** as any goods or electricity, and includes a product that is comprised in another product. The producer of the product is the manufacturer of the product (**s 1(2)(a)**),[2] and a person holds himself out as being the producer if he puts his name or trademark on the product or uses some other distinguishing mark: for example, a supermarket chain that sells its own-brand products (**s 2(2)(b)**). The supplier of the product, who is not an importer or own-brander, will be liable only where it is asked to identify the producer of the product and fails to do so (**s 2(3)**). The issue was recently the subject of a decision of the European Court of Justice. In Case C-358/08 *Aventis Pasteur v OB* (2009), it was held that to avoid liability it must provide the information about its own supplier or the actual producer quickly and by its own processes.

By **s 3**, a product contains a defect where 'the safety of the product is not such as persons generally are entitled to expect'. Thus, it can be argued that the **1987 Act** only requires the product to be reasonably safe; it does not impose a requirement of absolute safety. As almost any product is capable of being unsafe if misused (for example, a kitchen knife or an electric fire), the Act does not attempt to define safety, but instead provides a list of guidelines to be taken into account when considering what is meant by the term. So, by

---

1   With an essay question it is important to address the issues highlighted in the question, so some mention should be made of the reason why the change was 'feared'.

2   When writing an essay about a statute, it is important to be very careful to refer accurately to the relevant section, subsection and paragraph.

s 3(2), all of the circumstances shall be taken into account, including: (a) the way and purposes for which the product has been marketed and any instructions and warnings provided; (b) what might reasonably be expected to be done with the product. The Act also provides for certain defences, including the fact that the defect did not exist in the product at the relevant time, and the state-of-the-art defence – namely, 'that the state of scientific and technical knowledge at the relevant time was not such that a producer of products of the same description as the product in question might be expected to have discovered the defect if it had existed in his products while they were under his control'.[3]

This state-of-the-art defence permitted by s 4(1)(e) is wider than that allowed in Art 7(e) of the original EC Directive, giving rise to the possibility that, in appropriate cases, a claimant could claim that a defendant could only rely on Art 7(e), and not on s 4(1)(e), as the true state-of-the-art defence. However, in *EC Commission v UK* (1997), the European Court had to decide this very point and held that, in interpreting s 4(1)(e), there was nothing to suggest that the English courts would not arrive at the result that the Directive required. Indeed, *A v National Blood Authority* (2001) followed this case and adopted a purposive approach based on the Directive. In *A*, the court held that liability under the Directive is defect-based and that any question of fault by the manufacturer is irrelevant. Thus, a product is defective if it does not provide the level of safety that a person is entitled to expect, whether or not that level of safety could have been achieved by the manufacturer. The Art 7(e) defence will not be relevant where there are known risks or risks that can reasonably be ascertained. Thus, in *Abouzaid v Mothercare (UK) Ltd* (2001), a manufacturer was held liable where a defect could easily have been discovered. However, in *Abouzaid*, although the manufacturer was found liable under the Consumer Protection Act 1987, he was not liable in common law negligence as he had acted as a reasonably prudent manufacturer when the product was made. These cases make it clear that a manufacturer is in a worse position under the Act than at common law. One small relief for manufacturers is that in *Richardson v LRC Products Ltd* (2001), which concerned an allegedly defective condom, it was stated that in determining what persons were entitled to expect under s 3, all of the circumstances had to be taken into account, including any instructions or warnings, and the absence of any claim that the product was 100 per cent effective. Thus, if a manufacturer makes no claim that his product is 100 per cent effective, a failure does not necessarily prove the existence of a defect. However, in *Richardson*, it was reiterated that s 4 only affords a defence where the defect is one of which up-to-date scientific knowledge is ignorant. In *Pollard v Tesco Stores Ltd* (2006), the Court of Appeal could be said to be more sympathetic to manufacturers in that it held that despite the cap on the dishwasher powder not complying with BSI standards, it was not defective.

One very important point that should be noted is that for all of the defences contained within the Act, the burden lies on the defendant to prove the defence. This

3   Selective quotation from the Act will add to the quality of your answer.

could be seen as reversing the burden of proof from the previous situation under the common law.

To establish liability under the Act, it is necessary to show that the defect caused the damage, either wholly or in part. There is no requirement of foreseeability; only causation need be shown. The Act does not deal with the issue of causation, so the usual test in English law is applied: the 'but for' test (*Barnett v Chelsea and Kensington Hospital* (1969)). However, in reality, establishing the causal link between a product and damage suffered can be a difficult burden for the claimant to discharge, as cases concerning drugs such as the aborted MMR litigation have demonstrated.

Finally, it should be noted that the Act covers death or personal injury and damage to property. The property in question must be of the type that is normally intended for private use and which was intended for private use by the claimant. Consequently, damage to business property lies outside the scope of the Act. Damage to the product itself is excluded and there is a minimum value of £275 for property damage, below which damages cannot be awarded. By s 7, liability under the Act cannot be restricted or excluded, but under the **Unfair Contract Terms Act 1977**, it is also impossible for a negligent manufacturer to exclude liability for causing death or personal injury to a consumer (s 2(1)).[4]

To see to what extent this has changed the law, it is necessary to study the (still existing) common law. In *Donoghue v Stevenson* (1932), Lord Atkin stated:

> 'A manufacturer of products, which he sells in such a form as to show that he intends them to reach the ultimate consumer in the form in which they left him with no reasonable possibility of intermediate examination, and with the knowledge that the absence of reasonable care in the preparation or putting up of the products will result in an injury to the consumer's life or property, owes a duty to the consumer to take that reasonable care.'[5]

The first problem that a consumer had was to identify the manufacturer. This may have been impossible, so that a donee of goods as opposed to a purchaser could be without a remedy.

Additionally, the remedy may have been, in practice, worthless where the manufacturer was based entirely outside the jurisdiction. In such a case, under the **1987 Act**, the consumer could proceed against the importer of the goods into the EU (s 2(2)(c)), and one

---

4   This and the preceding paragraphs outline the structure of the Act, including case law which illustrates how the Act has been applied.

5   Being able to quote extracts from a leading judgment will add quality to your answer.

of the advantages of the Act from the consumer's point of view is the number of potential defendants that are available under s 2(2).

The next hurdle that a consumer had to overcome was to show the absence of reasonable care on the part of the manufacturer. It could be difficult to show that the defect arose in manufacture, especially where the product had left the manufacturer's control some time previously. Thus, in *Evans v Triplex Safety Glass* (1936), in which the owner of a car claimed that the windscreen was defective, he failed in his claim. The windscreen had been in use in the car for about one year and the plaintiff could not show that the defect in the glass was due to negligence on the part of the manufacturer. On the other hand, in *Mason v Williams and Williams* (1955), the plaintiff succeeded in proving that the manufacturers were negligent by showing that nothing had happened to the product after it left the manufacturers' possession that could have caused the defect. In practice, however, it was often very difficult for a claimant to fulfill the burden of proof in establishing who of several possible defendants in the chain of production and supply was actually doing less than other reasonable businesses of their type.

This problem for the consumer remains under the Act, as s 4(1)(d) provides that it is a defence for the manufacturer to show that the defect did not exist in the product at the relevant time, a defence successfully claimed by the defendant in *Piper v JRI Manufacturing Ltd* (2006) in relation to a defective prosthetic hip. However, there is a shift in the burden in that it is left for the defendant to establish this, rather than the claimant. Nevertheless, causation remains a problem for the consumer, both at common law and under the 1987 Act, but unlike the common law, there is no requirement of foreseeability of damage under the Act.

Liability under the Act does not extend to damage caused to the product itself (s 5(2)), whereas at common law, recovery for defective product economic loss was allowed by the House of Lords in *Junior Books v Veitchi* (1983). However, *Junior Books* has been subject to intense judicial criticism and later cases have tended to confine it within its specific facts. Practically, therefore, in this respect the common law and the 1987 Act are identical.

Thus, it can be seen that it is incorrect to state that manufacturers are in no worse a position since the Act than before. Although there are relatively few decided cases under the Act, research by consumers' organisations has suggested that companies are now more willing to settle claims where damage is caused by a defective product than before the introduction of the Act. It is suggested that the shift in the balance between the parties is due to the changes introduced by the Act. Thus, manufacturers are worse off in that a consumer has no requirements relating to establishing that the manufacturer was at 'fault' but only that the product was 'defective', foreseeability of damage is not an issue, and the defendant – that is, the manufacturer – will suffer the burden of any defence. In particular, it seems clear that recent cases have curtailed the extent of the state-of-the-art defence in s4(1)(e), so that manufacturers who would escape liability under common law negligence are now liable under the 1987 Act. However, apart from the lower limit of £275 for property damage, below which an action may not be brought, the manufacturer is in the same position as before as regards causation or defective product economic loss.[6]

Aim Higher

The statutory scheme under the **CPA** is rooted in EU law. If you are attempting an essay-type question in this area it may be useful to reflect on that fact, and the differences between the **CPA** and the product liability directive, noting the harmonising basis of it.

Common Pitfalls

In problem questions relating to this area, a common error is to forget the 'pure economic loss' exclusion. Remember, the defendant will be liable for personal injury and consequential damage caused by the defective product, but not for the value of the product itself.

QUESTION 18

Trudi bought her children – Andy and Bea – new laptop computers from a local dealer, Chipit, for £260 each. The laptops, exclusive to Chipit, were manufactured by Bytesize and made from components supplied by Ram Ltd, a company based in India. Trudi bought the particular model as it was rated as having low energy consumption and was described as an ideal, portable study tool.

A week after the purchases, Andy's computer overheated, due to a faulty internal fan. The computer caught fire, but he was there on hand to extinguish the flames and no further damage occurred. Bea took her computer away to university and was not aware of what had happened to her brother's computer. Bea's computer was left on standby for an evening while she went out with friends. The computer caught fire and the resulting blaze extensively damaged Bea's room, as well as causing significant smoke damage to the rest of the house. Chavez, a housemate, suffered minor burns as he attempted to extinguish the fire.

It transpired that Bytesize was aware of a potential fault in the fans but had not passed the information on to Chipit.

▶ Advise Andy, Bea and Chavez.

....

6   The concluding paragraph should seek to bring together arguments made in the body of the answer to address the question set.

How to Answer this Question

The question requires a relatively straightforward examination of the provisions of the Consumer Protection Act 1987 and the common law in relation to defective products.

The answer should contain:

❖ an explanation of the key terminology of the **Consumer Protection Act** – product, producer (s 2);
❖ an evaluation of the criteria necessary to show a defect (s 3);
❖ the nature of restrictions placed on property damage (s 5);
❖ common law under the rule in *Donoghue v Stevenson* (1932);
❖ consideration of the differences between this duty and the **Consumer Protection Act**;
❖ the need to demonstrate foreseeability of damage;
❖ the nature of restrictions placed on property damage.

Applying the Law

Strict liability

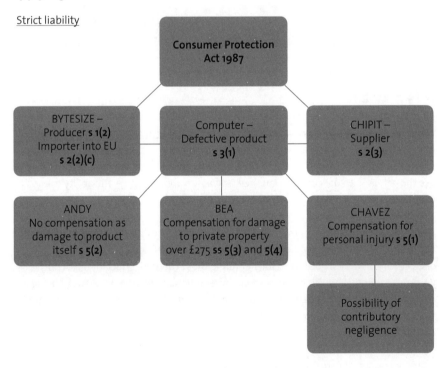

Fault liability

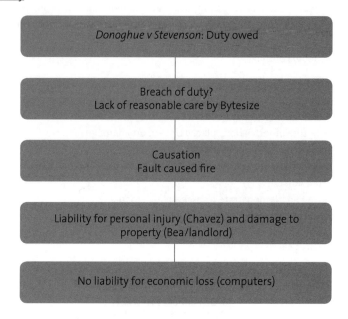

ANSWER

All of the parties should be advised that they might have a claim under the **Consumer Protection Act 1987**, which imposes a form of strict liability in relation to damage caused by defective products, as well as under the common law. Any person who suffers some form of personal injury or damage to their property caused by a defective product may use the Act: as with the common law (see *Stennet v Hancock* (1939)), the ability to sue extends to third parties who suffer damage as a result.[7]

Dealing with the **Consumer Protection Act**, first it must be established that the computer, and/or the faulty fan is a product. **Section 1(2)** of the Act defines a product as 'any goods or electricity' and then goes on to further refine those categories, including, for our purposes, 'a product which is comprised in other products, whether by virtue of being a component part . . .'. That definition would thus include the fan, were it to be separated from the computer. That done, the section also imposes liability upon the producer of that product.

A producer, according to s 1(2), is widely defined and liability is imposed by s 2 in respect of any damage caused wholly or partly by a defect in a product. It is not only the actual

....

7   Identifies and clarifies that the answer will involve consideration of both the common law and statute.

manufacturer who attracts liability, but also those who represent that they are the manufacturer, such as own-branders (s 2(2)). In that situation, Chipit could be held to be a manufacturer, but it would depend on the extent to which it identified Bytesize as the 'true' manufacturer of its exclusive product. So, for example, if Chipit were to state in its marketing that Bytesize made the model in question exclusively for Chipit, it would be less likely that it would be held to be the producer for the purposes of liability. Chipit might be liable as the supplier however, as provided for by s 2(3). That provision makes it clear that should a person suffering damage as a result of the defective product not be able to establish the actual producer, on reasonable inquiry and within a reasonable period of time, a position confirmed by the European Court of Justice in Case C-358/08 *Aventis Pateur v OB* (2009), by asking the supplier, the supplier assumes responsibility under the Act. In Chipit's case, it would seem that it would be able to identify Bytesize as the manufacturer and thus avoid this aspect of liability.

Bytesize is unquestionably a manufacturer within the meaning of the Act. Although Ram Ltd made the components, one of which was the ultimate cause of the defect, the Act provides in s 2(2)(c) that an importer into the European Union of a product manufactured outside will be held to be a producer. It would seem as though there is no way in which Bytesize can escape being held to be a producer.

The next step is to determine whether or not the product is defective. According to s 3(1), a product is defective if it is not as safe as persons generally are entitled to expect. The section extends this notion of safety to 'products comprised in that product', such as in our case, the fan. It is for Andy and Bea to prove the link between the defect and the damage suffered according to the decision in *Foster v Biosil* (2001), in which, in a first instance case involving breast implants, it was held that it was up to the claimant to prove that the product was defective by demonstrating what caused the failure. In determining whether a product is in fact safe, the Act provides that all of the circumstances should be taken into account and includes a list of indicators in s 3(2), which are to be used as guidelines for determining whether the product is reasonably safe. These relate to the marketing of the product, instructions and/or warnings (*Richardson v LRC Products* (2000)), what might reasonably be expected to be done with the product (*Bogle v McDonalds Restaurants Ltd* (2002)) and the time at which the product was supplied by the producer to another. Thus it does not mean that a product must be 100 per cent safe; merely that it should, according to all of the circumstances, be reasonably so. A computer is marketed to be used by its purchaser and it is inevitable that people, particularly if the product is marketed with a low energy rating, will leave the computer on standby at one time or another. Both Andy and Bea were using the computers as they were intended to be used, and it would appear that the computers overheated and caught fire because of a faulty component. On that basis, the computers were not as safe as a person would be reasonably entitled to expect (*A v National Blood Authority* (2001)) and are therefore defective. The strict liability nature of the Act means that Andy and Bea need only prove a causal link between the defect and the damage suffered in order to claim; there is no requirement that the damage be foreseeable. They are also not obliged to show that it was the fault of the defendant in that it had used less than reasonable care, so the fact that Bytesize was aware of the fault would be irrelevant in a case under the Act.

Section 5(1) sets out the type of damage giving rise to liability under the Act. Death, personal injury and property damage are all expressly permitted; thus, at first glance, Andy, Bea and Chavez would not have a problem in claiming against Bytesize for their losses and injury. As above, a third party can claim for damage caused by a defective product. Chavez's claim could be affected by s 6(4), which states that contributory negligence might apply. That would ultimately be a question of fact as we are not clear whether Chavez had acted in a way that contributed to his own harm. There are, however, limitations. So far as property damage is concerned, there is a monetary threshold of £275, so that if damage to property does not exceed that amount, there can be no claim (s 5(4)). This will exclude Andy, as we are told that there was no further damage except the computer catching fire. Bea's situation is likely to be different as we are informed that there is extensive damage and so a claim would be likely to succeed if above that threshold amount. Another factor will limit Andy's ability to claim, however, and would also affect the amount of Bea's claim. The Act excludes damage to the defective product itself (s 5(2)), so neither of the computers would be able to be claimed for because it was these that were defective. This raises an interesting point because we are told that it is merely the fan that is defective; however, s 5(2) states that the exclusion will apply to any product in which the defective product is comprised.

We are not told whether Bea owns or rents her property. On the assumption that she is renting, the landlord may have a problem in relation to a claim for the smoke damage, as s 5(3) of the Act does not permit recovery for damage to property that is not ordinarily used for private use or consumption. Essentially, this is not personal property within the terms of the Act and so therefore would fall within the exemption.[8]

At common law, the remedy for all of the parties would be in negligence. Each of the claimants would need to demonstrate that he or she was owed a duty of care by the manufacturer of the product, that the manufacturer was in breach of its duty and that the breach caused foreseeable damage to the claimant.[9]

---

8   The preceding paragraphs clarify the relevant law and applies it to the facts of the question. When applying statute law, ensure that you are accurate in your citation of the section numbers and subsections.

9   When applying the common law, it should be remembered that it will almost certainly be more difficult to establish liability in negligence as that involves proving fault, while the **Consumer Protection Act** involves strict liability.

The classic duty case in relation to defective products is, of course, *Donoghue v Stevenson* (1932). Lord Atkin made specific reference to the fact that a manufacturer of products owes a duty to the ultimate consumer of them, stating that: 'A manufacturer of products, which he sells in such a form as to show that he intends them to reach the ultimate consumer in the form in which they left him with no reasonable possibility of intermediate examination, and with the knowledge that the absence of reasonable care in the preparation or putting up of the products will result in an injury to the consumer's life or property, owes a duty to the consumer to take that reasonable care.' All of the parties would be able to establish that Bytesize, as the manufacturer, owed them a duty of care. Unlike the **Consumer Protection Act**, there is no possibility of imposing a duty on the supplier, unless it can be shown that the supplier was at fault by, for example, not checking their supplier sufficiently (*Fisher v Harrods* (1966)), which there is no evidence of here.

The mere fact of the defect would probably enable the breach element to be satisfied. A breach of duty requires a person to fall below the standard of the reasonable person (*Blyth v Birmingham Waterworks* (1856)) and, in this situation, Bytesize would have fallen below that threshold by permitting the defective computers to enter circulation, particularly given its suspicion of the potential fault. At this point, the parties would then be required to demonstrate that there was a causal connection between the manufacturer's breach and the damage that they suffered. The classic formulation is the application of the 'but for' test elaborated by Denning J in *Cork v Kirkby MacLean Ltd* (1952), in which he stated: 'Subject to the question of remoteness, causation is a question of fact. If the damage would not have happened BUT FOR a particular fault, then that fault is the cause of the damage; if it would have happened just the same, fault or no fault, the fault is not the cause of the damage.'[10] The last hurdle is for the parties to demonstrate that the damage was of a type or kind that was reasonably foreseeable, and thus not too remote a consequence of the breach (*The Wagon Mound (No 1)* (1961)). The damage that has been suffered due to a faulty fan, which caused overheating and a fire, would certainly be reasonably foreseeable. As a result, Bea would be able to claim for the damage to her property, and Chavez and the landlord would be able to claim for their injury and losses, respectively, noting here that *Stennet v Hancock* (1939) would extend the duty to third parties. As with the Act however, common law will not provide a remedy for damage to the computers themselves. This would be regarded as pure economic loss for which no remedy in negligence exists; the issue was made slightly unclear by the decision in *Junior Books v Veitchi Ltd* (1983), but the subsequent retreat from this case in a series of authorities has reinstated the traditional view that negligence does not permit recovery for pure economic loss comprised in a defective product. Thus, neither Andy nor Bea would have a claim.

----

10 Including a quote from a leading case will add quality to your answer.

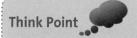

Think Point

Had Bea spent money on downloading music or other media onto her computer, would she be able to claim damages in respect of the fact that these would have been lost?

QUESTION 19

Dee goes to a café bar, Minchelli, with her friend, Cheryl. Cheryl buys them both bottled lager brewed by Stevensons. Dee drinks the beer straight from the bottle, but when she later pours the dregs into a glass, she finds the remains of a decomposing spider. Dee is immediately sick over her friend's designer handbag, and subsequently suffers from gastroenteritis for several days, requiring time off work and causing her considerable discomfort.

▶ Advise Dee and Cheryl.

Would it make any difference to your answer if you knew

(a) that Stevensons has gone out of business; or

(b) that the beer was imported by Stevensons from (i) Germany or (ii) America?[11]

How to Answer this Question

This question involves product liability, and is obviously closely based on the facts in *Donoghue*, but it will necessitate applying current law, i.e. the **Consumer Protection Act 1987**. It gives the opportunity for students to demonstrate that they appreciate how much better the position is for Dee than Ms Donoghue, but as this is not an essay question asking to 'compare and contrast' their positions, too much time should not be given to this aspect.[12]

You will need to establish:

❖   who was the producer, or other party liable under **s 2(2)**;

❖   that the product was defective;

❖   that the defect caused their injuries.

....

11   Where a question asks if something will make a difference to your answer, it usually will! When a question is broken down into different parts, as here, it is advisable to assess the relative worth, and therefore the attention to be given to each part, if the marks have not been broken down by the examiner.

12   A useful exercise might be to compare this answer to a problem question with the answer to an essay question on the same area of law to note the different uses of the same basic material, so see Question 17.

Applying the Law

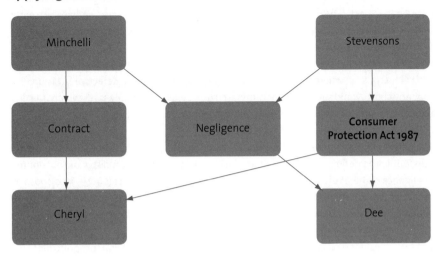

ANSWER

The facts of this problem clearly bear a close similarity to the leading negligence case of *Donoghue v Stevenson* (1932). However, whereas Ms Donoghue had to rely on a majority decision in the House of Lords to establish her right to a remedy, Dee and Cheryl can rely on the **Consumer Protection Act 1987 (CPA)**,[13] which imposes strict liability on the producer of a defective product. Dee therefore only has to prove the identity of the producer, that the product was defective and the causal[14] link between the defect and her injury to obtain compensation.

In *Donoghue*, it was never finally established whether there was a snail in the ginger beer, as the question for the courts was solely whether a duty was owed by a manufacturer to the ultimate consumer, but we are told here that the spider exists.

The producer under the **CPA** is defined in s 1(2)(c) to include the processor, so this would encompass brewing. Stevensons is thus the producer, and by virtue of s 2(1) will be strictly liable for damage caused by their defective product. (Unlike Ms Donoghue, there is no requirement to prove a breach of duty, or fault, which would have involved showing how and why the snail got into the bottle and whether reasonable care would have prevented it from doing so.)

13   Most examiners will be happy for you to abbreviate the names of statutes in exam conditions, but it is essential to give the full title initially, and show your chosen abbreviation.

14   Beware the simple error of writing this as CASUAL.

A defective product is one which by virtue of s 3(1) is not 'as safe as persons generally are entitled to expect',[15] bearing in mind such factors as how it is marketed and any warnings and instructions given with it. The courts have had relatively few chances to interpret the CPA, but see *Abouzaid v Mothercare* (2000) and more recently *Pollard v Tesco Stores Ltd & ors* (2006). Although the section does not impose absolute liability (see *Bogle v McDonalds* (2002), where it was held that very hot coffee was not 'defective'), it is unlikely that any court would say that a contaminated drink was 'reasonably safe', which is likely to be the minimum that persons generally are 'entitled to expect'.

The only remaining hurdles for Dee would seem to be to prove causation; that the harm falls within the definition of damage for the purposes of the CPA; and lack of contributory negligence on her part, a defence specifically provided for in the Act (s 6(4)). To dispose of the latter point, it might be argued by Stevensons that to drink directly from the bottle added to her harm, but given modern habits this is unlikely to succeed.

The CPA does not deal with causation specifically, so applying general tort principles of the 'but for' test in *Barnett v Chelsea and Kensington Hospital* (1969), it can be said that the fact that she was immediately sick suggests that 'but for' the sight of the spider she would not have vomited or become subsequently ill. (As a practical point, Dee or Cheryl could be advised to photograph the insect as evidence of both the existence of the defect and causation, as in many cases the absence of such evidence is a weakness of product liability cases.) Her vomiting and gastroenteritis, as personal injury, would fall within s 5(1).[16]

Stevensons could try to plead one of the statutory defences in s 4, but the most common, that the defect was undiscoverable scientifically (s 4(1)(e)) is unlikely to apply in this fact situation, and the fact that the bottle was sealed makes it unlikely that the defect occurred after it left Stevensons (s 4(1)(d)).

The introduction of strict liability under the CPA therefore makes it highly unlikely that Dee would have to rely on her common law rights under *Donoghue*.[17] However, as there are a few minor exclusions from the Act, such as liability for private property under £275 (s 5(4)), it may be that Cheryl may have to establish fault to recover for her designer handbag if it is valued at less than £275. If it is over this figure, she could claim as damage to property from Stevensons under s 5(1), or alternatively from Minchelli for breach of contract.

....

15   Including a short extract from a statute will increase the quality and accuracy of your answer.
16   Students sometimes feel that loss of earnings, as here as a result of her illness, amount to *economic* loss, as it will be a financial loss. However, this would be part of the assessment of her loss due to personal injury.
17   Here the fact that the common law right still exists is acknowledged, but little time is given to it as in practice it will no longer be necessary to rely on it. To have begun this answer with the common law would have suggested that this point was not fully appreciated.

Neither the CPA nor the common law gives a right to recover the cost of the lager, i.e. damage to the defective product itself (s 5(2) and despite *Junior Books v Veitchi* (1983), which has not been followed,[18] respectively), and Cheryl would be left to pursue this case against Minchelli for breach of her contractual implied rights under the **Sale of Goods Act 1979**, s 14, as the lager is not of satisfactory quality.[19]

Thus although some commentators have argued that there has been little advantage to consumers from the introduction of the CPA,[20] it is likely that Dee and Cheryl's cases in the 21st century would be settled quickly because of the move to strict liability, provided the difficult factual questions of causation could be established, and unlike Ms Donoghue would not have to resort to the highest court for a remedy.

(a) If Stevensons had gone out of business, liability under the CPA will not transfer to anyone else in the supply chain. The retailer, Minchelli, will only be liable under the CPA if it had put its own brand name on it or in some other way held itself out as the producer (s 2(2)(b)) or was unable to provide the name of the producer or other party in the supply chain (s 2(3)). At common law a retailer who should have spotted the defect or been suspicious of the manufacturer may be in breach of duty, *Fisher v Harrods* (1966), but if as here the lager was in a sealed opaque bottle there would be no chance of intermediate inspection, and if Minchelli had had no problems with Stevensons' products in the past it is highly unlikely that there has been a lack of reasonable care.

(b) (i) If the lager was imported from Germany, Dee would have to sue the German manufacturer (s 2(2)(c)). As the CPA was based on an EU Directive, the law in the UK and Germany should be harmonised, but doing so would not be straightforward because of language differences etc.

(ii) If the lager was imported from America, outside the EU, then Stevensons will be held liable, in effect standing in for the producer, CPA s 2(2)(c). As this is strict liability, it does not matter how much, or little, care Stevensons has taken when selecting the manufacturer.

---

18 This alerts the examiner that you appreciate the issue surrounding this area, but without going into it in more detail, as more is not really required in this question.

19 Although answering a Tort exam paper, it will not hurt, if there is time, to include information about the contractual position for the sake of completeness. In an Obligations paper, the relationship between contract and tort in product liability could receive more emphasis.

20 See Question 17 further on this point.

Occupiers' Liability

7

INTRODUCTION

Occupiers' liability is a specialised branch of the tort of negligence and is tested in most examinations year after year. The area is governed by statute – namely, the **Occupiers' Liability Act 1957** and the **Occupiers' Liability Act 1984**. Thus, in addition to the common law concepts of duty, breach, causation and remoteness, attention must be paid to the statutes and the exact words used therein.

The **1984 Act** is also frequently tested. Be aware that in moving around premises, a person may well change in status from a visitor to a non-visitor – that is, from being subject to the **1957 Act** to being subject to the **1984 Act**. By doing so, it will be much more difficult for that person to demonstrate that they are owed a duty of care, and this difference should be brought out in the answer.

Occupiers' liability is also likely to occur as an element of questions which are mainly concerned with other areas of tort law; see, for instance, Questions 15, 25 and 28, so look out for that possibility.

Checklist ✔

Students must be familiar with the following areas:

(a) the definitions of occupiers, visitors and non-visitors;

(b) the duty regarding children, warnings and independent contractors;

(c) the exclusion of duty;

(d) the circumstances under which a duty to a non-visitor arises and the nature of this duty.

Aim Higher ★

Strong candidates elaborate on the simple aspect of what 'premises' are. Given that it's one subsection, all encompassing and has several authorities, including the bizarre, as in *Gwilliam*, this is always a way to show that you are conversant with what is being regulated.

Common Pitfalls ✗

Weak candidates fail to remember that, ultimately, occupiers' liability is a specialist application of the tort of negligence and, therefore, operates within the same strictures of duty (albeit statutory), breach and damage, meaning that the usual rules apply once a duty is established. Also, there is a tendency not to differentiate clearly enough between the two Acts.

QUESTION 20

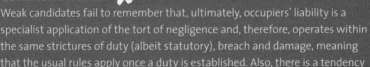

Harry inherits a large and dilapidated house from his mother. He moves in and decides to have substantial renovations carried out by Askew Alterations Ltd, a local company that specialises in renovating old property. Whilst these alterations are in progress, Harry decides to hold a party to welcome his new neighbours.

Barney and his five-year-old daughter Clara attend. Clara becomes bored and wanders into a room marked 'Danger – do not enter', where she is injured. Barney, while looking for Clara in that room, turns on a light switch that has not been completely finished and suffers an electrical shock.

Danny, who is aware that Harry's mother kept a good wine cellar, goes down to the cellar intending to help himself to some wine, but slips on a cork on the steps and breaks both his legs.

▶ **Advise Barney, Clara and Danny.**

How to Answer this Question

This is a standard occupiers' liability question, in that it involves the areas of independent contractors, children and visitors becoming non-visitors. The following points need to be discussed:

- ❖ occupiers and visitors;
- ❖ Harry's duty to visitors generally;
- ❖ Harry's duty to Clara;
- ❖ the effect of the warning notice;
- ❖ Harry's duty to Danny.

Applying the Law

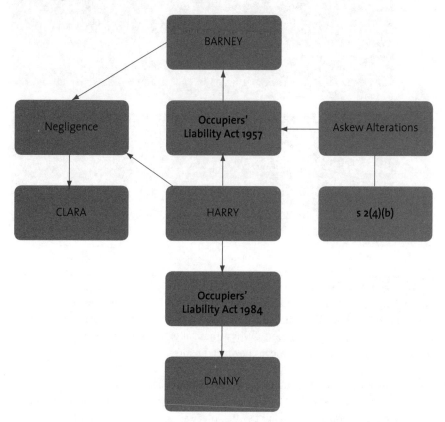

BARNEY

Negligence

Occupiers' Liability Act 1957

Askew Alterations

CLARA

HARRY

s 2(4)(b)

Occupiers' Liability Act 1984

DANNY

*This diagram demonstrates Harry's liability under the **Occupiers' Liability Acts**.*

ANSWER

Harry is the occupier of his house, as he has 'sufficient control over the premises that he ought to realise that any failure on his part to use care may result in injury to a person coming lawfully there' (*Wheat v Lacon* (1966), *per* Lord Denning). Barney, Clara and Danny are Harry's visitors (*Wheat*), and we must ascertain the nature of the duty that Harry owes to each of his visitors and decide whether he is in breach of that duty.

Harry owes each of his visitors the common duty of care (s 2(1) of the **Occupiers' Liability Act 1957**) and this duty is to take such care as in all of the circumstances is reasonable to see that the visitor will be reasonably safe in using the premises for the purposes for which he is invited or permitted by the occupier to be there. It should be noted that it is the visitor who must be reasonably safe and not the premises (see, for example, *Ferguson v Welsh* (1987)). Thus, the fact that repairs are being carried out to Harry's house, which is in a dilapidated condition, does not (without more) constitute a breach of duty.

CLARA[1]

Turning now to Clara, by s 2(3)(a) of the 1957 Act, Harry must be prepared for children to be less careful than adults. In *Latham v Johnson and Nephew Ltd* (1913), Lord Hamilton stated that there may be a duty not to lead children into temptation. Having said this, if the danger is obvious, even to a child, the occupier will not be liable (*Liddle v Yorkshire (North Riding) County Council* (1934)). With very young children, of course, almost anything can be a danger, but here an occupier will be able to rely on the decision of Devlin J in *Phipps v Rochester Corp* (1955). It was held that reasonable parents would not allow small children to go unaccompanied to places that may be unsafe for them, that both parents and occupiers must act reasonably, and that each is entitled to assume that the other has so acted. In *Bourne Leisure Ltd v Marsden* (2009), a tragic case involving the drowning of a toddler in a pond at a caravan park, it was held that an occupier owed a duty of reasonable, not absolute, care. A warning given of the presence of dangers did not have to be precise.

Considering all of the circumstances of the case, it should have been clear to Barney that Harry's house was in the process of redecoration and would hence contain danger that might not be obvious to a small child. Following *Phipps*, it would seem that Barney has not acted reasonably and that Harry was justified in relying on Barney to look after Clara. Harry could also argue that the sign 'Danger – do not enter' is a warning that discharges his duty under s 2(4)(a), but to achieve this, the warning must in all of the circumstances be enough to enable the visitor to be reasonably safe. The sign does not seem to be a warning at all, in that it makes no attempt to describe the danger. It is rather a prohibition on the spatial extent to which the visitor is entitled to be on the premises, which the occupier is entitled to do (*The Carlgarth* (1927)). In any event, it would not be enough in all of the circumstances to discharge the duty owed to a small child, nor to turn the small child into a non-visitor. It would also be pertinent to consider whether injury was sustained as a result of the state of the premises or as a result of any activity she undertook there: *Revill v Newberry* (1996) and recently *Siddorn v Patel* (2007). In the latter case, it was held that the statute would not apply and ordinary negligence principles would apply.

Hence, our advice to Clara is that she may not have a very strong case against Harry, but that she could sue Barney in negligence.[2] Barney owes Clara a duty of care under normal *Donoghue v Stevenson* (1932) principles. As a duty of care has previously been established, there is no need to proceed to the modern incremental formulation of a duty of care that was preferred by the House of Lords in *Caparo Industries plc v Dickman* (1990) and *Murphy v Brentwood District Council* (1990). Barney is in breach of his duty in allowing Clara to wander off in a house that was still being renovated, as this would not have been the action of a reasonable parent placed in Barney's position (*Blyth v Birmingham Waterworks* (1856)).

....

1   Dealing with each claimant in turn can help with the clarity of the answer.
2   There might be practical difficulties in suing her father, of course, and Barney may not have insurance coverage.

Finally, the harm that Clara has suffered was caused by Barney's breach of duty, as shown by applying the 'but for' test of Lord Denning in *Cork v Kirby MacLean* (1952). This damage was also reasonably foreseeable, as required by *The Wagon Mound (No 1)* (1961).

BARNEY

We have discussed the duty that Harry owes to Barney and must now consider whether Harry is in breach of this duty. *Prima facie*, it is a breach of duty to allow persons to come into contact with unsafe light switches, but Harry has attempted to discharge his duty via the notice. The notice seems to be insufficient as a warning notice, as it does not describe the nature of the danger in any way and so, by s 2(4)(a), would not be enough to make the visitor reasonably safe. In *Rae v Mars UK* (1989), it was held that where an unusual danger exists, the visitor should not only be warned, but a barrier or additional notice should be placed to show the immediacy of the danger; in this regard, see also *Moon v Garrett* (2006). Harry has not complied with this condition and, therefore, it seems that the notice is insufficient as a warning notice. However, Harry could rely on s 2(4)(b). This section states that where damage is caused to a visitor by a danger due to the faulty execution of any work of construction, maintenance or repair by an independent contractor employed by the occupier, the occupier is not to be treated, without more, as answerable for the danger.[3] This applies if, in all of the circumstances, the occupier had acted reasonably in entrusting the work to an independent contractor and had taken such steps (if any) as he reasonably ought in order to satisfy himself that the contractor was competent and that the work had been properly done.

The renovation is covered by s 2(4)(b), as it is reasonable to entrust it to independent contractors, and as we are told that Askew Alterations specialises in renovating old property, it would seem that it is competent. The question, therefore, is what (if any) steps Harry ought reasonably to have taken to satisfy himself that the work had been properly done. Despite the words 'had been properly done', it was held by the House of Lords in *Ferguson v Welsh* (1987) that it could apply where the work was still being done and had not been completed. The rule is that the more technical the work, the less reasonable it is to require the occupier to check it (*Haseldine v Daw* (1941); *Woodward v Mayor of Hastings* (1945)). In Harry's circumstances, it would seem that as the work is technical, there is no requirement to check that the work had been properly done and Harry has discharged his duty by employing reasonable independent contractors, if this is indeed the case.[4]

One could consider whether Askew Alterations is also an occupier. Although Harry is an occupier, an independent contractor may also be an occupier, for control need not be

---

3   Accurate citation of the statute will add quality to the answer.

4   As we are not specifically told whether Harry has checked out the contractors, it is preferable not to assume that the defendant would be able to rely on s 2(4)(b), and raising it as an issue demonstrates understanding of the provision.

exclusive (*Wheat v Lacon* (1966)). The question that has to be decided is whether the independent contractors have sufficient control, as in *AMF International v Magnet Bowling* (1968). In the present case, although we are told that renovations are continuing, it seems unlikely that Harry would hold a party while the contractors are physically present and working. Although physical possession is not a necessary ingredient of control (*Harris v Birkenhead Corp* (1976)), it would seem that at the relevant time Askew Alterations was not in sufficient control to make it an occupier.

Hence, our advice to Barney is that he may not be able to sue Harry, if **s 2(4)(b)** applies, but that he could sue Askew Alterations in negligence. Askew Alterations owes Barney a duty of care under normal *Donoghue* principles. Also, as a duty of care has previously been established, there is no need to proceed to the modern incremental formulation of a duty of care that was preferred by the House of Lords in *Caparo* and *Murphy*. Askew Alterations is probably in breach of its duty in leaving the switch in an unsafe condition, as this would not have been the action of a reasonable electrician placed in Askew Alterations' position (*Blyth v Birmingham Waterworks* (1856)). Finally, the damage that Barney has suffered was caused by Askew Alterations' breach of duty, as shown by applying the 'but for' test of Lord Denning in *Cork v Kirby MacLean* (1952), and this damage was reasonably foreseeable, as required by *The Wagon Mound (No 1)* (1961).

DANNY

Finally, we must consider advising Danny. Although Danny was initially a visitor, on entering the cellar, he became a non-visitor.[5] An occupier may place a spatial limitation on the visitor's permission to enter (*The Carlgarth* (1927)), but in such a case the limitation must be brought to the visitor's attention (*Gould v McAuliffe* (1941)). By implication, Danny must have known that he did not have Harry's permission to enter his wine cellar. Consequently, Danny became a trespasser when he entered that part of the premises. Even if Danny had had permission to visit the wine cellar, as he went there to steal Harry's wine, Danny must have known that he was entering the cellar in excess of the permission given to him and consequently became a trespasser.

Any duty now owed to Danny is governed by the **Occupiers' Liability Act 1984**. By **s 1(3)** of the **1984 Act**, an occupier will only owe a duty to a non-visitor if all three of the following are satisfied:

(a)   the occupier is aware of the danger or has reasonable grounds to believe that it exists;
(b)   the occupier knows or has reasonable grounds to believe that the non-visitor is in the vicinity of the danger or may come into the vicinity; and

---

5   Note that the **1984 Act** does not refer to 'trespassers', but 'non-visitors'.

(c)   the risk is one against which, in all of the circumstances, he may reasonably be expected to offer the non-visitor some protection.

It seems unlikely that requirement (a) is satisfied as there must actually be a danger (*Keown v Coventry Healthcare NHS Trust* (2006)) and actual knowledge of the danger is required: *Ratcliff v McConnell* (1999); *Rhind v Astbury Water Park Ltd* (2004); *Donoghue v Folkestone Properties Ltd* (2003).

Requirement (b) is not satisfied, as Harry had no reason to suspect that his guests would go down to the cellar. Hence, no duty arises in respect of Danny's accident in the cellar: see, for example, *Tomlinson v Congleton Borough Council* (2003); *Rhind v Astbury Water Park Ltd* (2004); *Donoghue*. In addition, Harry would have the defence of *ex turpi causa non oritur actio* (*National Coal Board v England* (1954)). Danny's claim is based directly on the illegality, and is not merely incidental, to use the test preferred by the majority in the Court of Appeal in *Pitts v Hunt* (1990) and by the House of Lords in *Tinsley v Milligan* (1993). However, in *Revill v Newberry* (1996), a trespasser was allowed to recover, subject to a large deduction for contributory negligence, when he was injured during his criminal activity. The Court of Appeal stated that 'an occupier cannot treat a burglar as an outlaw'. However, as Danny is unlikely to be able to establish a duty was owed, Harry will not have to rely on a defence.[6]

QUESTION 21

Eric owns a waxworks museum in the seaside town of Westsea. He decides to have a new air conditioning system installed in the museum by Coolit plc, but Coolit can only carry out this work at the height of the tourist season. Rather than delay the job until winter, or shut down while the work is being done and lose income, Eric decides to allow the public into the museum while the new air conditioning system is being installed. He places notices around the museum stating 'Danger – Work in Progress'. While the employees of Coolit are working in one part of the museum, some scaffolding that they have erected in another part of the museum collapses. The scaffolding injures Florence, who paid to enter the museum, and George, who entered without paying through the open back doorway that Coolit's employees were using to bring in equipment.

⬧   Advise Florence, who has suffered a fractured skull and had her spectacles broken, and George, who has suffered a broken shoulder and has had his new suit ruined.

How to Answer this Question

This is a straightforward occupiers' liability question involving two occupiers, an independent contractor, a visitor and a non-visitor.

....

6   Liability under the **1984 Act** is very difficult to establish because of the difficulty of satisfying **s1(3)** of the **1984 Act**, in contrast to the situation under the **1957 Act** where all visitors are owed the 'common duty of care'.

The following points need to be discussed:

- ❖ the likelihood of Eric and Coolit both being occupiers;
- ❖ the applicability of **s 2(4)(b)** of the **Occupiers' Liability Act 1957** to Eric;
- ❖ the liability of occupier to non-visitor;
- ❖ the damages recoverable.

Applying the Law

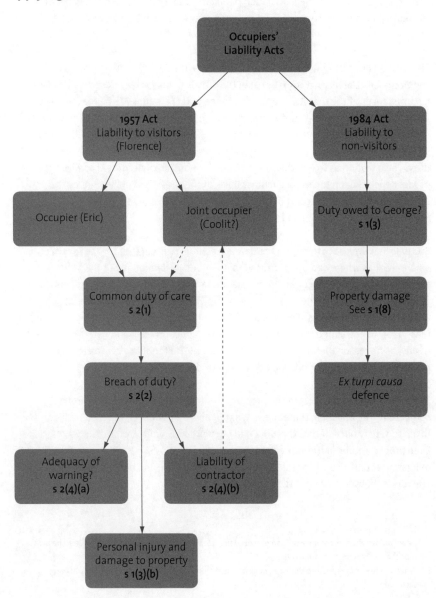

ANSWER --

Eric is the occupier of the museum as he has, *per* Lord Denning, sufficient control over the premises that he ought to realise that any failure on his part to use care may result in injury to a person coming lawfully there (*Wheat v Lacon* (1966)). In addition, Coolit may also be an occupier of the museum, for there is no need for control to be exclusive (*Wheat*). The question is whether Coolit, as an independent contractor, has sufficient control, as in *AMF International v Magnet Bowling* (1968). This is, of course, a question of fact and, as presumably the installation of an air conditioning system in a waxworks museum would involve extensive work, Coolit may well be held to be an occupier and so also be liable together with Eric.[7]

Florence is Eric's visitor (*Wheat*). Eric owes Florence the common duty of care by **s 2(1)** of the **Occupiers' Liability Act 1957**. By **s 2(2)**, the duty is to take such care as in all of the circumstances of the case it is reasonable to see that the visitor will be reasonably safe in using the premises for the purposes for which he is invited or permitted to be there. It should be noted that it is the visitor who must be reasonably safe and not the premises, so the fact that renovations are taking place does not, by itself, constitute a breach of duty. The question as to whether the occupier is in breach of his duty is always a question of fact depending on the exact circumstances of the case. This can be seen by the differing decisions of the court in the factually similar cases of *Murphy v Bradford Metropolitan Council* (1992) and *Gitsham v Pearce* (1992).

Eric will, however, seek to rely on the defence contained in **s 2(4)(b)**[8] of the **1957 Act** – namely, that where damage is caused to a visitor by a danger due to the faulty execution of any work of construction, maintenance or repair by an independent contractor employed by the occupier, the occupier is not to be treated without more as answerable for the danger. This applies if, in all of the circumstances, the occupier acted reasonably in entrusting the work to an independent contractor and had taken such steps (if any) as he reasonably ought in order to satisfy himself that the contractor was competent and that the work had been properly done.

There is nothing in the facts of the problem to suggest that Coolit is anything but competent. The question, therefore, is what (if any) steps Eric ought reasonably to have taken to satisfy himself that the work had been properly done. Despite the words 'had been properly done' in the subsection, it was held in *Ferguson v Welsh* (1987) that the obligation could arise where the work was still being done and had not been completed. The rule is that the more technical the work, the less reasonable it is to require the

----

7 Establishing who the occupier is, is an essential first step in a case of occupiers' liability, and be aware that there might be more than one.

8 When citing statutes, ensure that the section, subsection and (if appropriate) the paragraph are accurate.

occupier to check the work (cf *Haseldine v Daw* (1941) and *Woodward v The Mayor of Hastings* (1945)).

The work of installing an air conditioning system is certainly technical, but we are told that the damage was caused by scaffolding collapsing. If this danger was obvious to a reasonable observer, Eric should have been aware of the danger and cannot bring himself within **s 2(4)(b)**. However, if the careless work of Coolit was not apparent upon such examination, Eric will not be in breach.

Next, we need to consider whether the notices stating 'Danger – Work in Progress' discharge any duty owed by the occupier. By **s 2(4)(a)** of the **1957 Act**, where damage is caused to a visitor by a danger of which he has been warned by the occupier, the warning is not to be treated without more as absolving the occupier from liability, unless in all of the circumstances it was enough to enable the visitor to be reasonably safe.[9] The notices do not indicate the nature of the danger and it is a question of fact whether they were enough to allow a visitor to be reasonably safe. In *Rae v Mars UK* (1989), it was held that where an unusual danger exists, the visitor should not only be warned, but a barrier or additional notice should also be placed to show the immediacy of the danger (see also *Moon v Garrett* (2006)). On the facts of the present case, this had not been done. As the scaffolding fell on Florence, it seems that, in addition to the notice, the area should have been roped off to keep visitors away from any possible danger.

Hence, our advice to Florence is that Eric may be able to avail himself of this statutory defence, so she would be better advised to sue Coolit under the **Occupiers' Liability Act 1957** as occupiers and/or in negligence. Florence can recover for both the injury to her person and the damage to her property: **s 1(3)(b)** of the **1957 Act**.

George is clearly not a lawful visitor of Eric or Coolit. George comes within the definition of a trespasser as laid down by Lord Dunedin in *Addie v Dumbreck* (1929) as a person who goes onto land without invitation and whose presence is either unknown to the proprietor or, if known, is objected to. The duty owed to George is covered by the **Occupiers' Liability Act 1984**. By **s 1(3)** of this Act, an occupier will only owe a duty to a non-visitor if:

(a) he is aware of the danger or has reasonable grounds to believe that it exists;
(b) he knows or has reasonable grounds to believe that the non-visitor is in the vicinity of the danger or may come into the vicinity;
(c) the risk is one against which, in all of the circumstances, he may reasonably be expected to offer the non-visitor some protection.

....

9   Accurate citing of the words of the statute will add authority to your answer.

If the duty does arise then, by **s1(4)**, an occupier is to take such care as is reasonable in all of the circumstances to see that the non-visitor does not suffer injury.

In George's case, requirement (a) is satisfied as Eric was aware of the danger (as can be shown by his placing of the warning notices: *Woollins v British Celanese* (1966); *Rhind v Astbury Water Park Ltd* (2004); *Keown v Coventry Healthcare NHS Trust* (2006)).

Requirement (b) is not satisfied, as Eric has no reason to anticipate George's presence. In *White v St Albans City and District Council* (1990), it was argued that the very presence of a warning notice showed that the occupier had reason to suspect someone was likely to come into the vicinity of the danger, but this was rejected by the Court of Appeal. In both *Donoghue v Folkestone Properties Ltd* (2003) CA, and *Tomlinson v Congleton Borough Council* (2003) HL, the position of trespassers was considered and it was held in both cases that there was no duty owed in respect of obvious dangers. It was also held in both cases that no duty was owed where persons freely and voluntarily undertook an activity that involved some risk. In George's case, it could be argued that the danger from the activity involving scaffolding is obvious and that using the back door to enter the premises involved an element of risk in that any warnings would not be apparent to George.

Even if the duty does arise, it can be discharged by a reasonable warning: **s1(5)** (but see the discussion above). By **s1(9)**, injury only includes personal injury, and damage to property is expressly excluded (**s1(8)**). Thus, in the unlikely event of George being able to establish liability under the **1984 Act**, the damage to his suit would be irrecoverable.

The question that arises is if George could establish any liability, whether he would be met by the *ex turpi causa non oritur actio* defence as in *National Coal Board v England* (1954). The scope of this defence is difficult to ascertain from the decided cases. In *Euro-Diam v Bathurst* (1988), it was said that the defence rests on a public policy that the courts will not assist a claimant who has been guilty of illegal or immoral conduct of which the court should take notice, and the defence will apply if it would be an affront to the public conscience to grant the claimant relief. This test was used in *Thackwell v Barclays Bank* (1986) and in *Saunders v Edwards* (1987), and by Beldam LJ in *Pitts v Hunt* (1990). However, in *Pitts*, Dillon and Balcombe LJJ preferred to base their decisions on whether the plaintiff's claim was based directly on his illegal conduct or whether the illegal conduct was merely incidental. More recently, the House of Lords in *Tinsley v Milligan* (1993) rejected the affront to public conscience test. The test would now seem to be whether the claim is based directly on the illegal conduct (*Vellino v Chief Constable of Greater Manchester* (2002)). In George's case, it would seem that the *ex turpi* defence would succeed, so George should be advised that his chances of any recovery are extremely slim.

QUESTION 22

Gordon is the landlord of the Tamar public house and family restaurant, owned by Pilgrims Brewery. Recently some refurbishment was undertaken, and Gordon engaged Cowboys Limited (CL) to carry out the work. He had never used them before, but they were recommended to him by a customer as being cheap and cheerful. Work was completed in the dining area first and the premises were reopened. Bharat, a customer, tripped over a poorly secured floorboard, on his way to the salad bar, breaking his arm and smashing his glasses. In the commotion that followed, Bharat's young son managed to slip away and walked out of the door. He was attracted to the children's play area, which was adjacent to a landscaped water feature. He slipped on the edge, fell in the water and drowned.

CL were also contracted to upgrade the wiring and fusebox. Gordon had warned CL that the wiring was in poor condition. Sparkie, an employee of CL, was put in charge of the work in the cellar. She cut the wrong wire, received an electric shock and suffered severe burns to her hands.

Meanwhile, Wesley, a regular customer, wanted to have a look at the progress of the work in what was formerly the lounge bar. He squeezed through some plastic fencing that was used as a barrier to keep people out of the area, ignoring a sign stating: 'Danger – Keep Out – No Persons Beyond This Point Without Permission of the Contractors. No Liability for Injury is Accepted, Howsoever Caused'. The area was not properly lit and he tripped over some tools left on the floor. As a result he cut open his head and broke his watch.

▶ **Advise the parties as to their potential liabilities by reference to the duty owed by an occupier of premises.**

How to Answer this Question

This is a wide-ranging question on occupiers' liability which engages a number of issues. It is fairly typical in that it requires an evaluation of both **Occupiers' Liability Acts**, and introduces some complexity surrounding recent case law.

The following points need to be discussed:

- ❖   the **OLA 1957** and its application to visitors;
- ❖   the potential for any of the duties imposed to be delegated;
- ❖   the situation relative to children and parents;
- ❖   the position of visitors in the exercise of their calling;
- ❖   adult trespassers and warnings.

Applying the Law

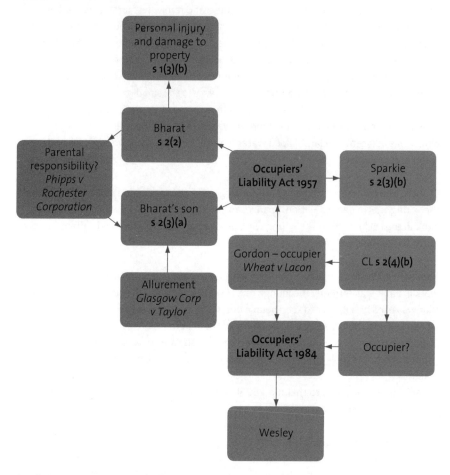

This diagram points out Gordon's and CL's potential liability.

ANSWER

The question is concerned with the liability of an occupier for harm suffered by people while on the occupier's premises. The law is shaped by the application of two Acts of Parliament, the **Occupiers' Liability Acts of 1957 and 1984** (hereafter the **1957 Act** and the **1984 Act**), which make provision for a duty of care to be owed in relation to lawful visitors and non-visitors (trespassers), respectively. Somewhat bizarrely neither Act defines the term 'occupier', so recourse must be made to the common law rules. In *Wheat v Lacon* (1966), Lord Denning identified several categories of what might be termed occupation. This includes shared occupancy, as may arise between Pilgrims Brewery and Gordon. The central test to determine occupancy is control (*Wheat*), and control may be exercised by an occupier not actually present on the site (*Harris v Birkenhead Corporation* (1976)). It is also possible for an independent contractor to be sufficiently in 'control' for them to be held to be an occupier (*AMF International v Magnet Bowling* (1968); *Gwilliam v West Herts Hospital NHS Trust* (2002)). The **1957 Act** does require an occupier to be in control of 'premises', which are extremely widely defined in **s 1(3)(a)** of the **1957 Act**, to include any fixed or moveable structure (*Wheeler v Copas* (1981) 3 All ER 405 (fixed ladder); *Gwilliam* ('splat wall')) or any vehicle, vessel or aircraft. It is clear that the Tamar fits the definition of premises and it would be a question of fact to determine which party had the necessary control to be an occupier. Given the facts, it is submitted that it would be likely to be Gordon, at least insofar as Bharat and Sparkie are concerned.[10]

The duty owed under the **1957 Act** is to visitors, generally understood to mean those with permission to be on the premises for the purpose that they are there. This would include licensees, invitees, or persons entering under a legal right. The duty is elaborated in **s 2(2)** of the **1957 Act** and is expressed as a duty to take such care as in all the circumstances is reasonable to see that the visitor will be reasonably safe in using the premises for the purposes for which he is invited or permitted by the occupier to be there. The extent of that duty, and the fact that it is the visitor and not the premises that has to be safe, was examined in the case of *Lewis v Six Continents plc* (2005).

Bharat is undoubtedly a visitor on premises occupied by Gordon and is owed a duty of care under the **1957 Act**. His injury stems from the state of the premises and thus it could be argued that Gordon has breached his duty of care, by failing to ensure Bharat's reasonable safety while on the premises, and is therefore liable. The damage suffered is of a type or kind that is foreseeable (*Jolley v Sutton LBC* (2000)) and thus the requirements for liability would be made out. Liability extends to both personal injury and damage to property under **s 1(3)(b)** of the **1957 Act**, so Bharat could be compensated for his broken arm and his broken glasses. The question of breach would of course be a question of fact – did Gordon take *reasonable* care to ensure Bharat was *reasonably* safe (**s 2(2)**)?

Gordon may wish to try and pass the liability on to CL; there is a statutory means by which an occupier can delegate his duty of care in limited circumstances where the injury on the property is caused by faulty workmanship. **Section 2(4)(b)** of the **1957 Act** sets out a three-part test to establish whether it is the occupier or an independent contractor employed by the occupier who is to owe the duty. First, there is a question as to whether the occupier acted reasonably in entrusting the work to an independent contractor. It would seem that this would be the case as a refurbishment would be reasonable to expect to be contracted out. Second, the occupier should take reasonable steps to satisfy themselves that the contactor was competent (in *Gwilliam* this competency requirement

---

10   The introduction includes consideration of the two Acts, and who is the occupier. Remember to distinguish clearly between the two Acts in the answer.

was extended to the adequacy of the contractor's insurance – although this decision has been subject to some criticism in the case of *Glaister v Appleby-in-Westmorland Town Council* (2009)). This factor is more open to debate. We are told that Gordon used them because they were 'cheap and cheerful', perhaps as opposed to professional and effective? That would ultimately be a question of fact. Finally, the occupier is required to take such reasonable steps as are necessary to satisfy himself that the work had been properly done. In law this has been taken to mean that the more complex the task being undertaken the less reasonable it is to expect the occupier to be able meaningfully to check the work. The leading cases on this issue are *Haseldine v Daw* (1941) (technical: a lift repair), where liability passed to the contractor, and *Woodward v Mayor of Hastings* (1945) (not technical: sweeping a snow covered step), where liability was retained by the occupier. The issue will turn on whether the loose floorboard would have been obvious on a reasonable inspection. If it was not, then it is likely that Gordon, subject to the finding that CL were competent contractors, could escape liability.

So far as the death of Bharat's son is concerned, the **1957 Act** states in **s 2(3)(a)** that an occupier should expect that children will be less careful than adults. This, effectively, imposes a higher duty of care on the occupier, in much the same way as the 'reasonable child' in determining standards of care in negligence is a different standard. This does not mean that an occupier has an absolute duty in relation to children on their premises; however, parental responsibility is also taken into consideration (*Phipps v Rochester Corporation* (1955); *Maloney v Lambeth LBC* (1966)). The recent case of *Bourne Leisure Ltd v Marsden* (2009) clarified the point further stating that an occupier owed a duty of reasonable, not absolute, care to children in situations where they could wander away from parental control and suffer harm from obvious dangers on the premises. The occupier would avoid liability if the basic parameters of any dangers on the premises had been pointed out to the parents. It is unclear whether Bharat was made aware of the water feature, although it could also be submitted that placing an obvious (to an adult) danger next to a play area, which would operate as an allurement (*Glasgow Corporation v Taylor* (1922)) to a child, would fall below the standard of care required of an occupier. Could Bharat have exercised any control over his son as the reasonable parent would have been expected to in that situation? Quite possibly the answer would be in the negative, but the question, then, of Gordon's liability would depend on the extent to which the broad range of dangers and the location of them was made clear to Bharat at the time.[11]

Sparkie would also be classed as a visitor on the premises, and would appear to have suffered an injury due to the state of the premises. However, Gordon is likely to be able to

---

11 Do not be afraid to leave the question of liability to Bharat's son uncertain, because often in a problem question you will have insufficient information (as here, as to the nature of any warnings given to Bharat) to be more definite.

avoid any liability in relation to her injuries. This is because in s 2(3)(b) of the 1957 Act it is provided that an occupier may expect that a skilled worker in the exercise of their calling will appreciate and guard against any special risks ordinarily incident to it, so far as the occupier leaves him free to do so (see also *Roles v Nathan* (1963)). Here, Sparkie, representing herself to be an electrician would be expected to take reasonable care of her own safety to the extent that it related to her job. An electrician would thus be expected to know which wire to cut, or at least to have ensured that the power was disconnected before attempting the operation. This would especially be so given Gordon's warning, which according to s 2(4)(a) would appear to satisfy the Act's requirement to be sufficient to ensure that the visitor was reasonably safe (*Roles v Nathan*).

It is clear that Wesley is not a visitor when he enters the former lounge bar. He probably was Gordon's visitor in the Tamar public house, but exceeded the terms of his permission to be there (*The Carlgarth* (1927)) by entering a prohibited area.[12] As above, in relation to the determination of who the occupier may be, the issue is one of control and it would thus be a question of fact to decide whether or not Gordon or CL exercised sufficient control. Given that there is a physical barrier and a warning sign expressly stating that permission to enter must be given by the contractor, there is, at least arguably, a presumption that, by virtue of *AMF v Bowling*, CL would be considered to be the occupier.

Whether Wesley is owed a duty of care depends on the test set out in s 1(3) of the 1984 Act which states that an occupier of premises owes a duty to a non-visitor if, first, the occupier is aware of the danger or has reasonable grounds to believe it exists; second, the occupier knows or has reasonable grounds to believe that the non-visitor is in the vicinity of the danger or may come into the vicinity; and third, the risk is one for which in all the circumstances he may reasonably be expected to offer the visitor some protection.[13] The fact that a warning notice was deployed by CL would be suggestive of the fact that they knew that a danger existed. However, it is unlikely that CL would be held to believe that Wesley would come into the area (*White v St. Albans City and District Council* (1990); *Donoghue v Folkstone Properties Ltd* (2003)). The question of obvious risk was discussed by the House of Lords in *Tomlinson v Congleton BC* (2003), and it was held that an occupier did not owe a duty in such circumstances to an adult trespasser. In a slightly different context that sentiment was echoed in *Poppleton v Trustees of the Portsmouth Youth Activities Committee* (2008), where Lord Justice May observed that adults who voluntarily engage in risky activities may find themselves uncompensated if the risk materialises.[14]

....

12 Look out for the possibility of a visitor in an occupiers' liability question becoming a non-visitor by 'straying' outside the area they were allowed to be in, as here with Wesley, and thus being subject to the **1984 Act.**

13 To be able to quote the words of the statute accurately will give extra authority to your answer.

14 Note how much more difficult it is to establish a duty of care under the **1984 Act** than the **1957** one.

In the unlikely event that a duty was held to exist, CL would probably escape liability by virtue of the fact that their warning was sufficient, according to s1(5) of the 1984 Act. Adult trespassers who have been provided with a warning but trespass nonetheless are usually held to have consented to run the risk of injury (*Ratcliffe v McConnell* (1999)). The attempt by CL to exclude liability would be irrelevant if no liability arose, but even if it did the attempt could be argued to be ineffective. There is some academic debate about whether the **Unfair Contract Terms Act 1977 s 2(1)** would apply, or whether the very low duty owed under the 1984 Act or the standard of 'common humanity' from *British Railways Board v Herrington* (1972) is so minimal as to be unexcludable.[15] Whatever the decision in relation to the injury suffered by Wesley he would not be able to make a claim in respect of his damaged watch as property damage is not recoverable under the 1984 Act s1(8).

---

15 Demonstrating awareness of elements of uncertainty in the law will add quality to your answer.

Vicarious Liability

INTRODUCTION

Vicarious liability is a topic that is regularly tested by examiners, either as a question in its own right or as part of a question on (say) negligence or employers' liability. Note that it is not a separate tort, but rather deals with who can be liable. Course of employment and express prohibitions are areas that are especially popular with examiners but, in all vicarious liability questions, it is vital to remember that a primary liability between the tortfeasor and the victim must be established before any liability can be transferred.

Checklist ✔

Students must be familiar with the following areas:

(a) the definition of 'employer' and 'employee';

(b) the course of employment and the close connection test laid down in *Lister v Hesley Hall Ltd* (2001);

(c) frolics and detours; and

(d) the courts' differing attitudes to careless and deliberate acts.

QUESTION 23

Factor X (FX), an events management company, was contracted to provide corporate hospitality by Womberfield Stadium for clients attending a sporting event. In order to exclude the general public from the exclusive corporate hospitality area, FX engaged its usual contactors, Crew Service (CS), to provide security for the day in question. The security staff's instructions from FX were detailed and included a specific instruction not to admit people without a ticket, along with an instruction that should there be any problem with a non-ticket holder trying to enter, the member of staff should radio a member of FX staff and wait for them to attend to resolve the situation.

The centrepiece to the hospitality buffet was an elaborate chocolate fountain. Paula, an FX employee, assembled the fountain incorrectly and did not test it as she had been instructed to do. As a result of the incorrect assembly, the fountain later toppled over, scalding several guests and knocking one unconscious. During the commotion, Scally tried to sneak into the event but was caught by Louie, one of the security staff. Louie violently twisted Scally's arm and threw him to the ground, breaking Scally's wrist and cutting his head.

▶ Advise FX.

How to Answer this Question

This question involves a consideration of the principles of vicarious liability in situations in which an employee has been negligent and also those in which the employee has committed a wilful act. It also involves the question of who may be held to be an employer in cases in which there is more than one possibility.

The following points require discussion:

❖   the liability of Paula to the guests;
❖   the liability of an employer for the negligence of employee;
❖   the basics of the tort of battery;
❖   the liability of an employer for deliberate torts committed by an employee;
❖   determining the employer for the purposes of liability.

Applying the Law

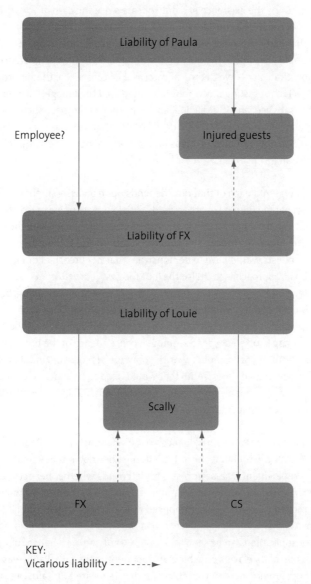

KEY:
Vicarious liability --------►

ANSWER

This question requires an application of the laws relating to vicarious liability – that is, making an employer liable for the tortious acts of his employees. As a result of Paula's failure to assemble the machinery correctly, people have been injured, and it first falls to be determined whether they could sue Paula and, if so, whether FX can be held vicariously liable. There should be no problem in demonstrating that Paula owed a duty of care. To determine the existence of a duty of care since the case of *Caparo Industries plc v Dickman* (1990) requires a consideration of the reasonable foreseeability of harm, the proximity of the relationship between the claimant and defendant, and whether it is fair, just and reasonable to impose the duty on the defendant. In the circumstances, it is highly probably that Paula owes a duty of care, as it is foreseeable that improper assembly and a lack of testing of the fountain could lead to damage; the proximity requirement is satisfied, and it is fair, just and reasonable to impose such a duty. It has also been noted (*B v Islington Health Authority* (1991)) that as far as personal injury cases are concerned, the duty remains as it was pre-*Caparo* – namely, the foresight of a reasonable person (*Donoghue v Stevenson* (1932)).[1]

Whether Paula was in breach of that duty depends upon an assessment of the reasonableness of her conduct: in other words, would a reasonable person have behaved in the way that she did (*Blythe v Birmingham Waterworks* (1856))? Given the facts, it is unlikely that she has performed to the required standard and is therefore in breach of her duty. Next, the guests would have to demonstrate that her breach of duty caused their injuries. The basic approach is to utilise the 'but for' test (*Barnett v Chelsea and Kensington Hospital Management Committee* (1969)), essentially meaning: but for the defendant's breach of duty, would the damage have occurred? Once again, the linkage is simple and can easily be attributed to Paula's negligence. Finally, it must be determined whether the damage suffered was too remote a consequence of the breach (*The Wagon Mound (No 1)* (1961)) – in other words, was the damage of a type or kind that was reasonably foreseeable? In this case, all that would need to be shown would be that personal injury was reasonably foreseeable. Clearly it was. Paula is therefore very likely to be held to have been negligent.[2]

Can FX be held liable for Paula's negligence? To be vicariously liable, Paula must be an employee of FX. We are told that she is. Next it must be shown that Paula is acting in the course of her employment. The basic test is to determine whether her act was something that was a wrongful or unauthorised manner of doing an authorised act, or whether it was so far removed from what was authorised as to be independent from it (*Century Insurance v Northern Ireland Road Transport Board* (1942); *Lister v Helsey Hall* (2001)). A contemporary application can be seen in *Grauil v Carroll* (2008) where a rugby club was held liable for one of its players punching an opponent in the face. Paula was clearly in the course of her employment while setting up the chocolate fountain; the fact that she did so wrongly, or in an unauthorised manner, is not sufficient to enable FX to escape

---

1 This establishes the parameters of the answer, showing that the vicarious liability of the employer depends on first establishing that the employee is liable for a tort.

2 Establishing Paula's liability in negligence is a crucial stage in a vicarious liability answer, and here we are told that she assembled the fountain incorrectly.

liability for her conduct. Accordingly, the advice to the injured guests would be to sue FX for the damage that they have suffered.[3]

As far as Louie is concerned, it is likely that he has committed battery, an element of the tort of trespass to the person. Battery is defined as a direct, intentional application of force by the defendant in the absence of the claimant's consent. The force must be direct (*Reynolds v Clarke* (1725)) and intentional (*Letang v Cooper* (1965)), so in the circumstances, Scally would have little trouble in proving these elements. Additionally, any form of touching or application of force is capable of being a battery (*Cole v Turner* (1704)): clearly, an arm twist and being thrown to the ground would suffice. There is an element of uncertainty as to whether the touching should be hostile or not (*Wilson v Pringle* (1987); *F v West Berkshire Health Authority* (1989)), but irrespective of that debate, there would be no problem in establishing a battery in this situation as the touching is undoubtedly hostile and falls well within the description of the tort. There would also be little chance of Louie being able to claim that he was acting in self-defence, as that particular defence would require that the force used was reasonable (*Turner v MGM* (1950); *Cross v Kirkby* (2000)); additionally, the defence of protecting a third party's property is also limited by the same requirement. Louie, it would appear, has definitely committed the tort of battery; he is also likely to have committed a criminal offence for which he could be charged, but it would be in Scally's interests to seek to sue Louie's employer for the tortious act. The case of *Majrowski v Guy's and St Thomas' NHS Trust* (2006) has extended an employer's liability to harassment, under the **Protection from Harassment Act 1997**, committed by an employee in the course of his employment.[4]

Battery

It now falls to consider whether Louie's employer could be held vicariously liable for his battery. The question to be determined is whether an employer can be held liable for the deliberate torts of an employee. Previously, the law sought to establish a link between the act of the employee and the nature of the employment that s/he was engaged in, or that there was attributable fault on the part of the employer, for example by not supervising the employee closely enough (*Lloyd v Grace, Smith & Co* (1912); *Warren v Henley's Ltd* (1948)). More recently, in *Lister v Helsey Hall* (2001), the House of Lords was asked to determine whether an employer, a boys' school, could be held vicariously liable for a series of sexual abuses perpetrated by one of its wardens. It was held that it could. The test according to the Lords was whether the nature of the employment was close to the wrongdoing perpetrated by the employee. Departing from earlier authority, the House of Lords held that there was no need for the tort to be committed in the furtherance of the employer's business. A similar case, involving an assault by a doorman at a nightclub, was also upheld against the employer in *Mattis v Pollock* (2003) and see also *Hawley v Luminar*

Application of V.L. Course of Employment

3   It is important to demonstrate that Paula is an employee, acting in the course of employment.
4   Demonstrates Louie's liability for a tort, in this case trespass to the person, and the implications of this being a deliberate act, rather than negligence.

Vicarious
Liability
Cause of
Employment

Leisure Ltd (2006), considered further below. In *Maga v Trustees of the Birmingham Archdiocese of the Roman Catholic Church* (2010) there was said to be a close enough connection between the work of a priest and a young boy in his neighbourhood for his abusive behaviour to have been regarded as in the course of his employment, even though the boy was not a member of the Church. It would therefore appear that an employer could be liable for Louie's actions, but the question remains, which one?[5]

Joint
Liability
for V.L.

Louie is employed by CS; however, it would appear from the facts that he has been 'lent' to FX by virtue of the fact that FX has hired-in security from CS. In such circumstances, you would perhaps think that the contract between the two companies would be decisive on the issue. Case law, however, has suggested that it is not that simple. In *Mersey Docks and Harbour Board v Coggins and Griffiths* (1947), the appellants lent a crane driver and crane to the respondents. Due to the crane driver's negligence, a third party suffered personal injury and it was therefore necessary to determine which employer was vicariously liable. The contract between the parties indicated that the hirer was liable, but the House of Lords held that in such circumstances the contract could not decide the issue. Instead, it created a presumption that the permanent employer would be liable unless it could overcome the burden of proving otherwise, which it could not. Two relatively recent decisions appear to have altered that position. In *Viasystems Ltd v Thermal Transfer Ltd* (2005), the Court of Appeal reviewed vicarious liability and concluded that the decision as to whether an employee remained an employee of the permanent employer, or was 'deemed to be the temporary employee of the hirer of his services', turned on the question of control. In that case, it was held that more than one employer could be vicariously liable, although that would depend on the facts of the case and in particular the integration of the employee into the business of both employers. The judgment was approved in *Hawley*, in which a nightclub doorman seriously assaulted a person outside a club. It was held that the nightclub was vicariously liable for his actions, even though he was deemed a temporary employee. Applying *Viasystems* and *Hawley* to the situation involving Louie, it would appear that FX may well be vicariously liable as it issued instructions and could be said to have control over the performance of the task; failing that, there is the possibility that both employers might share liability to Scally.[6]

QUESTION 24

Gamma plc employs David as a driver and Elaine as a salesperson. One day, Elaine has to call on a customer but, as her car is being serviced, she asks David if he can drive her to the customer's premises. David agrees, but when they are in the car, he tells Elaine that

---

5   Vicarious liability is important where the harm is caused by an employee who will probably not be in a position to pay compensation, unlike the employer(s).

6   Here it is important to demonstrate knowledge of recent cases showing that there can sometimes be joint liability and the important issue of control.

he must first call at his private house to collect a suit to take to the dry cleaners. Whilst on the way to the house, David sees a patch of oil that has been spilt on the road and says to Elaine: 'See that oil – I'll show you how to control a skid.' David then drives onto the patch of oil, but fails to control the subsequent skid and hits a wall, injuring Elaine and damaging beyond repair a valuable painting that Elaine is carrying in her briefcase.

▶ Advise Elaine.

How to Answer this Question

This question involves the area of frolics and detours, and the recent attitude of the courts when considering course of employment in situations involving deliberate acts by the employee, rather than negligent acts. As is typical of exam questions, however, an additional area is also tested – namely, the principle that a tortfeasor takes his victim as he finds him – and tests how that principle applies to property damage.

The following points need to be discussed:

❖ the liability of David to Elaine;
❖ the vicarious liability of Gamma plc for David's victim;
❖ consideration of course of employment as regards deliberate acts of the employee;
❖ the possibility of *volenti*; and
❖ that David takes Elaine as he finds her.

Applying the Law

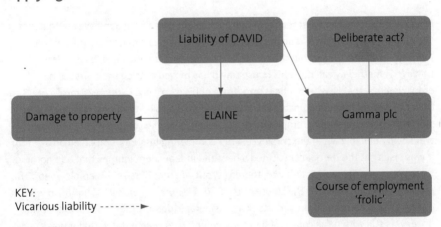

KEY:
Vicarious liability --------▶

ANSWER

We must first decide whether Elaine can sue David and, if so, whether Gamma plc is vicariously liable for David's actions. Elaine must first show that David owes her a duty of care. In those situations in which a duty of care has previously been found to exist, there

Tort of Negligence

is no need to apply the incremental formulation preferred by the House of Lords in *Caparo Industries plc v Dickman* (1990) or *Murphy v Brentwood District Council* (1990). We could note here the statement of Potts J at first instance in *B v Islington Health Authority* (1991), in which he stated that in personal injury cases, the duty of care remains as it was pre-*Caparo* – namely, the foresight of a reasonable man (*Donoghue v Stevenson* (1932)) – a finding that does not appear to have been disturbed on appeal (1992). In fact, a duty of care has been found to exist in a number of cases involving drivers and their passengers: for example, *Nettleship v Weston* (1971). However, even without knowledge of such cases, we could deduce the existence of a duty of care, as it is reasonably foreseeable that, by driving carelessly, a passenger may suffer injury.

Next, Elaine must show that David was in breach of his duty – that is, that a reasonable person or rather a reasonably competent driver in David's position would not have acted in this way (*Blyth v Birmingham Waterworks* (1856); *Nettleship v Weston* (1971)). It seems clear that a reasonable driver would not drive deliberately onto a patch of oil and so David is in breach of his duty. Elaine will also have to show that this breach caused her injuries and the 'but for' test in *Cork v Kirby MacLean* (1952) proves the required causal connection. Finally, Elaine will have to prove that the harm suffered was not too remote – that is, that it was reasonably foreseeable (*The Wagon Mound (No 1)* (1961)). This should give rise to no problems, as all that Elaine will have to show is that some personal injury was foreseeable. Elaine will not have to show that the extent of the injury was foreseeable or the exact manner in which the injury was caused (*Smith v Leech Brain* (1962); *Hughes v Lord Advocate* (1963)). Elaine could therefore sue David.[7]

Next we must consider whether Gamma plc is liable for David's actions. We are told that the employer/employee relationship exists and it seems clear that, at the start of the journey, David is acting within the course of his employment. We need to consider, however, whether by calling at his house David has moved outside the course of his employment – that is, whether he is on a 'frolic of his own'. In *Whatman v Pearson* (1868), a driver who went home for lunch, contrary to his employer's instructions, was held to be still within the course of his employment. However, in *Storey v Ashton* (1869), employers were held not liable when the employee, after completing his work, embarked on a detour. It was held that this detour constituted a new and independent journey that had nothing to do with his employment and was, therefore, outside the course of his employment. This problem was considered by the House of Lords in *Williams v Hemphill Ltd* (1966), in which a driver carrying some children undertook a considerable detour. The House held that the driver was still within the course of his employment. Lord Pearce stated that it was a question of fact in each case whether the deviation was so unconnected with the employer's business that the employee was on a 'frolic of his own' and, in *Williams*, the

---

7   The introductory paragraphs clarify that Elaine has the choice whether to sue David and/or Gamma, thus demonstrating understanding of the concept of vicarious liability.

presence of the boys on the bus showed that it was not a frolic of the driver's own. Lord Pearce stated that had the driver in *Storey* been carrying some property of his employers, for instance, he might have remained in the course of his employment. Having considered *Joel v Morrison* (1834) and *Storey*, Lord Pearce stated that to constitute a frolic of his own, the employee's journey had to be entirely unconnected with the employer's business, as opposed to a mere detour for the employee's selfish purposes. However, on the facts of *Williams*, Lord Pearce held that the presence of passengers whom the employee had to take to their destination made it impossible to say that the detour was entirely for the employee's purposes. Applying this criterion to our case, the presence of Elaine will make it impossible to say that the detour was undertaken entirely for David's selfish purposes and thus David is likely to remain in the course of his employment.[8]

The next question we must consider is whether David remains in the course of his employment when he drives onto the patch of oil. The court has taken a much more restrictive approach to course of employment where 'deliberate' wrongful acts have occurred, as can be seen by decisions of the Court of Appeal in *Heasmans v Clarity Cleaning Co Ltd* (1987) and *Irving v Post Office* (1987). In *Heasmans*, an employer was held not to be vicariously liable for the actions of an employee who was employed to clean telephones, but who made unauthorised telephone calls costing some £1,400. The Court noted that the employee was employed to clean the telephones and that in using them he had not cleaned them in an unauthorised manner, but had done an unauthorised act that had taken him outside the course of his employment. In *Irving*, the employee, who worked for the Post Office and was employed to sort mail, wrote some racial abuse concerning the plaintiff upon a letter addressed to the plaintiff. The employee was authorised to write upon letters, but only for the purposes of ensuring that the mail was properly dealt with. It was held that the employers were not vicariously liable for the actions of the employee, as in writing racial abuse he was doing an unauthorised act and not an authorised act in an unauthorised manner. The Court stated, *per* Fox LJ, that limits had to be set to the doctrine of vicarious liability, particularly where it was sought to make employers liable for the 'wilful wrongdoing' of an employee. Thus, in *General Engineering Services v Kingston and St Andrews Corp* (1989), firemen who drove very slowly to a fire were held not to be in the course of their employment in so doing. The firemen were employed to travel to the scene of fire as quickly as reasonably possible and in travelling slowly they were not doing an authorised act in an unauthorised manner, but an unauthorised act. Given the attitude of the courts to deliberate acts, it is submitted that in carrying out this deliberate act, David has moved outside the course of his employment and that Gamma plc will not be liable for his action. The fact that, in driving onto the oil, David was not acting for the benefit of his employer is not necessarily

---

8   Always consider whether vicarious liability is an option, as here, when an employer is involved. In many cases, an individual such as David would be unable to pay damages and Gamma would be in better position to do so.

relevant to taking the act outside the course of his employment (*Lloyd v Grace, Smith & Co* (1912); *Century Insurance v Northern Ireland Road Transport Board* (1942)).

V.L &
The Close
Connection
Test.

In *Lister v Hesley Hall Ltd* (2001), the House of Lords, in reviewing the law on course of employment, held that an employer will also be liable for unauthorised acts that are so connected with authorised acts that they may be regarded as modes, albeit improper modes, of doing authorised acts. Their Lordships held that it was necessary to concentrate on the relative closeness of the connection between the tort and the nature of the employment, taking a broad approach to nature of employment. The close connection approach was also used by the House of Lords in *Dubai Aluminium Co v Salaam* (2003) and the Court of Appeal in *Mattis v Pollock* (2004) and recently examined by the Court of Appeal in *Gravil v Carroll* (2008) and *Maga v Roman Catholic Archdiocese of Birmingham* (2010), where a priest assaulted a juvenile who was not a memeber of his congregation.

VL
The Close
Connection
Test.

Although *Lister* may seem at first glance to suggest that David is acting in the course of his employment when driving onto the patch of oil, it should be remembered that in *Lister* there was a very close connection between the tort and the course of employment. *Lister* is therefore not a general authority for widening the course of employment to cover deliberate acts, but *Maga* could be said to widen the test of close connection, in that it was through his work that the priest had the opportunity to commit the tort. A court would have to decide whether the connection to David's work was sufficient using this test.9

The Voluntary
defense
of
Volenti

David may seek to raise the *volenti* defence against Elaine. To do this successfully, David will have to show that Elaine voluntarily assented to the risk of damage, which seems unlikely (*Dann v Hamilton* (1939)). Although the defence of *volenti* succeeded in *Morris v Murray* (1990), this was a case in which the risk was glaringly obvious from the outset. In any event, s149(3) of the **Road Traffic Act 1988** precludes reliance on *volenti* in road traffic situations (*Pitts v Hunt* (1990)).10

Eggshell
Rule

As regards the damage to the valuable painting, David (and Gamma plc, if he is still within the course of his employment) will be liable. David may not have foreseen that Elaine would be carrying such valuable property, but he could have foreseen that Elaine would be carrying some property and this will be sufficient (*Vacwell Engineering v BDH Chemicals* (1971)). When considering damage to property, a narrower attitude to foreseeability is taken than with harm to the person (*The Wagon Mound (No 1)* (1961)), and the 'eggshell skull' rule in *Dulieu v White* (1901) cannot be applied without great caution. However, Elaine should be able to recover for the damage to her painting on the authority of *Vacwell*.11

....

9 The preceding paragraphs demonstrate the importance of considering the leading cases in detail, and quoting from the judgment and/or identifying the individual judge will add to the quality of your answer.

10 It is always worthwhile to consider any possible defences, even if not specifically asked for in the question.

11 Here the fact that the painting is *valuable* should lead to consideration of the 'eggshell skull' theory – facts such as this should not be overlooked.

QUESTION 25

Delta plc owns a small office. Delta asks Frank, an electrician, to undertake various works at the company premises and tells Frank that his work will take about one week.

While Frank is working in Delta's offices, he carelessly rewires a switch and Gloria, an employee of Delta, is injured when she uses the switch. Henry, who is visiting Delta in an attempt to sell some office equipment, is also injured when he trips over a length of electrical cable that Frank has left in a corridor.

▶ Advise Gloria and Henry.

How to Answer this Question

This question involves a consideration of the liability of an employer for the acts of an independent contractor. As such, it is less run of the mill than standard vicarious liability questions and the answer will be shorter, provided that the student is aware of the relevant legal principles.

The following points need to be discussed:

❖ the differentiation between employees and independent contractors;
❖ the liability of the employer for an independent contractor;
❖ the non-delegable duties of the employer; and
❖ the liability of the employer for acts of collateral negligence.

Applying the Law

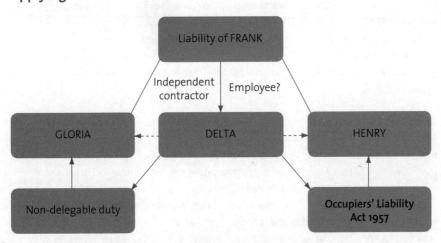

KEY: --------► possible vicarious liability

ANSWER

We must decide whether Gloria and Henry could sue Frank and, if so, whether Delta plc is liable for Frank's actions. Gloria must first show that Frank owes her a duty of care. In those situations in which a duty of care has previously been found to exist, there is no need to apply the incremental formulation preferred by the House of Lords in *Caparo Industries plc v Dickman* (1990) or *Murphy v Brentwood District Council* (1990). We could note here the statement of Potts J at first instance in *B v Islington Health Authority* (1991), in which he stated that in personal injury cases the duty of care remains as it was pre-*Caparo* – namely, the foresight of a reasonable man (*Donoghue v Stevenson* (1932)) – a finding that does not appear to have been disturbed on appeal (1992). In fact, a duty of care has been found to exist in a similar situation in *Green v Fibreglass Ltd* (1958). However, even without knowledge of this case, we could deduce the existence of a duty of care as it is reasonably foreseeable that, by carelessly rewiring the switch, a person who subsequently uses it may suffer injury.[12]

Next, Gloria must show that Frank was in breach of this duty – that is, that a reasonable person, or rather a reasonably competent electrician, in Frank's position, would not have acted in this way (*Blyth v Birmingham Waterworks* (1856); *Bolam v Friern Hospital Management Committee* (1957)). It seems clear that a reasonable electrician would not rewire a switch carelessly and so Frank is in breach of his duty. Gloria will also have to show that this breach caused her injuries and the 'but for' test in *Cork v Kirby MacLean* (1952) proves the required causal connection. Finally, Gloria will have to prove that the damage she has suffered was not too remote – that is, that it was reasonably foreseeable (*The Wagon Mound (No 1)* (1961)). This should give rise to no problems, as all that Gloria will have to show is that some personal injury was foreseeable; she will not have to show that the extent was foreseeable, or the exact manner in which the injury was caused (*Smith v Leech Brain* (1962); *Hughes v Lord Advocate* (1963)).

Given then that Frank is negligent, can Delta plc be held liable for his negligence? It seems clear that Frank was acting within the course of his employment. Provided that the relevant act (that is, the rewiring of the switch) was an authorised act, the fact that Frank has carried it out in a wrongful and unauthorised manner will not take the act outside the course of his employment (*Century Insurance v Northern Ireland Road Transport Board* (1942)). Consequently, we need to decide whether Frank is an employee of Delta plc, or whether he is an independent contractor. It is extremely difficult to formulate a universal test for an employee. The original test, laid down in *Yewens*

---

12 Always consider whether vicarious liability is an option, as here, when an employer is involved.

The following handwritten annotations appear in the left margin:

Negligence
The Duty of Care

Damage:
Breach &
Causation

V.L
Being on
authorised
act in an
unauthorised
way.

Employee

v Noakes (1880), was the 'control' test: the employer had the right of control as to the way in which the employee carried out his work. This test has obvious problems when the person concerned has a particular skill, especially if the employer himself does not possess that skill.

Employer Test. The Control Test.

In *Stevenson, Jordan and Harrison Ltd v MacDonald* (1952), Denning LJ (as he then was) proposed the 'business integration' test: does the person do his work as an 'integral part of the business', when he will be an employee, or is he merely 'accessory' to it, when he will be an independent contractor? However, the test is just as difficult to apply as the control test and, in *Market Investigations v Minister of Social Security* (1969), it was held that a person was an employee because she was not in business on her own account. This test also seems vague, although in *Andrews v King* (1991) it was described by Browne-Wilkinson VC as the 'fundamental test'. The modern approach of the courts is to eschew any single test and examine all of the facts of the case. Looking at the facts of Frank and Delta plc, it would seem that Delta plc has the right to tell Frank what work is to be done, but not how to do it, so that Frank is an independent contractor. In *Ready Mixed Concrete v Minister of Pensions* (1968), MacKenna J laid down several conditions for a contract of employment, one of which was that the worker agrees to be directed as to the mode of carrying out the work. MacKenna J held that this right of control was a necessary (although not sufficient) condition of an employment contract and it was said to be particularly important in cases of temporary employment in *Interlink Express Parcels Ltd v Night Trunkers Ltd* (2001). However, this condition seems to be lacking in Frank's case, leaving him as an independent contractor. Thus, *prima facie*, Delta plc is not liable for Frank's actions.[13]

The integration test.

Employee status.

Applied on

However, as regards Gloria, Delta plc, as Gloria's employer, is under a non-delegable duty to take reasonable care for the safety of its employees (*Wilsons and Clyde Coal v English* (1938)). By the phrase 'non-delegable', one does not mean that the employer cannot delegate performance to an independent contractor, but that the employer cannot delegate responsibility for performance. Thus, although the standard rule is that an employer is not liable for the actions of an independent contractor (*Morgan v Girls Friendly Society* (1936); *D and F Estates v Church Commissioners* (1989)), Delta plc will be liable to Gloria for failing to take reasonable care for her safety.[14]

Employers liability

As regards Henry, as he is not an employee of Delta plc, he cannot claim on this basis. He may have to rely on suing frank in negligence.

Liability or.

However, there are some situations in which an employer is liable for the torts of an independent contractor. The employer is so liable in the following situations: if it has

---

13 This demonstrates how the facts of the case in hand can be applied to the relevant law. By referring to named judges and including short quotations, the quality of the answer is improved.

14 You need to distinguish clearly between the employer's vicarious liability (through Frank's negligence) and Delta's direct liability to Gloria as an employee.

authorised the independent contractor to commit the tort (*Ellis v Sheffield Gas Consumers Co* (1853)); if it is negligent in choosing an independent contractor who is not competent (*Pinn v Rew* (1916)); and if a non-delegable duty is imposed upon it by common law – that is, a duty the performance of which can be delegated, but not the responsibility. Neither of the first two situations are relevant here, but one of the situations that may be relevant as regards common law non-delegable duties is that in which the independent contractor is employed to carry out work that is extra-hazardous (*Honeywill and Stein Ltd v Larkin Bros* (1934); *Alcock v Wraith* (1991)). In *Alcock*, the Court of Appeal held that a crucial question was: 'Did the work involve some special risk or was it from its very nature likely to cause damage?' It is submitted that the work in question was not extra-hazardous and so Delta plc will not be liable (*Salsbury v Woodland* (1969)).

Independent Contractors [margin annotation]

If it were decided that Frank's work was extra-hazardous, Delta plc might be able to claim that Frank's negligence was merely collateral to the performance of his work and that it was not liable (*Padbury v Holliday and Greenwood* (1912)). Whether the negligence was in fact collateral would depend on the particular facts of the case and we are not given sufficient details to come to any firm conclusion.

OLA [margin annotation]

If Henry were to sue Delta plc under the **Occupiers' Liability Act 1957**, he would be met with the defence in s 2(4)(b) that Delta plc acted reasonably in entrusting the work to an independent contractor, and took such steps as were reasonable to satisfy itself that the contractor was competent and that the work had been properly done. In *Haseldine v Daw* (1941), it was held that there was no need to check the work of contractors employed to repair a lift as the work was technical. In *Woodward v Mayor of Hastings* (1945), it was held that, as the work was non-technical, there was a need to check that it had been properly done. In Henry's situation, although the wiring of a switch is a technical task, Henry's injury arose because Frank left some electrical cable on the floor, which is not a technical matter. This situation seems closer to the carelessly cleaned step in *Woodward* than the carelessly repaired lift in *Haseldine*, so it is submitted that Henry could successfully sue under the **Occupiers' Liability Act 1957**.[15]

Aim Higher

Make sure you can differentiate between independent contractor and employee, or 'hired out' employee. As cases such as *Viasystems* and *Hawley* have examined these relationships quite closely, it is worth getting familiar with the tests.

---

15 Be aware of other possibilities, not just the main thrust of the questions, and be prepared to consider other issues, such as the **Occupiers' Liability Act** here, when advising claimants. See Chapter 7 for more on occupiers' liability.

Common Pitfalls ✘

You are most likely to encounter vicarious liability as a problem question, sometimes mixed up with other areas of negligence. Do not forget to determine whether the 'other' negligence will satisfy the tests for liability before addressing the vicarious liability aspect. The other major pitfall is to muddle an employers' liability *to* an employee and their vicarious liability *for* an employees' negligence.

Nuisance

INTRODUCTION

Questions on nuisance are popular with examiners, possibly because nuisance is a complex topic with several unresolved areas. Much of this complexity is due to the fact that there are few hard-and-fast rules as to what constitutes a nuisance; instead, there are a number of guidelines that the court may or may not decide are relevant in deciding whether a particular activity amounts to a nuisance.

Recently, a number of nuisance cases have involved the provisions of the **Human Rights Act 1998** and candidates should be aware of the importance of this rapidly developing area of law.

Checklist ✔

Students must be familiar with the following areas:

(a)   the types of activity capable of constituting a nuisance;

(b)   the factors indicating whether an interference is unreasonable and the relative importance of these factors *inter se*;

(c)   the possible defendants in a nuisance action;

(d)   the defences and especially the invalid defences;

(e)   the undecided point regarding recoverability of damage for personal injury and economic loss;

(f)   public nuisance;

(g)   the relevance of the **Human Rights Act 1998**, especially **s 6**, and **Arts 2** and **8** of the **European Convention on Human Rights (ECHR)**.

In addition, a nuisance question may contain elements of negligence or *Rylands v Fletcher* (1868).

QUESTION 26

Sarah owns a house in a small village that she leases to May. May owns four dogs, which she keeps in kennels in the garden. The dogs spend large amounts of the day and night barking, and this annoys her neighbours, Terence and Ursula. Victor, another neighbour, finds the noise during the day particularly annoying, as he works nights and has to sleep during the day. All of the neighbours complain to May, who refuses to do anything. Consequently, Ursula lights a large bonfire in her garden in the hope that the smoke will stop the barking. Terence, whose hobby is woodworking, takes the television suppressor off his electric drill and uses it in the evenings to interfere deliberately with the reception on May's television.

▶ **Discuss the legal situation.**

How to Answer this Question

The following points need to be discussed:

* whether the barking of the dogs is a nuisance;
* the liability of landlord and tenant in nuisance;
* whether Victor is a sensitive claimant;
* the liability of Ursula in nuisance for the bonfire;
* the liability of Terence in nuisance for the interference with the television reception;
* the liability of the local authority under the **Human Rights Act 1998**.

Applying the Law

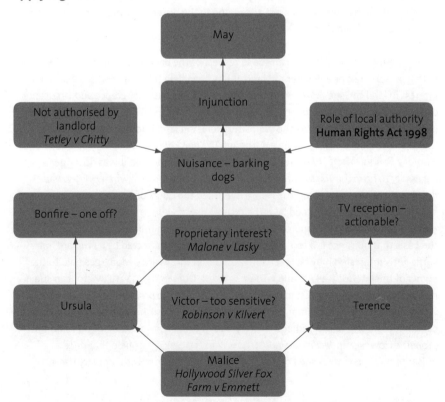

This diagram demonstrates May's, Ursula's and Terence's potential liability in Nuisance.

ANSWER

We must first decide whether the barking of the dogs constitutes a nuisance. A nuisance is an unreasonable interference with a person's use or enjoyment of land or some right over or in connection with it. It is well established that noise can constitute a nuisance (*Halsey v Esso Petroleum* (1961); *Tetley v Chitty* (1986)), but not all interference gives rise to liability. There must be give and take between neighbours, and the interference must be substantial and not fanciful (*Walter v Selfe* (1851)). As we are told that the dogs spend large amounts of the day and night barking, this noise would probably amount to a nuisance. Duration of the interference is one of the factors that a court would take into account in deciding whether a noise amounts to a nuisance. The shorter the duration of the interference, the less likely it is to be unreasonable (*Harrison v Southwark and Vauxhall Water Co* (1891)).[1]

Given that the barking of the dogs constitutes a nuisance, we must next decide who is the proper defendant in respect of this nuisance. As May is responsible for the dogs, she will be a defendant. The landlord, Sarah, will not be liable: the nuisance did not exist before she leased the premises; the premises have not been let for a purpose that constitutes a nuisance (as in *Tetley*); any right that Sarah has reserved to enter and repair is irrelevant, as the nuisance has not arisen due to the disrepair of the premises. Hence, May is the only defendant.

Finally, we must ascertain who can sue in respect of the barking. As nuisance is concerned with a person's use or enjoyment of land, it has been held that only persons with an interest in land can sue (*Malone v Laskey* (1907)). On this basis, if Terence and Ursula are owners or tenants of the property, they can sue but if, for example, Terence is the sole owner, Ursula would not have the requisite interest in land traditionally required to found an action in private nuisance. Although in *Khorasandjian v Bush* (1993) and *Hunter v Canary Wharf Ltd* (1996), the Court of Appeal found that it was no longer necessary to have the classic interest in land required by *Malone*, when *Hunter* was decided in the House of Lords, the House overruled the Court of Appeal on this point and held that *Malone* was still good law. The recent case of *Dobson v Thames Water Utilities* (2009) has confirmed this approach, while also considering human rights arguments, on the basis that nuisance is a tort affecting land. The people affected by it who are not sufficiently interested may be taken into account in the award of damages paid to the owner of the interest (see *Dobson v Thames Water Utilities No 2* (2011)). Victor can sue if he has the traditional interest in land, but may run into the problem that being a night worker, he is a sensitive claimant. In *Robinson v Kilvert* (1889), it was held that a claimant cannot recover where the damage is solely due to the sensitive nature of the claimant's property. However, in *McKinnon Industries v Walker* (1951), it was held that once a nuisance has been established on the grounds of interference with ordinary use, a

---

1   Explanation of the tort of nuisance in relation to noise interference requires citing relevant case law.

claimant can recover for interference with a sensitive use. Hence, if Victor can establish that the barking constitutes an unreasonable interference with his use or enjoyment of property, he will have full remedies. Any harm caused must be foreseeable (*The Wagon Mound (No 2)* (1967); *Cambridge Water Co v Eastern Counties Leather plc* (1994)), but this requirement gives rise to no problems for the claimants.

The remedies[2] available against May would be damages to compensate for past nuisance and an injunction to prevent further nuisance. The court does have power, under **s 50** of the **Senior Courts Act 1981**, to award damages in lieu of an injunction, but this power is used very sparingly. In *Shelfer v City of London Electric Lighting Co* (1895), the Court of Appeal held that damages should only be awarded where:

(a)   the injury to the claimant's legal rights is small;

(b)   the damage is capable of being estimated in money;

(c)   the damage can be adequately compensated by a small money payment;

(d)   the case is one in which it would be oppressive to the defendant to grant an injunction.

In *Jaggard v Sawyer* (1995), the Court of Appeal stated that these criteria provided a good working rule, but that the basic question was whether, in all of the circumstances, it would be oppressive to the defendant to grant the injunction. The question has recently been considered in *Regan v Paul Properties* (2007) and the *Shelfer* tests reaffirmed. On the facts that we are given, there seems no good reason for the court to diverge from the normal practice and thus an injunction should be granted against May.

We must next consider the actions of Ursula and Terence. Ursula has lit a large bonfire in her garden. This of itself may not constitute a nuisance – the interference must be substantial and not merely fanciful (*Walter v Selfe* (1851)). In deciding whether a particular interference is unreasonable or not, the court will rely on a series of guidelines, rather than on any rigid rules. In Ursula's case, the court would consider the duration of the interference, as the shorter the duration of the interference, the less likely it is to be unreasonable (*Harrison v Southwark and Vauxhall Water Co* (1891)). In particular, it seems that an isolated event is unlikely to constitute a nuisance. In *Bolton v Stone* (1951), it was stated that a nuisance must be a state of affairs, however temporary, and not merely an isolated happening. Thus, although Ursula might claim that the bonfire is an isolated event, it does constitute a temporary state of affairs and is capable, in law, of being a nuisance: see, for example, *Crown River Cruises v Kimbolton Fireworks* (1996). A possible argument that Ursula might employ is that she only lights a bonfire on rare occasions and that this is a reasonable use of her land. However, the fact that a defendant is only making reasonable use of his land is not, of itself, a valid defence in nuisance

---

2   Remember to consider remedies, especially as here when it can demonstrate the importance of injunctions in relation to nuisance.

(*AG v Cole* (1901); *Vanderpant v Mayfair Hotel* (1930)). As regards any interference with health and comfort, the court will take into account the character of the neighbourhood (*Bamford v Turnley* (1860)), as 'what would be a nuisance in Belgravia Square would not necessarily be so in Bermondsey' (*Sturges v Bridgman* (1879), *per* Thesiger LJ).[3] A contemporary application can be seen in the recent case of *Watson v Croft Promo-Sport Ltd* (2009). There it was held that a motor racing circuit in a rural location did constitute a nuisance, although it was only partly restricted by an injunction. However, in *Coventry Promotions v Lawrence* (2012) an action for nuisance by noise from motor-racing failed, as it was held that pre-existing motor-racing activities that had lawfully carried on for more than a decade, had become part of the 'character of the neighbourhood'. Thus, as Ursula lives in a rural area, the occasional lighting of a bonfire might not constitute a nuisance, as there must be an element of give and take between neighbours. However, if Ursula by her lack of care allowed an annoyance from the bonfire to become excessive, she would become liable in nuisance (*Andreae v Selfridge* (1938)). The character of the neighbourhood is not relevant, however, if the nuisance causes physical damage to the property (for example, if smoke from the bonfire discolours paintwork etc: *St Helen's Smelting Co v Tipping* (1865)). The real problem that Ursula faces, however, is that she is activated by malice. Although malice is not a necessary ingredient of nuisance, its presence is not only a factor to be taken into account (*Christie v Davey* (1893)), but may even turn an otherwise non-actionable activity into a nuisance (*Hollywood Silver Fox Farm v Emmett* (1936)), where it seems clear that in the absence of malice no action would have arisen. Ursula cannot claim to be making a reasonable use of her land if she intends to cause damage. Hence, May could sue Ursula in nuisance (May having the necessary interest in land, being a tenant) and obtain damages and an injunction.

Terence is deliberately interfering with May's television reception. This interference is presumably not of limited duration, which is a factor mitigating against unreasonableness of any interference (*Harrison v Southwark and Vauxhall Water Co* (1981)). Terence is clearly activated by malice, as in *Hollywood Silver Fox Farm* and *Christie*, so *prima facie* he would seem to have committed a nuisance. However, May has a problem, in that, in *Bridlington Relay v Yorkshire Electricity Board* (1965), Buckley J held that interference with purely recreational facilities, such as television reception, did not constitute an actionable nuisance and stated that 'at present' the ability to receive interference-free television signals was not so important a part of a householder's enjoyment of his property as to be protected in nuisance. The phrase 'at present' has been quoted by later claimants and, in the Canadian case of *Nor-Video Services Ltd v Ontario Hydro* (1978), it was held that interference with television reception could amount to a nuisance, and the High Court in *Hunter* took a similar view. Unfortunately for May,

---

3   This short phrase is easily remembered (just remember which way round the two very different areas in London appear in it!), and will come in useful in most questions on private nuisance.

both the Court of Appeal and the House of Lords in *Hunter* rejected this approach, holding that interference with television reception did not constitute an actionable nuisance. Thus, May has no remedy in respect of Terence's actions.[4]

Finally, we should consider any remedies that might be available to Terence, Ursula and Victor under the **Human Rights Act 1998**. Under **Art 8** of the **European Convention on Human Rights (ECHR)**, brought into UK law by **s 1** of the **1998 Act**, Terence, Ursula and Victor have the right to respect for private and family life. In *López Ostra v Spain* (1995), it was held that the construction of a waste treatment plant next to the applicant's house that caused local pollution and health problems was a violation of the applicant's rights. In this case, the Spanish government did not own the plant, but it was sufficient that the local authority had allowed the plant to be built. Under **s 6(1)** of the **1998 Act**, it is unlawful for a public authority to act in contravention of a **Convention** right. Also, and by **s 6(6)**, 'act' includes a failure to act. Consequently, it could be argued that by failing to institute proceedings for statutory nuisance, the local authority has failed to protect the rights that Terence, Ursula and Victor have under **s 6** and is thus liable in damages to these parties, although there is no indication given that the local authority is or should be aware of the situation. In *Baggs v UK* (1987) and *Hatton v UK* (2003), it was taken for granted by the European Court of Human Rights that noise came within **Art 8**.[5]

QUESTION 27

Beta Products plc owns a factory set in the centre of a manufacturing town and employs a considerable number of people. One day, the factory emits a quantity of acid fumes that damage the paintwork of the neighbouring houses and some residents' cars. In addition, Beta has recently installed some machinery that is considerably more noisy than the machinery it replaced and which annoys its immediate neighbours.

▶ Discuss any potential liability of Beta both at common law and under the **Human Rights Act 1998**.

How to Answer this Question

At first sight, this question seems only to cover a few issues of nuisance. However, careful study will show that it raises a number of common law issues, as well as the rapidly developing area of **Human Rights Act** actions.

---

4   Here there is consideration as to whether the actions taken against May constitute actionable nuisances themselves, with consideration of how the ancient law of nuisance deals with modern phenomena like TV reception.

5   When you have not been asked in the question to advise anyone in particular, as here, it is important to consider all possible claimants/defendants. This last part of the answer demonstrates an awareness of the effect of the **Human Rights Act 1998** in this area, which has become crucial in recent years.

The following points need to be discussed:

- ❖ the utility of Beta's conduct;
- ❖ the relevance of neighbourhood to interference with health and comfort and physical damage;
- ❖ whether an isolated event can constitute a nuisance;
- ❖ the possibility of action in public nuisance;
- ❖ additional actions in *Rylands v Fletcher* (1868) and negligence;
- ❖ the situation under the **Human Rights Act 1998**, with especial reference to **Art 8** of the **European Convention on Human Rights**.

Applying the Law

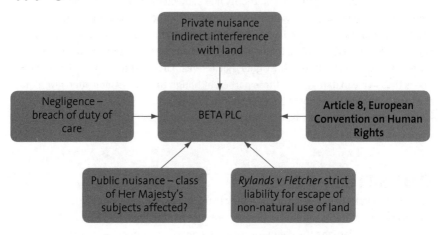

ANSWER

We shall first consider whether Beta plc has incurred any liability in private nuisance.[6] A nuisance is an unreasonable interference with a person's use or enjoyment of land, or of some right over or in connection with it. However, not all interference necessarily gives rise to liability and there must be give and take between neighbours. Also, the interference must be substantial and not fanciful (*Walter v Selfe* (1851)). The courts have developed a number of guidelines that are used to determine whether any particular interference is unreasonable, but each test is only a guideline and not a condition, and the court has to evaluate the defendant's behaviour in all of the circumstances of the case. In Beta's case, the court will consider whether the emission was an isolated event. In *Bolton v Stone* (1951), it was stated that a nuisance could not arise from an isolated

---

6   This question requires coverage of a huge swathe of law, and thus a brief overview of each is required, starting with private nuisance. In such questions, careful planning is required to avoid omitting anything (see diagram).

happening, but had to arise from a state of affairs, however temporary. Thus, in *Midwood v Manchester Corp* (1905), a gas explosion was held to be a nuisance because, although it was an isolated event, it was due to a pre-existing state of affairs – namely, the build-up of gas. On this basis, it could be argued that the escape of acid smut was due to a build-up of this material on Beta's premises and thus the emission can constitute an actionable nuisance. The damage suffered is not due to any sensitive use of the neighbours' property (as in *Robinson v Kilvert* (1889)) and, although the premises are in the centre of a manufacturing town, the character of the neighbourhood is not to be taken into account where physical damage to property has been caused (*St Helen's Smelting Co v Tipping* (1865)). We are told that Beta employs a considerable number of people, but the utility of the defendants' conduct, although a factor to be taken into account, seems to be a factor of lesser importance in the overall assessment (*Adams v Ursell* (1913); Irish case of *Bellew v Cement Co* (1948)). Thus, the fact that Beta provides employment is not a conclusive factor. Note that it would not be necessary to show that Beta was negligent, as negligence is not an essential ingredient of nuisance. Indeed, it would be no defence to Beta to show that it took all reasonable care and even all possible care, provided that it caused the nuisance, that is sufficient. Thus, taking all of the circumstances into account, a court would find that the emission constituted an actionable nuisance. Traditionally, an interest in the land in question was required as a prerequisite for an action in nuisance (*Malone v Laskey* (1907)) and, although this requirement was relaxed by the Court of Appeal in *Khorasandjian v Bush* (1993) and *Hunter v Canary Wharf Ltd* (1996), it was reimposed by the House of Lords in *Hunter* (1997). Hence, only owners and tenants of the properties affected may sue, and not their guests or lodgers. The owners and tenants could obtain damages for the loss (apart from any personal injuries) that they have suffered, together with an injunction to prevent future emissions. The case of *Dobson v Thames Water Utilities* (2009) confirms this view. There the claims of children and other non-interested parties were not considered, despite a strong argument based on human rights considerations. The tort, according to the Court of Appeal, affects land, and damages reflect the loss of value of the land. However, such loss of value could also take account of interferences with other people residing on the property without a proprietary interest. This was confirmed in *Dobson v Thames Water Utilities No 2* (2011) where the court held that Thames Water were liable for breach of duty in relation to nuisance caused by odour and that there had been a breach of human rights. It applied the principle set down in *Dobson and others v Thames Water Utilities Ltd* [2009] that the award of damages in nuisance to the property owners was relevant when considering an award of damages under the **Human Rights Act 1998** for a non-property-owning claimant. However, having taken into account all the circumstances of the case, it was not satisfied that an award of damages to non-property-owning claimants, such as children, was in fact necessary as this had been accounted for in the owners' damages for nuisance. As regards the noisy machinery, it is well established that noise can constitute a nuisance (*Halsey v Esso Petroleum* (1961); *Tetley v Chitty* (1986)). In deciding whether the noise from the machinery amounts to a nuisance, it is clearly not an isolated event of limited duration, nor is there any evidence of sensitivity on the part of the neighbours. However, as the noise is an interference with health and comfort, the character of the neighbourhood must be taken into account (*Bamford v Turnley* (1860)). As Thesiger LJ stated in *Sturges v Bridgman* (1879), 'what would be a nuisance in Belgravia Square would not necessarily be so in Bermondsey'. As we are told that Beta's factory is in the centre of a manufacturing town, the neighbours would have to accept a certain amount of noise as part of everyday living. However, in *Roshner v Polsue and Alfieri Ltd* (1906), in which a person lived in an area devoted to printing, he obtained an injunction to prevent the use of a new printing machine that interfered with his sleep. Thus, it will be a question of fact for the court to decide whether or not the increased noise amounts to a nuisance in all of the circumstances of the case. Again, only persons with an interest in land could sue in respect of this noise (*Malone*; *Hunter*). It should also be noted that foreseeability of harm is a necessary ingredient of nuisance (*The Wagon Mound (No 2)* (1967); *Cambridge Water Co v Eastern Counties Leather plc* (1994)), but harm is foreseeable for both the fumes and the noise.

Beta might also, as regards the emission, be liable in public nuisance (*Halsey v Esso Petroleum* (1961)). Similar considerations will apply as for private nuisance, but some additional factors must be shown. Firstly, the persons affected by the nuisance must consist of the public or a section of the public (*AG v PYA Quarries* (1957)). Secondly, the claimant must have suffered damage over and above that suffered by the public at large. A highly significant decision was taken in *Corby Group Litigation Claimants v Corby BC* (2008), which permitted the recovery of personal injury for public nuisances. This currently makes public nuisance the only form of the tort which permits such recovery. In *Halsey*, it was held that where acid smuts damaged washing hung out to dry and a car, the owner of the damaged property could sue in public nuisance. Thus, the car owners whose car paintwork is damaged could sue in public nuisance and they would not have to have any interest in land. Whether those persons whose paintwork was damaged could sue would depend on their being able to prove damage over and above that suffered by the public at large.[7]

An additional cause of action that might lie against Beta is under the rule in *Rylands v Fletcher* (1868). According to this case, a person who 'for his own purposes, brings onto his land and collects and keeps there anything likely to do mischief if it escapes, must keep it in at his peril and, if he does not do so, he is *prima facie* answerable for all the damage which is the natural consequence of its escape'.[8] In addition, there must be a non-natural user of land and the damage must be foreseeable (*Cambridge Water Co*). Again, in *Halsey*, the defendants were liable under *Rylands* for the damage caused by the acid smuts to both the washing and the car. A problem that could arise is whether Beta has made a

---

7   Here, application of relevant cases on public nuisance to Beta's use of the land is required, especially in relation to personal injury.

8   When applying *Rylands* it is advisable to be able to cite the words of the original judgment, as here.

non-natural use of its land. After *Halsey*, it was held in *British Celanese v Hunt* (1969) that factories in industrial parks were a natural use of land. More recently, however, in *Cambridge Water Co*, the House of Lords took a more restrictive approach as to what constitutes natural use and in particular stated that the provision of employment did not, of itself, constitute a natural or ordinary use of land. In *Transco v Stockport Metropolitan Borough Council* (2004), the House of Lords undertook an extensive, in-depth review of the rule in *Rylands* and held that the requirement that the thing is likely to do mischief if it escapes should not be easily satisfied. It must be shown that the defendant has done something that he recognised or ought to have recognised as giving rise to an exceptionally high risk of danger or mischief if it escapes, however unlikely such an escape might have been thought to be. The acid fumes and noise could come into this category. In addition, their Lordships considered the non-natural use requirement and held that the defendant's use of the land must be extraordinary and unusual. The House doubted whether the test of reasonable use was helpful, since a use may be very out of the ordinary but still reasonable, such as the storage of chemicals in an industrial park. Thus, the fact that Beta's factory is situated in a manufacturing town, which might be relevant to reasonable use, still does not stop the use from being extraordinary and unusual. Hence it seems likely that Beta could be liable in a *Rylands* action.

It would also be possible for those persons affected by the emission to sue in negligence. The claimants will have to show that Beta owes them a duty of care. In a novel fact situation, the court will apply the test favoured by the House of Lords in *Caparo Industries plc v Dickman* (1990) and *Murphy v Brentwood District Council* (1990) – namely, to consider the foreseeability of damage, proximity of relationship and the reasonableness or otherwise of imposing a duty of care. If a duty is found to exist, it must be shown that Beta was in breach of that duty by failing to act as a reasonable factory owner would (*Blyth v Birmingham Waterworks* (1856)). It must also be shown that this breach caused the damage and that the damage was not too remote, in that it was reasonably foreseeable (*The Wagon Mound (No 1)* (1961)). The problem in a negligence action will be in proving that Beta was in breach of its duty for, if it followed the standard procedure of its trade, that is good evidence that it was not in breach (see, for example, *Knight v Home Office* (1990)).

Finally, we must consider any causes of action that might arise under the **Human Rights Act 1998**. **Article 8** of the **European Convention on Human Rights (ECHR)**, which was brought into UK law by s1 of the **Human Rights Act 1998**, establishes the right to respect for private and family life and home. Also, **Art 1** of the **First Protocol** to the ECHR states that persons are entitled to the peaceful enjoyment of their possessions and **Art 2** establishes a right to life.

As regards **Art 8**, in *López Ostra v Spain* (1995), it was held that the construction of a waste treatment plant next to the applicant's house, which had caused local pollution and health problems, was a violation of **Art 8**. In this case, the Spanish government did not own the plant, but it was held to be sufficient that the local authority had allowed it to be built on their land and the government had subsidised it. As s 6(1) of the 1998 Act makes it unlawful for a public authority to act in any way incompatible with a Convention right, and by s 6(6) an 'act' includes a failure to act, both the government and local authorities could be held liable for breaches of Art 8. Article 8 has also been held to apply to toxic emissions from a factory (*Guerra v Italy* (1998)), so clearly hazardous emissions could fall within Art 8 and even Art 2 if the emissions were sufficiently hazardous. However, in *Hatton v UK* (2003) and *Marcic v Thames Water Utilities Ltd* (2004), the fundamentally subsidiary nature of the Convention was emphasised. In *Hatton*, it was stated that national authorities have direct democratic legitimation and are well placed to evaluate local needs and conditions. Thus, if the local authority had canvassed opinions of persons affected by the activities of Beta and considered these opinions before allowing the activities, it is possible that the Convention action would fail: see *Hatton*.

An action under the Human Rights Act 1998 would raise no problems as regards interest in land (*McKenna v British Aluminium Ltd* (2002)), recovery of economic loss or application to personal injuries. Indeed, in *Marcic v Thames Water Utilities Ltd* (2001), the High Court judge found for the claimant under Art 8, while dismissing the claims based on nuisance and *Rylands v Fletcher*; although the House of Lords dismissed the claimants' actions in both nuisance and under Art 8 (following *Hatton*), it is clear from the High Court decision that much of the detailed law of nuisance is irrelevant in considering a breach of Art 8 (see also *Dennis v MOD* (2003)). Thus, an action under the Human Rights Act 1998 would be available to a considerable range of claimants who suffer personal injury due to Beta's factory (subject to the subsidiary nature point discussed in *Hatton* and *Marcic*), and the possible defendants to such an action could be the local authority under s 6(1) and (6) of the 1998 Act, or the UK government.[9]

QUESTION 28

Ricardo has recently bought an old manor house in the heart of the countryside which he intends to open to the public when it has been restored. The necessary building work caused considerable noise, dust and fumes to spread over the neighbouring district. The villagers nearby suffered disruption to their sleep on several occasions and they were unable to go into their gardens during the summer months because of the smells. They also found that their cars and paintwork were covered with grime. Additionally, the parish council had received a number of letters expressing fears that the visitors to the manor would disrupt the villagers' tranquillity in future, particularly in blocking the narrow streets with their cars. The council passed on these concerns, and the fact that

9   It is essential nowadays to consider Human Rights Act implications in relation to claims which might previously have been restricted to nuisance and negligence.

the villagers were very angry, to Ricardo, but he failed to respond. He is in financial difficulties, and spends long periods away from the site.

During the building work, Dan, a specialist pipe-layer, is employed to replace the old drains. While digging a trench, he pierces an electricity cable and receives a severe electric shock. Dan has to have his arm amputated and he can no longer work.

That night, Marco, one of the villagers, organises a protest against the building work outside the boundary wall. During the course of the protest, he climbs over the wall, intending to place one of his protest banners directly under Ricardo's window. On the way back from doing this, he falls down the unfinished trench which had been left uncovered after Dan was rushed to hospital. Marco is a keen footballer but he has now badly damaged his legs and is unlikely to play again.

(i)   Discuss the rights of the villagers in tort in connection with the disturbances, both current and potential, and indicate what remedies might be available to them. To what extent does it make a difference to your answer to know whether planning permission had been granted for this project?

(ii)   Explain to Ricardo whether Dan and Marco are likely to have a successful claim against him in tort, and what their remedy might be. He also wishes to know if he may take a civil claim against Marco.

How to Answer this Question

This question requires consideration of three different topics which may not have been taught together. Students should be alert for this possibility, about which they may have been forewarned. This requires the student to identify the relevant material, and apply it as appropriate. As it is in two parts, an assessment will have to be made as to the relevant weight to be given to each part of the question in terms of how much time to spend on each. For this question, as no indication is given, it might be appropriate to assume that they are of roughly equal weight.

The following points need to be discussed:

❖   whether the villagers have any rights in public or private nuisance;
❖   the effect of planning permission;
❖   Ricardo's potential liability under the **Occupiers' Liability Acts**;
❖   Liability of Marco in trespass;
❖   Any remedies or defences.

Applying the Law

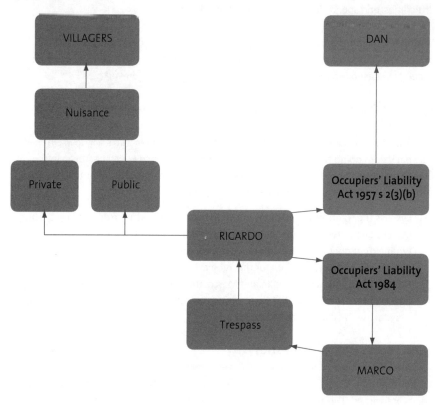

This diagram shows Ricardo's potential liability under nuisance and the Occupiers' Liability Acts.

ANSWER

The villagers are concerned about the interference with their property and so would be able to consider taking action against Ricardo in either public or private nuisance. They might also consider an action based on the **European Convention on Human Rights (ECHR)**, incorporated into English law by the **Human Rights Act 1998**, because **Article 8** gives a right to respect for private life.[10]

Private nuisance is 'an unlawful interference with persons' use or enjoyment of land or some right over or in connection with it' (Winfield & Jolowitz, *Tort*).[11] The first important thing for the villagers is to establish whether they have the right to sue in private

---

10   As the specific tort actions were not referred to in the question, identifying what they are is a crucial part of answering the question, and one that will earn relatively 'easy' credit.
11   Tort is an ancient common law tort, so a referenced textbook definition is acceptable.

nuisance, because the House of Lords in *Hunter v Canary Wharf* (1997) confirmed the old principle of law in *Malone v Lasky* (1907) that only those with a proprietary interest in the land can claim. So only owners and tenants can sue, not, for example, others in the houses such as children, visitors or lodgers such as au pairs, who might be equally affected. The argument that this might be inconsistent with these individuals' **Article 8** rights has been considered by the courts in cases like *Dobson v Thames Water* (2008), but when the High Court re-examined the position in *Dobson v Thames Water* (2011), the children did not receive separate compensation as it was held that this had been accounted for in the owners' damages.

Assuming that at least some of the villagers fulfil this criterion, they would need to establish that the indirect interference (here noise, fumes and smells which have long been recognised as being capable of constituting a nuisance in cases such as *Halsey v Esso Petroleum* (1961) etc) was unreasonable. In relation to the material property damage to their cars, there should be no difficulty in establishing this as in *St Helens Smelting Co v Tipping* (1865), but in relation to amenity damage the courts might require a balancing of factors between the claimants and the defendants because as was said by Thesiger LJ in *Sturges v Bridgman* (1879) 'what might be a nuisance in Belgravia Square would not necessarily be so in Bermondsey'.[12] It would be taken into account that this was a rural area, which is described as previously 'tranquil', so it could be seen as unreasonable. However, the building work is likely to be temporary and the duration of the nuisance is an important factor. The courts have held though that even temporary disruption can be actionable (*De Keysers Royal Hotel v Spicer Bros* (1914)). Ricardo might try to argue that he is providing employment and that the public good of this outweighs the private harm, but the courts are unlikely to accept this as in *Dennis v Ministry of Defence* (2003). If he had obtained planning permission for this enterprise, that would not in itself be a defence to creating a nuisance (*Wheeler v Saunders* (1996)), unless it could be said to have changed the whole nature of the neighbourhood, which is unlikely here with the relatively small scale of the project (*Gillingham BC v Medway Docks* (1993)).[13]

The villagers might wish to try to obtain an injunction to restrict the noise and dust etc to particular times, and to prohibit the Manor from being opened to the public. The granting of an injunction is discretionary as it is an equitable right, and so the courts might decide to award damages instead (*Shelfer v City of London Electric Lighting Co* (1895)), although this is for the defendant to argue, not the claimants (*Regan v Paul Properties* [2006]). As we know Ricardo is already in financial difficulties, this might be enough to bring the

---

12 This is a useful quote for any question on nuisance, but ensure you get the areas of London the right way round!

13 Always remember to apply the law to the facts in the problem, and say as much as possible about why it applies; as here, by drawing attention to the small scale.

project to an end anyway.[14] However, this will obviously be a costly procedure for the villagers, and as always with neighbour disputes it might be preferable to try to negotiate a settlement rather than resorting to a court battle which would sour relationships for the future. Nevertheless, a knowledge of their legal position would enable the villagers to negotiate from a position of strength.[15]

The concerns about the blocking of the highway are likely to amount to public nuisance which requires there to be '... an act or omission which materially affects the reasonable comfort and convenience of life of a class of Her Majesty's subjects' (*Attorney General v PYA Quarries* (1957), Romer LJ) and in order to sue for tort the claimant must be affected more than others in the class. In this case therefore, unless there are individuals who fulfil this requirement, it may be best to leave this to be dealt with as the crime of public nuisance, or to other powers that the Council might have over the highway system. However, if the cars which were damaged were on public roads, as in *Halsey*, the owners could recover under public nuisance.

Dan could possibly sue Ricardo under the **Occupiers' Liability Act (OLA) 1957**. As a visitor, he is owed the 'common duty of care' by virtue of **s 2(1)** by Ricardo, who would qualify as the occupier as he would seem to have sufficient 'control' over the property as we are told he is the owner (*Wheat v Lacon* (1966)). This is so unless his trips away are significant enough to mean that somebody else has control. The duty is to take 'reasonable care to ensure that visitors are reasonably safe' (**s 2(2)**), and is by no means absolute liability as demonstrated in such cases as *Bowen v National Trust* (2011) where the defendant was not liable for a branch which fell on and injured children in a school party. Here, Ricardo could rely on **s 2(3)(b)**, which states that 'those in the exercise of their calling' should in effect take care of themselves, and as long as Ricardo has not interfered with the way Dan works, it would seem that he has been injured in the course of his specialist work and therefore no liability attaches to Ricardo.

Incidentally, Dan may have a claim against his employer for, maybe, not training him sufficiently, or alternatively under the **OLA 1957** if his employer is an occupier, but as the question asks us to advise Ricardo, this need not detain us longer.[16]

Marco is clearly a trespasser as he has no right to be on Ricardo's land. Thus if Ricardo owes him a duty at all it will fall to be determined under the **Occupiers' Liability Act 1984, s 1(3)** which covers liability to 'non-visitors'. All three parts of the subsection have to be met, and it is much more difficult to establish than the duty in the **1957 Act**. Marco would

---

14 Again, try to use all the information given to make relevant points based on the legal situation.

15 It can be valuable to point out any practical implications of legal advice in answering a question, provided that the legal position is clarified first.

16 This is the type of information which may be included if there are no time constraints.

have to show that (a) Ricardo knew of the danger (here, the uncovered ditch); (b) knew or had reasonable grounds to suspect he was in the vicinity of the danger; and (c) it was reasonable in the circumstances for something to have been done to protect Marco from the danger.[17] Given that we are told that Ricardo is often away, and that the ditch had been left open very recently due to an emergency, it is highly unlikely that Ricardo will owe Marco a duty. If however, he does, then the duty is very similar to that under the **1957 Act**, to take reasonable care (**s1(4)**). Alternatively it could be argued, as it very often successfully is against adult trespassers, that he knew he was running a risk by going at night onto property where building work was going on and so the defence of *volenti* would apply (**s1(6)** and cases such as *Tomlinson v Congleton BC* (2003) and *Ratcliff v McConnell* (1999)).

Marco could be sued by Ricardo as he has committed the tort of trespass to land by coming directly on to land where he is not permitted to be. This ancient tort is actionable *per se*, so even though it appears Marco has done no damage, he could be sued. Ricardo should be told however that he could only be granted nominal damages to mark the breach, so this is unlikely to be worthwhile.

Neither Dan nor Marco appear to have a strong claim against Ricardo, but if they were to be successful they would be awarded damages, which would seek to put them in the position they would have been in had the tort never occurred, insofar as money can do that, and would mainly cover costs like loss of earnings and medical expenses, and non-tangible losses such as suffering pain and loss of amenity such as playing football. Considering Ricardo's financial position however, he may not be in a position to pay any claim unless he is adequately insured.

QUESTION 29 --

'The difficulties of proceeding with an action in private nuisance are grave, but the prospects of potential claimants have increased with the coming into force of the **Human Rights Act 1998**.'

▶ **Discuss the above statement.**

How to Answer this Question

This question calls for a discussion of some of the problems that would be encountered in successfully running an action in private nuisance.

In particular, the following points need to be discussed:

❖ the guidelines in determining whether any particular interference is unreasonable;

17 Here the opportunity is taken not just to recite or copy the statute, but to apply it directly to the facts.

* possible defendants;
* the defences available to a defendant;
* the scope of the action as regards personal injury and economic loss;
* nuisance and the **Human Rights Act 1998**.

Answer Structure

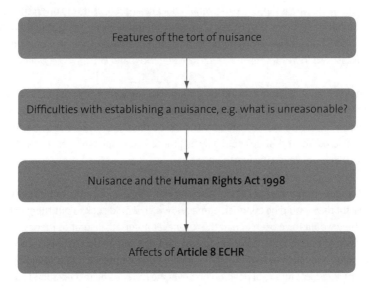

Features of the tort of nuisance

Difficulties with establishing a nuisance, e.g. what is unreasonable?

Nuisance and the **Human Rights Act 1998**

Affects of **Article 8 ECHR**

ANSWER

The law on private nuisance, or nuisance as we shall henceforth call it, gives rise to a number of difficulties in its application to factual situations. This is due not to any conceptual difficulty, but rather to the variety of circumstances in which nuisances have been held to exist and to the flexible approach that the courts adopt in deciding in any given case whether or not a nuisance exists. In addition, the exact scope of the tort is shrouded in uncertainty. Therefore, we shall examine these uncertainties.[18]

A nuisance can be defined as an unreasonable interference with a person's use or enjoyment of land, or some right over or in connection with it. It was previously held from this definition that only persons with an interest in the land affected can sue (*Malone v Laskey* (1907)) and, although this requirement was relaxed by the Court of Appeal in *Khorasandjian v Bush* (1993), it was reimposed by the House of Lords in *Hunter* (1997). Although this has narrowed the range of potential claimants, it has reintroduced some certainty back into nuisance, as the exact link between the person affected and the land was somewhat uncertain following the Court of Appeal decision and *dicta* in *Hunter*. The

---

18 This opening paragraph succinctly addresses the issues to be discussed.

decision in *Dobson v Thames Water Utilities* (2009) has further clarified this point, confirming the need for a link with the property, due to the fact that nuisance is a tort that protects interests in land, either the land itself, or the value of its amenity. It should also be noted that foreseeability of damage is a necessary ingredient of nuisance (*The Wagon Mound (No 2)* (1967); *Cambridge Water Co v Eastern Counties Leather plc* (1994)), although this is unlikely to be a problem in practice. It also seems, from the decision in *Bridlington Relay Ltd v Yorkshire Electricity Board* (1965), that interference with purely recreational facilities lies outside the tort of nuisance. In *Bridlington*, the court was concerned with the reception of interference-free television signals. Despite the use of the phrase 'at present' by Buckley J in his judgment and the willingness of the High Court in *Hunter* (1994) to allow an action in nuisance for interference with television signals, both the Court of Appeal (1996) and the House of Lords (1997) in *Hunter* held that an action did not lie for such interference. Thus, an uncertainty has been removed, in that the possibility of an action in such circumstances certainly does not arise, although the exact extent of purely recreational facilities is not clear.

Moving on to what constitutes an unreasonable interference, we meet a major area of uncertainty. The courts have laid down a series of guidelines as to what constitutes an unreasonable interference but, as in any situation in which it has to be decided whether or not some particular conduct is reasonable, the courts' decisions cannot amount to binding precedents. The total circumstances of the case must always be taken into account in deciding this question. What gives rise to particular uncertainty in nuisance is that the courts seem willing, when the circumstances require it, to either disregard a particular guideline or to assign it less importance in some cases than in others. Nevertheless, there is one guideline that the courts seem willing to follow on almost all occasions – namely, the rule that not all interference gives rise to liability, that there must be give and take between neighbours, and that the interference must be substantial and not merely fanciful (*Walter v Selfe* (1851)). When we consider the guidelines that the courts adopt, we shall see that there are three that the courts tend to apply in the majority of cases, and three that the courts consider, but to which they seem more willing to attach a lower importance if the circumstances so require.

Turning now to the first category, we have the duration of the interference. The shorter the duration of the interference, the less likely it is to be found unreasonable. So, in *Harrison v Southwark and Vauxhall Water Co* (1891), temporary work in sinking a shaft was held not to constitute a nuisance because of the temporary nature of the work. Given that a short interference is not likely to give rise to liability, the question arises as to whether an isolated event is capable of constituting a nuisance. In *Bolton v Stone* (1951), it was held that an isolated happening could not constitute a nuisance, but that what was required was a state of affairs, however temporary. Thus, in *Midwood v Manchester Corp* (1905), a gas explosion was held to constitute a nuisance, even though it was an isolated event, because it was due to a pre-existing state of affairs – namely, a build-up of gas.

One factor that the courts seem to always take into account is whether the claimant is abnormally sensitive. The rule is that a person cannot increase his neighbour's possible legal liability just because he puts his land to some special use. Thus, in *Robinson v Kilvert* (1889), a plaintiff could not recover for damage caused by heat from the defendant's heating pipes to his stock of 'exceptionally sensitive' brown paper, as the heat would not have interfered with a normal use of the property. However, once a nuisance has been established, full remedies are available in respect of any unusually sensitive use that the claimant makes of his property (*McKinnon Industries v Walker* (1951)).

The character of the neighbourhood is also a relevant factor where the interference is with health and comfort (*Bamford v Turnley* (1860)). This is also illustrated by the famous statement of Thesiger J in *Sturges v Bridgman* (1879), in which he said 'what would be a nuisance in Belgravia Square would not necessarily be so in Bermondsey'.[19] It should not be thought that this criterion means that if an area is industrialised or built up, then no nuisance can take place there; the question that has to be decided is whether the interference is unreasonable or not, having regard to the general area. Thus, in *Roshner v Polsue and Alfieri Ltd* (1906), a plaintiff who lived in an area that was mostly given over to printing successfully claimed that the noise of a new printing machine constituted a nuisance, as it was held that the noise of this machine was excessive even for an area largely devoted to printing. Clearly, therefore, whether a particular interference with health and comfort is actionable will depend on the exact nature of the area and the interference in question, making the chances of success at trial difficult to predict with any confidence. In *Coventry Promotions v Lawrence* (2012) an action for nuisance by noise from motor-racing failed, as it was held that pre-existing motor-racing activities that had lawfully carried on for more than a decade had become part of the 'character of the neighbourhood'.[20] It should be noted, however, that the character of the neighbourhood is not relevant where property damage has been caused (*St Helen's Smelting Co v Tipping* (1865)).

Now we come to those guidelines to which the courts are ready to attach a lesser importance when the circumstances of the case demand it. Firstly, there is the utility of the defendant's conduct, as the more useful it is, the less likely it is that the resulting interference with the claimant's land is unreasonable. This would be especially true in, for example, construction work where in addition the interference will be temporary. However, if the circumstances so require, the court will override this guideline. So, in the Irish case of *Bellew v Cement Co* (1948), the court decided that the only cement works in Ireland constituted a nuisance and granted an injunction that closed it down for a period of time, despite the fact that the supply of cement was vitally important. In

---

19 This quote, correctly remembered, is nearly always useful in a nuisance question.
20 A modern case example will add authority to the answer.

Adams v Ursell (1913), an English court also rejected the defence that the defendant's activities were useful.

Secondly, the courts may take into account any malice on the part of the defendant. Malice is not an essential ingredient of nuisance but, if the defendant is acting maliciously, any interference caused thereby is more likely to be unreasonable. Thus, in *Christie v Davey* (1893), in which the defendant's acts were totally malicious, they were held to constitute a nuisance. In *Christie*, it is quite likely that the acts of the defendants would have been held to constitute a nuisance even in the absence of malice but, in *Hollywood Silver Fox Farm v Emmett* (1936), the presence of malice converted what probably would not have been a nuisance into a nuisance. There, the defendant fired some guns at the boundary of his land, adjacent to the plaintiff's land, where foxes that were sensitive to noise were breeding. It was held that this constituted a nuisance, although it seems clear that in the absence of malice, no nuisance would have been committed.

The final guideline to which the courts look is whether there has been some fault on the part of the defendant. Negligence is not an essential ingredient of nuisance, although it may often be present in practice, as it is no defence to an action in nuisance for the defendant to show that he took all reasonable care or even all possible care. Provided that the defendant caused (or continued) the nuisance, he is liable. However, the defendant's lack of care in allowing an annoyance to become excessive may give rise to liability in nuisance (*Andreae v Selfridge and Co* (1938)).

It can be seen from the above discussion that whether the court will decide in any particular case that the interference suffered was unreasonable is difficult to predict and tends to support the statement that forms this question. There are, however, additional areas of uncertainty within the law of nuisance. One problem concerns who can be sued in respect of any particular interference. There is no problem where the creator of the nuisance can be identified, but problems may arise where the occupier of land from which the nuisance emanates did not create the thing that causes the nuisance. If the relevant device was created by a trespasser, the occupier will only be liable if he continues or adopts the device (*Sedleigh-Denfield v O'Callaghan* (1940)). If the occupier does neither of these things, it may be impossible to identify the trespasser, leaving the claimant without a remedy. If the nuisance arose from an act of nature, then, by the authority of *Goldman v Hargrave* (1967) and *Leakey v National Trust* (1980), the occupier must take reasonable steps to minimise foreseeable damage to others. Again, what a court will think is reasonable in any set of circumstances can be difficult to predict. If a tenant causes a nuisance on demised premises and is not worth suing because he will be unable to satisfy judgment, the landlord may be liable if he knew of the nuisance before the start of the tenancy, or if he knew the purposes for which the tenancy was created would give rise to a nuisance as an 'ordinary and necessary' consequence of the use (*Tetley v Chitty* (1986)).

It is generally not a valid defence to show that the claimant came to the nuisance (*Sturqes v Bridgman* (1879)). However, in *Miller v Jackson* (1977), in which some houses were built at the edge of a village green on which cricket was played and cricket balls landed in the plaintiff's garden, Lord Denning stated that *Sturges* was no longer binding today, but this was not the view of the other members of the Court of Appeal. Lord Denning also stated in this case that where there was a conflict between public and private rights, public rights should prevail. This was exactly opposite to the view taken in the earlier case of *Pride of Derby v British Celanese* (1953), in which it was held that private rights should prevail. However, in the later case of *Kennaway v Thompson* (1981), the Court of Appeal refused to follow Lord Denning's *dicta* and held that where there was a clash between private and public rights, private rights should prevail. This represents a further area of uncertainty in the law of nuisance, but it is submitted that Lord Denning's *dicta* regarding the priority of public rights do not represent the correct view of the law at present and that his *dicta* regarding *Sturges*, a long-established case, must await confirmation by the House of Lords.

We should note that one important area of former uncertainty has been considered recently – namely, whether recovery is possible in nuisance in respect of personal injuries. In *Cunard v Antifyre* (1933), it was stated that recovery for personal injury is not possible. Also, in *Cambridge Water Co v Eastern Counties Leather plc* (1994), the House of Lords, when considering an action under the rule in *Rylands v Fletcher* (1868), referred with approval to a 'seminal' article by Professor Newark ('The boundaries of nuisance' (1949) 65 LQR 480), in which he argued that recovery for personal injury should not be possible in nuisance. Although the House did not decide the situation regarding recovery in respect of personal injury in *Rylands*, let alone in nuisance, their Lordships' wholehearted acceptance of Professor Newark's article suggests that a future court will not allow such recovery. Thus, it came as no surprise when the House of Lords in *Hunter v Canary Wharf Ltd* (1997) followed their reasoning in *Cambridge Water Co* and declared that actions for personal injury should not be brought in nuisance. Despite the decisions in *Hunter* and the *dicta* suggesting non-recovery under *Rylands* in *Transco v Stockport MBC* (2004) it was held in *Corby Group Litigation v Corby BC* (2009) that damages for personal injury *were* available in public (but not private) nuisance.

Another debatable point is whether economic loss can be recovered in nuisance. Although there exist *dicta* in *British Celanese v Hunt* (1969) and *Ryeford Homes v Sevenoaks District Council* (1989) that suggest that economic loss is recoverable, the whole tenor of the judgments of the House of Lords in *Cambridge Water Co* and *Hunter* is against such recovery.

It should also be noted that if the activity that it is claimed constitutes a nuisance is regulated by statute, a common law claim in nuisance will not be allowed if it is inconsistent with the statutory scheme (*Marcic v Thames Water Utilities Ltd* (2004)), but see *Barr & Ors v Bifffa Waste Services* (2012) where the Court of Appeal held that the permit under which the waste disposal company was operating did not amount to statutory authority and did not provide a defence to nuisance.

Finally, we should note the recent and possibly far-reaching effect of the Human Rights Act 1998 on the law of nuisance. Article 8 of the European Convention on Human Rights, brought into the law by s 1 of the 1998 Act, establishes the right to respect for private and family life and home. Article 1 of the First Protocol to the ECHR states that persons are entitled to the peaceful enjoyment of their possessions, and Art 2 of the Convention establishes a right to life.

As regards Art 8, in *López Ostra v Spain* (1995) it was held that the construction of a waste treatment plant next to the applicant's house, which had caused local pollution and health problems, was a violation of Art 8. In this case, the Spanish government did not own the plant, but it was held to be sufficient that the local authority had allowed it to be built on their land and the Spanish government had subsidised it. As s 6(1) of the 1998 Act makes it unlawful for a public authority to act in a way incompatible with a Convention right and by s 6(6) an 'act' includes a failure to act, both the government and local authorities could be held liable for breaches of Art 8. Article 8 has also been held to cover noise (*Baggs v UK* (1987); *Hatton v UK* (2003)) and toxic emissions (*Guerra v Italy* (1998)). Clearly, hazardous emissions could fall within Art 1 and even Art 2 if the emissions are sufficiently hazardous.

This new jurisprudence could have extensive effects on the law of nuisance. An action under the Human Rights Act 1998 would raise no problems of interest in land, recovery of economic loss or application to personal injuries. Indeed, in *Marcic* (2001), in the High Court, the judge found for the claimant under Art 8 while dismissing the claims based on nuisance and *Rylands*. Although the House of Lords dismissed the claimant's claims in both nuisance and under Art 8, it is clear from the judgments in both the High Court and the Court of Appeal that much of the detailed law of nuisance is irrelevant in considering a breach of Art 8. In *Dobson v Thames Water Utilities No 2* (2011) the court held that Thames Water were liable for breach of duty in relation to nuisance caused by odour and that there had been a breach of human rights. It applied the principle set down in *Dobson and others v Thames Water Utilities Ltd* [2009] that the award of damages in nuisance to the property owners was relevant when considering an award of damages under the Human Rights Act 1998 for a non-property-owning claimant. However, having taken into account all the circumstances of the case, it was not satisfied that an award of damages to non-property-owning claimants, such as children, was in fact necessary as this had been accounted for in the owners' damages for nuisance

However, the European Convention on Human Rights does not automatically provide a mechanism for bypassing much of the detailed common law of nuisance. In *Hatton* and *Marcic*, the fundamentally subsidiary nature of the Convention was emphasised. In *Hatton*, it was stated that national authorities have direct democratic legitimation and are well placed to evaluate local needs and conditions. A fair balance must be struck between the interests of the individual and the interests of the community as a whole. Thus, if the appropriate national or local authority consults widely and considers carefully all responses to its consultation, it will not be found in breach of the **Convention** (*Hatton*).

A further restriction on the use of the **Convention** is the existence of a detailed statutory regime in which the potential nuisance exists. Thus, in *Marcic*, the House of Lords held the contents of a statutory scheme for a statutory sewerage undertaker struck a reasonable balance between the needs of the individual and of the community. In *Hatton*, it was held that in matters of general policy, on which opinions might differ widely, the role of the domestic policymaker should be given special weight. So, given the fundamentally subsidiary nature of the **Convention**, **Art 8** could not override the statutory scheme. Additionally in *Dennis v MOD* (2003), a case involving noise nuisance caused by low-flying military aircraft brought on the basis of nuisance and **Art 8**, the court awarded substantial damages to compensate for the breach of the claimant's **Art 8** rights.

Thus, taking an overall view of the law of nuisance, we can see that, despite several recent decisions that have introduced greater certainty into the law of nuisance, there are a number of areas in which either the law is uncertain, or in which it would be difficult to predict with any confidence at all what decision a court would come to, faced with a particular set of facts, whether the common law of nuisance or the **European Convention on Human Rights** is invoked.[21]

---

21 Time should always be taken at the end of an essay to reach some conclusion on the question set.

INTRODUCTION

Questions on *Rylands v Fletcher* (1868) are popular with examiners as there are a number of undecided aspects to the rule and because it is very easy to combine a *Rylands* situation with elements of nuisance, negligence or liability for animals.

Checklist ✔

Students must be familiar with the following areas:

(a) the elements of the rule itself, with especial reference to:

- the non-natural user requirement;
- the decision of the House of Lords in *Transco v Stockport MBC* (2004);

(b) defences, and especially the independent acts of third parties.

QUESTION 30

Delta Manufacturing plc owns and operates a factory situated on an industrial estate on the outskirts of a small town. One day, the environmental control system malfunctioned for some unknown reason and large quantities of toxic fumes were emitted. These fumes damaged paintwork on some houses in the town and some inhabitants also suffered an allergic reaction to the fumes. As a result of the adverse publicity, the town has seen a reduction in its normal tourist trade and the local shopkeepers are complaining of loss of business.

▶ Advise Delta Manufacturing plc of any liability that it might have incurred. Would your advice differ if Delta operated its factory under statutory authority?

How to Answer this Question

It is important in answering this question to consider the possible causes of action in detail, paying particular attention to *Rylands v Fletcher* (1868) and nuisance, and the possibility of a negligence action. The defence of statutory authority must also be considered for these actions.

The following points need to be discussed:

- ❖ the ingredients of *Rylands v Fletcher* (1868), with especial reference to non-natural use;
- ❖ the recoverability for property damage by landowners and non-landowners;
- ❖ the ingredients of nuisance;
- ❖ negligence and the problem of proof of breach of duty;
- ❖ statutory authority as a defence to the above actions;
- ❖ action under the **Human Rights Act 1998**.

Applying the Law

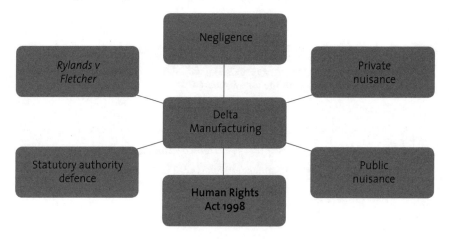

ANSWER

- -

We shall first[1] consider whether Delta has incurred any liability under the rule in *Rylands v Fletcher* (1868), which is that a 'person who, for his own purposes, brings onto his lands and collects and keeps there anything likely to do mischief if it escapes must keep it in at his peril, and if he does not do so, he is *prima facie* answerable for all the damage which is the natural consequence of its escape'. In addition, the defendant must have made a 'non-natural' use of his land and the harm caused must be foreseeable (*Cambridge Water Co v Eastern Counties Leather plc* (1994)). The whole area of *Rylands* was reconsidered by

....

1   As the question does not indicate which aspects of the law should be considered, credit will be given for correctly identifying, and giving relevant weight to the appropriate areas.

the House of Lords in *Transco v Stockport Metropolitan Borough Council* (2004) and we shall examine the effect of this case on Delta's liability.[2]

The fumes have been brought onto Delta's land for Delta's purposes. They have been brought onto Delta's land in the sense that they are not something that is there by nature, such as thistles (*Giles v Walker* (1890)) or rainwater (*Smith v Kenrick* (1849)). The toxic fumes are clearly likely to do mischief if they escape and there has been an escape from Delta's premises, as required by *Read v Lyons* (1947). As it is foreseeable that the fumes would cause harm, we must determine whether or not there has been a non-natural use of land, an aspect that has given rise to much confusion. In *Rylands* itself, the word 'natural' was used to mean something on the land by nature, but later cases have construed the word as meaning 'ordinary' or usual. In *Rickards v Lothian* (1913), Lord Moulton said of the use of land required to bring *Rylands* into operation: 'It must be some special use bringing with it   . increased danger to others, and must not merely be the ordinary use of the land or such a use as is proper for the general benefit of the community.' In *Read*, Viscount Simon described Lord Moulton's analysis of *Rylands* as 'of the first importance'. In *Transco*, the House of Lords considered in detail the non-natural requirement. Lord Bingham stated that the ordinary use test is to be preferred to the non-natural use test as this makes it clear that *Rylands* only applies where the use of land is extraordinary and unusual. Lord Bingham doubted that a test of reasonable use was helpful since a use may be out of the ordinary but reasonable: for example, the storage of chemicals on industrial premises as in *Cambridge Water*. It was also doubted that Lord Moulton's criterion of whether the use is proper for the general benefit of the community was helpful, echoing the criticism of this phrase by Lord Goff in *Cambridge Water*. Thus Lord Bingham stated that it was necessary to show that the defendant had brought onto or kept on his land an exceptionally dangerous or mischievous thing in extraordinary or unusual circumstances, which Delta has done.[3]

If the rule were to be applicable, then the houseowners could recover for damage to their paintwork (*Rylands*). However, houseowners could not recover for their allergic reaction, as the rule in *Rylands* does not cover personal injury (*Transco*). If any person suffered personal injury but had no interest in land, that lack of interest would itself rule out an action in *Rylands* (*McKenna v British Aluminium Ltd* (2002)). The local shopkeepers have suffered economic loss and, despite *Weller v Foot and Mouth Disease Research Institute* (1965), there seems to be no clear authority for recovery on their part, and the general tenor of *Cambridge Water Co* (and the analogous case of *Hunter v Canary Wharf Ltd*) is against such recovery.

We shall next consider whether any action will lie against Delta in nuisance. There would be no problem to houseowners or tenants recovering for the damage to their paintwork.

....

2 When dealing with *Rylands v Fletcher*, it is advisable to be able to quote the exact words used in the original judgment, as here.

3 The crux of a case on *Rylands v Fletcher* is often likely to be whether the use of the land is 'non-natural' or not 'ordinary'.

As this involves damage to property, the character of the neighbourhood is not a relevant factor (*St Helen's Smelting Co v Tipping* (1865)), although the persons affected will have to show that they have an interest in the land affected (*Malone v Laskey* (1907); *Hunter v Canary Wharf Ltd* (1997)). Even persons with an interest in land, however, will be unable to claim for any allergic reactions as, in *Hunter*, the House of Lords stated that actions for personal injury should not be brought in nuisance. Although there are *dicta* in *British Celanese v Hunt* (1969) and *Ryeford Homes v Sevenoaks District Council* (1989) that suggest that recovery for economic loss is possible, the tenor of the judgment of the House of Lords in *Hunter* is against such recovery.

An action in public nuisance may also lie against Delta. Here, the claimant will have to show that the nuisance affected a section of the public (*AG v PYA Quarries* (1957)) and that he suffered damage over and above that suffered by the public at large. The advantage to claimants in public nuisance is that no interest in land is required and both personal injury and economic loss are recoverable (*Rose v Miles* (1815)). Thus, those persons with no interest in land could sue in respect of the allergic reaction, which would constitute special damage, as could the shopkeepers.

Also, Delta may be liable in negligence. There would be no difficulty in showing the existence of a duty of care and causation and foreseeability, but there could be problems in proving breach, as we are told that the emission occurred for an unknown reason. A possible claimant might seek to rely on *res ipsa loquitur*, but this would not reverse the burden of proof, which lies on the claimant throughout (*Ng Chun Pui v Lee Chuen Tat* (1988)). If Delta could show that it had in place a proper system of inspection and control (*Henderson v Jenkins and Sons* (1970)), this would be sufficient to negate liability. If negligence could be proved against Delta, then of course any claimant who has suffered damage to property or to the person may sue, but the shopkeepers would be unable to recover for their economic loss, as the chances of a claimant now successfully relying on *Junior Books v Veitchi* (1983) seem non-existent.

If the factory had been operated under statutory authority, liability would not arise either under *Rylands* or nuisance unless negligence on the part of Delta could be shown (*Green v Chelsea Waterworks* (1894); *Allen v Gulf Oil Refining* (1981)). However, in *Barr v Biffa Waste Services* (2012) the Court of Appeal held that, short of express or implied statutory authority to actually commit a nuisance, there is no basis for using a statutory scheme (here granting of a Waste Permit) to cut down private law rights, and the claimants did not have to demonstrate negligence. Carnworth LJ stated that the 'fundamental principles [of nuisance] were settled by the end of the 19th century and have remained resilient and effective since then'.

In an action for nuisance by noise from motor-racing, the Court of Appeal held that pre-existing motor-racing activities, lawfully carried on for more than a decade, had become part of the 'character of the neighbourhood', against which the alleged nuisance must be judged (*Coventry Promotions v Lawrence* (2012)).

Finally, we must consider any causes of action that might arise under the **Human Rights Act 1998**.[4] Article 8 of the **European Convention on Human Rights**, brought into UK law by **s1** of the **1998 Act**, establishes the right to respect for private and family life. Also, **Art 1** of the **First Protocol** to the **ECHR** states that persons are entitled to the peaceful enjoyment of their possessions, and **Art 2** establishes a right to life.

As regards **Art 8**, in *López Ostra v Spain* (1995), it was held that the construction of a waste treatment plant next to the applicant's house, which had caused local pollution and health problems, was a violation of **Art 8**. In this case, the Spanish government did not own the plant, but it was held to be sufficient that the local authority had allowed it to be built on their land and the government had subsidised it. As **s6(1)** of the **1998 Act** makes it unlawful for a public authority to act in a way incompatible with a **Convention** right and by **s6(6)** an 'act' includes a failure to act, both the UK government and local authorities could be held liable for breaches of **Art 8**. **Article 8** has been held to cover toxic emissions from a factory (*Guerra v Italy* (1998)), so clearly the emissions from Delta's factory would fall within **Art 8** and even **Art 2** if the emissions are sufficiently hazardous.

An action under the **Human Rights Act 1998** would raise no problems as regards interest in land, recovery for economic loss or recovery for personal injuries. Indeed, in *Marcic v Thames Water Utilities Ltd* (2001), the High Court found for the claimant under **Art 8** while dismissing the claims based on nuisance and *Rylands*. Although the Court of Appeal (2002) held that the claimant could recover in nuisance while upholding the High Court's findings under the **Human Rights Act 1998**, subsequently overruled by the House of Lords in 2004, it is clear from the High Court decision that much of the detailed law on nuisance and *Rylands* is irrelevant in considering a breach of **Art 8**. However, in *Dobson v Thames Water (No 2)* (2011), although there had been a breach of **Convention** rights through smells and mosquito nuisance, children were not entitled to any compensation as their families had been adequately compensated for nuisance. Thus, an action under the **Human Rights Act 1998** may be available to a considerable range of persons who suffer injury due to Delta's factory, and the possible defendants could be the local authority under **s6(1)** and **(6)** of the **1998 Act**, or the UK government.

QUESTION 31

'Although the rule in *Rylands v Fletcher* has been subject to recent judicial scrutiny, there still remain areas of uncertainty and it is doubtful if it adds anything to existing English law.'

▶ Discuss the above statement.

---

4   **The Human Rights Act 1998** has had an important impact on land tort cases: see Chapter 14 for more on this.

How to Answer this Question

This is a general essay question requiring a discussion of the similarity and differences between *Rylands v Fletcher* (1868) and nuisance, especially since the decisions of the House of Lords in *Cambridge Water Co v Eastern Counties Leather plc* (1994), *Hunter v Canary Wharf* (1997) and *Transco v Stockport Metropolitan Borough Council* (2004).

The following aspects need to be discussed:

- ❖ the ingredients of an action in *Rylands*;
- ❖ the similarity with an action in nuisance;
- ❖ the problems raised by the requirement in *Rylands* for an escape and non-natural use;
- ❖ other actions that may reinforce *Rylands*, for example, animals, trespass or negligence.

Answer Structure

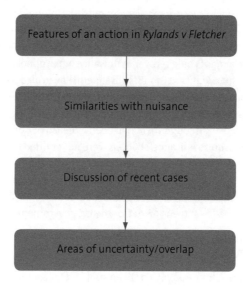

Features of an action in *Rylands v Fletcher*

Similarities with nuisance

Discussion of recent cases

Areas of uncertainty/overlap

ANSWER

In *Rylands v Fletcher* (1868), Blackburn J gave the classic statement of the law when he stated: 'We think that the true rule of law is that the person who, for his own purposes, brings onto his land and collects and keeps there anything likely to do mischief if it escapes, must keep it in at his peril, and, if he does not do so, he is *prima facie* answerable for all the damage which is the natural consequence of its escape.' This statement was approved when the case was appealed to the House of Lords, where Lord Cairns LC made the crucial addition that the defendant also had to make a 'non-natural' use of his land.[5]

The scope and certainty of the rule can be considered under the following headings.

ACCUMULATION

The rule refers to 'bringing' things onto the defendant's land and thus does not apply to things that are naturally on the land, such as thistles (*Giles v Walker* (1890)) or rainwater (*Smith v Kenrick* (1849)).

DANGEROUS THINGS

The rule refers to 'anything likely to do mischief if it escapes'. However, there are very few objects that do not give rise to some risk if they escape. In *Transco v Stockport Metropolitan Borough Council* (2004), the House of Lords stated that the mischief test should not be easily satisfied. It should be shown that the defendant had done something he recognised or ought to have recognised as giving rise to an exceptionally high risk of danger or mischief if it escapes, however unlikely such an escape may have been thought to be. In *Read v Lyons* (1947), Lord Macmillan stated that it would not be practicable to classify objects into dangerous and non-dangerous things. It is no longer considered necessary that the thing be dangerous, but danger is still relevant when considering non-natural use or foreseeability of damage.

ESCAPE

The rule clearly states that the thing must escape from the defendant's land and the necessity for this was emphasised by the House of Lords in *Read v Lyons* (1947) and in *Transco*.

HIS LAND

Although the rule refers to 'his land', there is no requirement that the defendant be the owner of the land – it would seem from the cases that it is enough that the defendant has control of the thing. This is similar to the position in nuisance and, indeed, the House of Lords in *Cambridge Water Co v Eastern Counties Leather plc* (1994) held that the rule in *Rylands* is basically the law of nuisance extended to cover an isolated escape.

HIS OWN PURPOSES

This requirement suggests that if the defendant brings the thing onto his land for some other person's purpose, the rule ceases to apply. This is often said to be supported by the decision of the House of Lords in *Rainham Chemical Works v Belvedere Fish Guano Co* (1921), although in that case liability was admitted at first instance, and the appeals to the

---

5   When dealing with *Rylands v Fletcher*, it is advisable to be able to quote the exact words used in the original judgment, as here. The elements of the tort can then be systematically addressed in the body of the essay.

Court of Appeal and the House of Lords were concerned solely with whether the directors of the company could be held personally liable. Thus, *Rainham* is very questionable support for this requirement.

NON-NATURAL USE

The original meaning of the phrase 'natural use' was something that was there naturally or by nature, but gradually the courts interpreted it to mean 'ordinary' or 'usual'. In *Rickards v Lothian* (1913), Lord Moulton stated: 'It must be some special use bringing with it increased danger to others, and must not merely be the ordinary use of land or such use as is proper for the general benefit of the community.' Although this was described in *Read* by Viscount Simon as 'of the first importance', it was criticised by the House of Lords in *Cambridge Water Co*. Lord Goff stated that the phrase 'ordinary use of land' was lacking in precision and that the alternative criterion, 'or such as is proper for the general benefit of the community', introduced doubt and might not keep the exception within reasonable bounds. In *Transco*, the House of Lords considered in detail the non-natural requirement. Lord Bingham stated that the ordinary use test is to be preferred to the natural use test, as this makes it clear that *Rylands* only applies where the use of land is extraordinary and unusual. Lord Bingham doubted that a test of reasonable use was helpful since a use may be out of the ordinary but reasonable: for example, the storage of chemicals on industrial premises, as in *Cambridge Water*. It was also doubted that Lord Moulton's criterion of whether the use is proper for the general benefit of the community was helpful, echoing the criticism of this phrase by Lord Goff in *Cambridge*. Thus, Lord Bingham stated that it is necessary to show that the defendant had brought an exceptionally dangerous or mischievous thing in extraordinary or unusual circumstances.

FORESEEABILITY OF DAMAGE

In *Cambridge Water Co*, after a thorough historical survey of the rule, it was held that foreseeability of damage following escape was a necessary ingredient of an action under the rule in *Rylands*.

DAMAGE COVERED

Property damage is clearly covered by the rule, but personal injuries are excluded, as personal injuries do not relate to any right in or enjoyment of land: *Transco*.

INTEREST IN LAND

Because of the similarity of *Rylands* and nuisance (*Cambridge Water Co*), it has been held that claimants under *Rylands* must have a proprietary interest in the land affected: *McKenna v British Aluminium* (2002).

It can be seen that *Rylands* bears a close resemblance to nuisance. Nuisance may be defined as an unreasonable interference with a person's use or enjoyment of land, or some right over it or in connection with it. It does not require an accumulation, as it applies, for example, to noise, and it applies to both dangerous and non-dangerous things. The relevance of the thing being dangerous is as to whether the defendant has made a reasonable use of his land. Nuisance differs from *Rylands*: in *Rylands*, there are defined ingredients to the tort; in nuisance, there are guidelines as to whether the interference with the claimant's land was unreasonable. Thus, in nuisance, the court will take into account the duration of the interference, whether it was of a temporary nature and whether it was an isolated event. It was held in *Bolton v Stone* (1951) that an isolated happening could not constitute a nuisance, whereas in *Cambridge Water Co*, it was held that such an isolated event could found an action under *Rylands*.

By the very nature of nuisance, the thing, be it noise or a physical thing, must escape from the defendant's land. Also in nuisance, there is no requirement that the defendant be the owner of the land, mere control being sufficient. There is no requirement in nuisance that there is a non-natural use of the land, only that it is unreasonable. It is, of course, possible that a natural use of land will be unreasonable due to (say) the presence of malice on the part of the defendant (*Hollywood Silver Fox Farm v Emmett* (1936)). In both torts, foreseeability of damage is required and neither of these torts cover personal injuries.

Despite the relaxation of the requirement that the claimant has an interest in land by the Court of Appeal in *Khorasandjian v Bush* (1993) and *Hunter v Canary Wharf* (1996), the House of Lords reinstated this requirement in *Hunter* (1997).

Thus, it can be seen that there is an overlap between *Rylands* and nuisance, and in many situations the two causes of action may coexist. *Rylands* does, however, fill one gap in the law, in that it does apply to an isolated event whereas nuisance does not. It has also been held that nuisance does not cover interference with purely recreational matters (*Bridlington Relay v Yorkshire Electricity Board* (1965)), whereas this restriction does not apply to *Rylands*.[6]

It could thus be said that in practice, the majority of cases in which *Rylands* applies will also give rise to causes of action in nuisance and possibly other torts such as negligence, animals or trespass. However, *Rylands* does cover some areas that other torts do not cover, such as the isolated event, which is not covered in nuisance, and the isolated event caused by the action of an independent contractor, which would be covered in neither nuisance nor negligence. In the case of *LMS International Ltd v Styrene Packaging Ltd* (2005), a *Rylands* action was successfully brought against a defendant in circumstances under which a fire spread from one industrial unit to another.

....

6   When answering an essay question, the actual question set should be borne in mind and addressed throughout the answer, so here to emphasise the unique properties of the tort addresses the issue of whether it 'add(s) anything to the existing law'.

It can also be seen that recent cases have brought an element of certainty into the law regarding *Rylands*. It is now clear that foreseeability of damage is an essential ingredient, as is an interest in land, and that judicial opinion considers that *Rylands* is not applicable to personal injuries.[7] However, the discussion of the phrase 'natural use' in *Transco* and the use of the phrase 'extraordinary and unusual' use does not seem to have introduced much certainty into this area. Similarly, the suggestion that the 'mischief' criterion should not be at all easily satisfied and that the test that the defendant has done something that he recognised or ought to have recognised as giving rise to an exceptionally high risk of danger or mischief if it escapes seems also to lack certainty.[8]

QUESTION 32

One evening, Henry lights a bonfire in his garden in order to burn some garden rubbish. The smoke and smell from the bonfire annoy his neighbours, who are watching television with the windows open, and sparks from the fire damage some clothing that one of his neighbours has hung out in his garden to dry. The smoke from the bonfire drifts onto the road and is so thick that it obstructs the vision of a passing motorist who, as a result, runs into a lamp post. Henry goes indoors to listen to the radio and, some time later, the bonfire spreads to his neighbour's property, destroying a garden shed.

▶ **Advise Henry of his legal liability.**

How to Answer this Question

This is a question that requires a discussion of Henry's liability in nuisance, the relationship of nuisance to an action in *Rylands v Fletcher* (1868), and any liability Henry might incur in negligence and under the special rules that govern fires.

The following points need to be discussed:

- ❖ liability in nuisance for the smoke and smell;
- ❖ liability in nuisance for the damage to the clothing;
- ❖ the possibility of liability arising under the rule in *Rylands v Fletcher* (1868);
- ❖ liability in negligence;
- ❖ liability for the fire under the **Fires Prevention (Metropolis) Act 1774**.

---

7 Here the emphasis is on the relative certainty in the law.
8 This addresses the question set, as to how/why the situation is still uncertain, despite recent high level judicial scrutiny.

Applying the Law

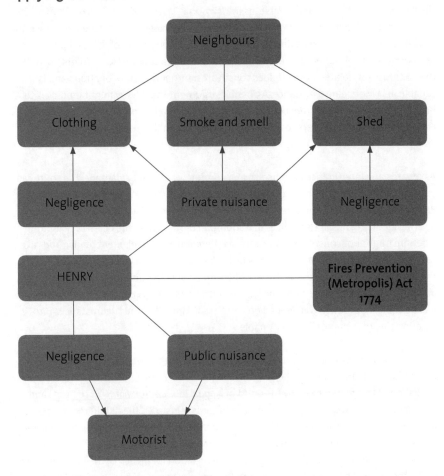

This diagram illustrates Henry's liability in negligence and nuisance.

ANSWER

We shall first consider any liability that Henry may have incurred in private nuisance (which we shall henceforth simply refer to as nuisance) for the smoke and smell from his bonfire. A nuisance consists of an unreasonable interference with a person's use or enjoyment of land, or of some right over or in connection with it. However, not all interference will necessarily give rise to liability: the harm must be foreseeable (*The Wagon Mound (No 2)* (1967); *Cambridge Water Co v Eastern Counties Leather plc* (1994)), and the interference must be substantial and not merely fanciful (*Walter v Selfe* (1851)). In deciding whether a particular interference is unreasonable or not, the court will rely on a series of guidelines rather than on any rigid rules. In Henry's case, the court would consider the duration of the interference, as the shorter the duration of the interference, the less likely it is to be unreasonable, as in *Harrison v Southwark and Vauxhall Water Co* (1891). In particular, it seems that an isolated event is unlikely to constitute a nuisance. In *Bolton v Stone* (1951), it was stated that a nuisance must be a state of affairs, however temporary, and not merely an isolated happening. Thus, although Henry might claim that the bonfire is an isolated event, it does constitute a temporary state of affairs and is capable in law of being a nuisance. A possible argument that Henry might employ is that he only lights a bonfire on rare occasions and that this is a reasonable use of his land. However, the fact that a defendant is only making reasonable use of his land is not, of itself, a valid defence in nuisance (*AG v Cole* (1901); *Vanderpant v Mayfair Hotel* (1930)).

As regards any interference with health and comfort, or 'amenity' damage, the court will take into account the character of the neighbourhood, as 'what would be a nuisance in Belgravia Square would not necessarily be so in Bermondsey' (*Sturges v Bridgman* (1879), *per* Thesiger LJ).[9] Thus, if Henry lives in a suburban or rural area, the occasional lighting of a bonfire might not constitute a nuisance, as there must be an element of give and take between neighbours. However, if Henry by his lack of care allowed an annoyance from the bonfire to become excessive, he would become liable in nuisance (*Andreae v Selfridge and Co* (1938)). Hence, as regards the smoke and smell from his bonfire, whether Henry will be liable in nuisance will depend on whether, taking all of the circumstances into account, the interference is unreasonable.

As nuisance protects a person's use or enjoyment of land, then traditionally only those neighbours with an interest in the land can sue (*Malone v Laskey* (1907)). Despite the relaxation of this requirement by the Court of Appeal in *Khorasandjian v Bush* (1993) and *Hunter v Canary Wharf Ltd* (1996), the House of Lords reinstated the requirement when it heard *Hunter* (1997). Thus, only those neighbours with an interest in the property affected (for example, houseowners or tenants) can sue, and not merely members of their families or guests. These others may have a right to compensation for breach of their **Article 8** rights under the **European Convention on Human Rights**, see *Dobson v Thames Water* (2009).

It was also held in *Bridlington Relay v Yorkshire Electricity Board* (1965), and confirmed by the House of Lords in *Hunter* (1997), that interference with purely recreational facilities, such as television reception, would not constitute an actionable nuisance. However, the interference suffered by Henry's neighbours is not with the reception of their television programmes, but rather with their enjoyment of their property, for had they wished only to sit in their houses with the windows open, they would not have been able to do so without the discomfort from the smoke and smell of Henry's bonfire.[10]

....

9 This quote, properly remembered, is almost always useful in a nuisance answer.

10 Note that the question does NOT refer to interference with TV reception (which would not be actionable), but refers to general annoyance/interference. Noting this distinction allows the understanding of the meaning of 'amenity' damage to be demonstrated.

Turning now to the damage to the neighbour's clothing, where physical damage to property has been caused, the character of the neighbourhood is not relevant (*St Helen's Smelting Co v Tipping* (1865)) and a court would be far more likely to find that an interference is unreasonable where physical damage to property has occurred. Even if the bonfire did not originally constitute a nuisance, Henry's lack of care in allowing the interference to become unreasonable would make him liable (*Andreae*). It therefore seems likely that Henry would be liable for the damage to his neighbour's clothing, provided of course that his neighbour has the required interest in land.

Henry could also incur liability for the damage to his neighbour's clothing in negligence. Henry will owe his neighbour a duty of care under normal *Donoghue v Stevenson* (1932) principles. As a duty of care has already been held to exist in such circumstances, there is no need to go to the modern incremental formulation of the test for a duty of care that was preferred by the House of Lords in *Caparo Industries plc v Dickman* (1990) and *Murphy v Brentwood District Council* (1990). In allowing sparks to damage his neighbour's property, Henry has possibly not acted as a reasonable person would and so could be in breach of his duty (*Blyth v Birmingham Waterworks* (1856)), and the 'but for' test of Lord Denning in *Cork v Kirby MacLean* (1952) shows the required causal connection. Finally, the damage suffered by the neighbour is not too remote as it is reasonably foreseeable (*The Wagon Mound (No 1)* (1961)). Thus, Henry could be liable for the damage to the clothing in negligence and there would be no requirement for the neighbour to have any interest in land.

As regards the passing motorist, he could not sue Henry in nuisance, as he has no interest in the land. He may be able to sue Henry in negligence, as the required elements of duty, breach and damage appear to be present (see the above discussion regarding the neighbour and his damaged clothing). The motorist may also have a cause of action in public nuisance, in that Henry has created a danger close to the highway (*Tarry v Ashton* (1876); *Castle v St Augustine's Links* (1922)).

We shall next consider whether Henry has incurred any liability for the fire and the damage that it has caused to the garden shed.[11] Liability could arise in a number of ways: the first possibility is an action under the rule in *Rylands v Fletcher* (1868). However, in *Mason v Levy Auto Parts* (1967), MacKenna J held that liability for fire cannot be based on *Rylands* because the 'thing' has not escaped from the defendant's land as required by *Rylands* (see also *Johnson v BJW Property Developments Ltd* (2002)). Instead, Henry may be liable under common law liability for fire. Here the claimant will have to show: firstly, that Henry brought onto his land things likely to catch fire and kept them there in such condition that, if they did ignite, the fire would be likely to spread to the claimant's land; secondly, that he did so in the course of some non-natural use of the land; finally, that the

---

11   The question requires careful consideration of a specialist area of tort relating to fire damage.

things ignited and the fire spread, as determined in *LMS International Ltd v Styrene Packaging Ltd* (2005). Although these are different criteria from those used in *Rylands*, similar considerations will apply in deciding whether these criteria have been satisfied in any particular case. The only element that would appear to give rise to any problems here is the requirement that the use of land be non-natural. In *Rylands* itself, the word 'natural' was used to mean something that was there by nature. However, in *Rickards v Lothian* (1913), Lord Moulton stated that a non-natural use must be 'some special use bringing with it increased dangers to others, and must not merely be the ordinary use of the land or such a use as is proper for the general benefit of the community'. In *Transco v Stockport Metropolitan Borough Council* (2004), the House of Lords considered in detail the non-natural use requirement. Lord Bingham stated that the ordinary use test is to be preferred to the non-natural use test as this makes it clear that *Rylands* only applies where the use of land is extraordinary and unusual. He doubted that a test of reasonable use was helpful since a use may be out of the ordinary but reasonable: for example, the storage of chemicals on industrial premises as in *Cambridge Water v Eastern Counties Leather plc* (1994). It was also doubted that Lord Moulton's criterion of whether the use is proper for the general benefit of the community was helpful, echoing the criticism of this phrase by Lord Goff in *Cambridge Water*. Thus, Lord Bingham stated that it is necessary to show that the defendant had brought or kept on his land an exceptionally dangerous or mischievous thing in extraordinary or unusual circumstances, and this Henry has done (see further *LMS International Ltd v Styrene Packaging Ltd* (2005)). Henry would thus be liable in a common law action for fire.[12]

In addition, Henry would also incur liability at common law in nuisance, as the fire has damaged his neighbour's property (*Goldman v Hargrave* (1967)), assuming that his neighbour has the necessary interest in the land. Liability could also attach in negligence, as there is no problem in establishing a duty of care, causation and damage that is not too remote and, by leaving the fire to go indoors and listen to the radio, Henry has failed to take reasonable care to prevent the fire from causing damage (*Musgrove v Pandelis* (1919); *Ogwo v Taylor* (1987)).

Now we must consider whether Henry could escape liability by relying on the provisions of the **Fires Prevention (Metropolis) Act 1774**. **Section 86** of that Act provides (in archaic language) that no action shall be brought or damages recovered in respect of a fire that starts accidentally. So Henry will not be liable for the consequences of the fire if it began accidentally. The meaning of 'accidentally' was considered in *Filliter v Phippard* (1847), in which the defendant deliberately lit a fire to burn some weeds and then neglected the fire, which spread to the plaintiff's land and damaged his hedge. It was held that the

---

12 The crux of a case on *Rylands v Fletcher* is often likely to be whether the use of the land is 'non-natural' or not 'ordinary', and careful consideration of the leading cases, as here, with reference to the differing viewpoints of the judges, will add to the quality of the answer.

defendant could not rely on the Act, because the fire did not begin 'accidentally' – it began negligently. The court held that a fire only began accidentally where it began by mere chance or was incapable of being traced to any cause (see also *Johnson*). As *Filliter* is legally indistinguishable from Henry's situation, it follows that Henry cannot rely on the 1774 Act as a defence. In *Johnson*, it was held that 'accidentally' applied to the escape of fire, rather than the manner in which the fire started, but even on this interpretation, Henry would not be able to rely on the 1774 Act.

Thus, Henry should be advised that he will be liable for the damage to the clothing and to the shed, and for the damage suffered by the motorist.

Aim Higher ★

Being aware of some of the recent debates in *Rylands*, such as the undecided point on personal injury (it is not conclusive at the moment and is only *obiter* – although very persuasive), will help your answer.

Common Pitfalls ✗

A common error is often made in relation to the *'non-natural use'* aspect. Familiarising yourself with Lord Hoffmann's speech in *Transco* will help you get a grip of what this actually means in contemporary usage.

Trespass to the Person, to Land and to Goods

INTRODUCTION

Trespass is an area that may be tested by the examiner either in its own right or as part of a question, mostly involving, for example, occupiers' liability or nuisance.

There have, however, been a number of recent developments in the law of trespass, such as hostile touching, trespass to airspace and false imprisonment of prisoners, which may jog the examiner's mind on the topic of trespass.

Checklist ✔

Students must be familiar with the following areas:

(a)   the definition and elements of, and defences to, assault;

(b)   the definition and elements of, and defences to, false imprisonment;

(c)   the rule in *Wilkinson v Downton* (1897);

(d)   the definition and elements of, and defences to, trespass to land and especially trespass to airspace;

(e)   the definition and elements of, and defences to, trespass to goods, and in particular title to lost goods and the allowance for improvement of goods.

QUESTION 33

Arthur, who had been drinking heavily, entered Billie's pizzeria to buy a takeaway pizza. Billie took the order and requested payment. Arthur then discovered that he did not have the money to pay for the pizza and so Billie asked him to leave. Arthur picked up a chair and waved it above his head, shouting 'Give me the pizza'. Billie retreated to the back of the shop, scared and unable to escape. After five minutes or so of Arthur waving the chair and ranting, Chris the delivery driver returned, having made a delivery. Seeing Arthur, he said, 'Okay mate, put down the chair, eh?', and took a step towards him, holding out his hand. Arthur swung the chair at Chris, hitting him and cutting his arm. Chris wrestled the chair from Arthur, smashed it over Arthur's head and then ran out of the door to get help. Hearing the commotion, Daisy, a passerby, assumed that the pizzeria was being robbed. She tripped Chris, who hit his head on the pavement and was knocked semi-conscious. Daisy then sat on Chris and called the police on her mobile phone. Billie, meanwhile, grabbed a pizza slicing wheel and approached Arthur. She said: 'If you don't leave now I'm going to slice you with this.' Arthur fled the pizzeria.

▶ Advise the parties as to their liabilities and remedies in tort.

How to Answer this Question

The question involves assault, battery and false imprisonment, as well as requiring the candidate to consider aspects of the defences that might apply to trespass to the person. The answer should contain, at least, a consideration of the following potential areas of liability. (It should be noted that there is often a considerable overlap of criminal and tortious liability in relation to trespass to the person. When attempting a tort question, avoid the temptation of including criminal law principles unless they are directly applicable, such as in relation to 'arrest'.)

❖ The status of Arthur as a trespasser.
❖ The assault by Arthur (and Billie).
❖ The battery by Arthur, Chris and Daisy.
❖ The false imprisonment by Arthur and Daisy.
❖ Defences?

Applying the Law

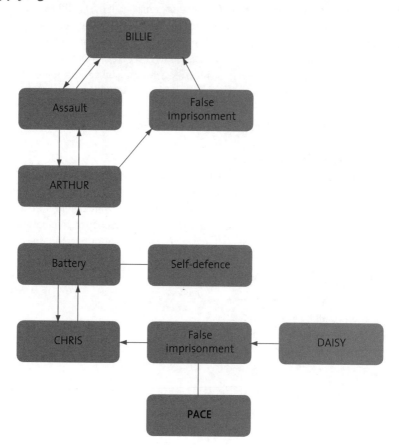

This diagram demonstrates the liability of the parties to each other in trespass to the person.

ANSWER[1]

When Arthur entered the premises, he was a lawful visitor under licence to be on the premises (see, for example, *Robson v Hallett* (1967)), but at the point that Billie asked him to leave, he was required to leave the pizzeria, as his licence to be present had been revoked. A bare licence, such as that to enter the shop to make a purchase or communicate with the owner, may be revoked at will provided that notice is given (*Stone v Taffe* (1974)) and after a reasonable time, the licensee, Arthur, becomes a

....

1   This is a complex question that needs careful planning (see diagram). Time spent planning a problem
     question will not be wasted, as it will help to ensure a logical structure to the answer and that nothing is
     overlooked.

trespasser by virtue of his continued presence in the pizzeria having been asked to leave.

In picking up the chair and shouting at Billie, Arthur is clearly committing an assault. An assault can be defined as conduct that makes the claimant have reasonable apprehension of an immediate battery (application of force) or the threat to commit a battery. The immediacy of the threatened battery is relevant. Willes J in *Osborn v Veitch* (1858) noted that immediate in this context meant 'a present ability of doing the act threatened, for it can be done in an instant'.[2] Although the fear must be reasonably held, the claimant must also have a reasonable belief that the battery is able to be and will be committed (*Thomas v NUM (South Wales)* (1985)). In this case, while Arthur has not expressly stated that he will do anything to Billie, the threatening nature of his behaviour would suggest that Billie could reasonably believe that Arthur would apply some force to her and was sufficiently close for this to be an immediate application. It is highly probable in this situation that Arthur has committed an assault. Trespass is actionable *per se*, meaning that a person is able to sue despite not actually having suffered damage. The cause of action accrues on the interference, for example the touching, should the case involve a battery. It is unlikely that a person would be awarded anything but nominal damages however, unless they were able to prove that they had suffered real damage.

Arthur is also likely to have committed false imprisonment by acting in such a way as to ensure that Billie remained at the rear of the premises. False imprisonment requires that the defendant directly and intentionally confines the claimant without the claimant's consent or without other lawful excuse. It does not matter how long the confinement is, so long as it is total (*Bird v Jones* (1845)). The House of Lords evaluated the law on false imprisonment in *R v Bournewood Community and Mental Health NHS Trust* (1998), a case in relation to the detention of an autistic patient that was subsequently considered to be unlawful by the European Court of Human Rights (see *HL v United Kingdom* (2005)). In *Austin v Commissioner of Police of the Metropolis* (2007), the Court of Appeal held that the police practice of 'kettling' demonstrators did not amount to false imprisonment. There is no lawful excuse that Arthur could rely on in this situation, although he might subsequently argue that he was unaware of the effect of his actions due to his intoxication (although this is no defence) and he is very likely to have satisfied the tests for false imprisonment.

In relation to Arthur hitting Chris with the chair, it would appear that he has committed a battery. A battery is a direct (*Reynolds v Clark* (1725)) and intentional (see *Letang v Cooper* (1964)) application of force to which the claimant does not consent. It may be committed by a person touching the claimant, throwing something at the claimant or through the agency of another object, such as a weapon or other substance or object. Case law has

2   Use of a direct quote in an answer will add to its quality.

suggested that the touching should be of a malicious or hostile character (*Wilson v Pringle* (1986); see also *F v West Berkshire Health Authority* (1989)), rather than, for example, constituting horseplay, Chris did not consent to being hit with the chair and Arthur's behaviour could not be described as anything other than hostile. The magnitude of the injury suffered by Chris does not have to have been intended by Arthur, as battery requires only that the act itself was intentional: it does not matter if the perpetrator intended the full consequences of what then resulted.

The fact that Chris then responded with violence himself, essentially committing a battery on Arthur, necessitates consideration of the defence of self-defence. The defence entitles a person to use force to defend themselves, their property or another person, even in a pre-emptory sense, such as a response to a perceived threat of, rather than actual, battery. The defence exists alongside s 3 of the **Criminal Law Act 1967**, which provides for the same result. The person must honestly believe that force is necessary and then use only such force as is reasonable. What is reasonable force will depend upon the circumstances and is nicely encapsulated by the *dicta* of Lord Oaksey in the case of *Turner v MGM* (1950). His Lordship stated that, 'if you are attacked by a prize fighter you are not bound to adhere to the Queensbury Rules. It is clear, however, that even in the lowest of brawls any force used in self defence must be both reasonable and proportionate to the threat of, or actual, violence offered by the plaintiff.'[3] The burden of proving the defence falls on the defendant who claims it. The issue was clarified by the House of Lords in *Ashley v Chief Constable of Sussex Police* (2008). To satisfy the requirement the defendant must prove two things: an honest belief of a threat of imminent attack; and that the belief was reasonable. In this case Chris would likely be able to satisfy this burden.

We need therefore to determine whether or not Chris's action is able to be categorised as reasonable force. Actual violence was perpetrated against Chris by Arthur. He responded in kind with the same weapon, so it might seem as though his response was reasonable and proportionate. The relatively recent case of *Cross v Kirkby* (2000) considered whether a defendant who had fractured a claimant's skull by hitting him with a baseball bat, with which he had himself first been struck by the claimant, had acted in self-defence. The Court of Appeal held that he had (see also *Lane v Holloway* (1968) for an example in which the reaction was held to be disproportionate to the force applied and thus self-defence did not arise). *Cross* also confirmed that the defence of *ex turpi causa* would also apply in cases of battery in which the claimant him- or herself had been guilty of criminal behaviour in perpetrating the violence. It would appear on balance that Chris would be able to rely on self-defence and perhaps the general defence of *ex turpi causa* as a means to avoid any liability to Arthur for striking him with the chair.[4]

---

3   A quote such is this is likely to be helpful in many questions on trespass to the person.
4   For further information on *ex turpi causa* see Chapter 15.

Daisy's actions in relation to Chris would almost certainly constitute battery, by reference to the tests explained above. Her trip was a direct application of force and was unarguably of a hostile character. It is irrelevant that she made a mistake as to the nature of what Chris was doing. As above, the magnitude of the injury suffered by Chris is irrelevant in determining Daisy's liability for this incident. Daisy may also be liable for false imprisonment. She is undoubtedly restraining Chris's movement. Chris's imprisonment as such is both intentional and direct (see, for example, *Sayers v Harlow UDC* (1958) for an example of unintentional and indirect 'imprisonment'). Chris is described as being 'semi-conscious' and so may not be fully aware of the fact that his movement is being restricted by Daisy. The courts have considered this issue on more than one occasion and have established the view that persons need not be aware of their 'confinement' for the tort to be made out. Lord Atkin's statement in *Meering v Graham White Engineering* (1919) that, 'It appears to me that a person could be imprisoned without his knowing it. I think a person could be imprisoned while he is asleep, while he is in a state of drunkenness, while he is unconscious, and while he is a lunatic', was approved by Lord Griffiths in *Murray v Ministry of Defence* (1988). It is presumed, however, that if a person were unaware of their false imprisonment, any damages award would be nominal. Taking the above into consideration, it would seem that Daisy has falsely imprisoned Chris, and so he would be able to maintain actions against her for both battery and false imprisonment.

Daisy obviously was mistaken; however, mistake is not an applicable defence in trespass to the person cases (*R v Governor of Brockhill Prison ex p Evans* (2001)). A defence does exist in limited circumstances under the **Police and Criminal Evidence Act (PACE) 1984**, which permits a citizen a limited power of arrest. This is a codification of a long-existing common law power of arrest, which was dependent upon the actual (past) or continuing commission of an offence. **Section 24A** of that Act limits this power of arrest without warrant for non-police officers to situations in which a person knows or reasonably suspects that an indictable offence has been or is being committed. So, for example, if a citizen effects an arrest in the mistaken belief that an offence has been committed, the arrest will be unlawful (*Walters v WH Smith* (1914) and *R v Self* (1992)). The latter case was a criminal case involving a charge of shoplifting: when the defendant was subsequently acquitted of the shoplifting charge, a conviction for assault when resisting arrest was also quashed. By extension, the same principles would apply to a civil claim for trespass to the person. A further limitation restricts non-police action in arrests to situations in which the person reasonably believes that the intervention is necessary to prevent any of the situations in **s 24A(4)** occurring. These situations include preventing the person injuring themselves or others, damaging property or evading police capture. Daisy may claim that she reasonably suspected a robbery (an indictable offence) and that she reasonably believed that she was preventing Chris from absconding. This would be a determination for a court on the evidence.[5]

---

5 Take care to distinguish between criminal and civil law.

The final consideration relates to Billie. By brandishing a weapon in the direction of Arthur and given the course of events to this point, it might well be that she is committing an assault. Arthur may well have a reasonable apprehension that he is about to be on the receiving end of a battery. There may, however, be a crucial difference here, as Billie has made the threat conditional on Arthur's leaving: by stating that, 'if you don't leave now', Billie has effectively stated that she will not harm Arthur unless he does not leave. A conditional threat may nullify the threat of a battery, as in the classic case of *Tuberville v Savage* (1669).

Aim Higher

For trespass to the person answers it is useful to keep in mind the statutory defences, such as **PACE**, and also the fact that there may be a human rights interface, particularly when considering false imprisonment.

Common Pitfalls

Do not forget that all trespasses require some 'direct' interference, but that trespass to the person and land differ in terms of whether they are capable of being able to be committed negligently.

QUESTION 34

Martin owns a house with a very large garden. Neil is taking his dog for a walk along the road bordering Martin's house when the dog jumps over Martin's fence and runs into his garden to eat some flowers. Neil enters the garden to retrieve his dog, which, by now, has run into Martin's greenhouse. While Neil is in the greenhouse, Martin sees him and shuts the door, saying: 'Stop there, you thief, I am phoning the police!' Neil, who knows that he can explain his presence to the police, is quite happy to stay in Martin's greenhouse, admiring Martin's collection of exotic plants. The police arrive in a few minutes and no charges are brought against Neil. Neil leaves his jacket in Martin's greenhouse, but Martin refuses to return it to Neil until Neil pays Martin compensation for damage that Martin claims was done to the plants in his garden by Neil.

▶ Advise Martin and Neil of any legal consequences of their actions.

How to Answer this Question

This question covers trespass to land and false imprisonment. The question as to whether trespass to land can be committed negligently must be discussed, together with the elements and defences to false imprisonment.

Thus, the answer should consider:

❖   Neil's trespass via the dog;

❖ Neil's trespass on Martin's property;
❖ false imprisonment by Martin, and the provisions of the **Police and Criminal Evidence Act (PACE) 1984** and common law defences;
❖ distress damage feasant;
❖ other causes of action, for example, negligence, nuisance, the **Animals Act 1971** and defamation.

Applying the Law

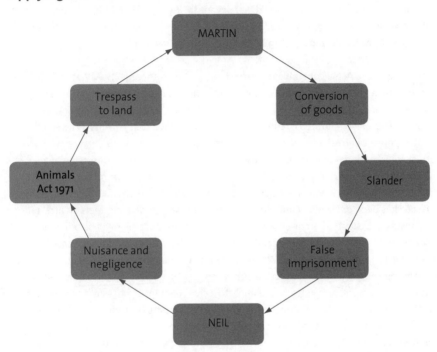

This diagram highlights Martin's and Neil's liability to each other.

ANSWER

When Neil's dog enters Martin's property, Neil has committed trespass to land through his dog and it seems, from *League Against Cruel Sports v Scott* (1985), that trespass to land through animals can be committed negligently. When Neil enters Martin's land to retrieve the dog, he too has committed trespass to land, as clearly Neil intended to enter upon Martin's land, which is sufficient – there is no need to show that Neil intended to trespass (*Conway v Wimpey* (1951)).

When Martin shuts Neil in the greenhouse, Martin has committed the tort of false imprisonment, which consists of the total deprivation of the freedom of a person for any period, however short, without lawful justification (see *R v Bournewood Community and Mental Health NHS Trust* (1998) for a restatement by the House of Lords of the elements of false imprisonment), although the position may change as a result of the ruling of the European Court of Human Rights in *HL v UK* (2005) which held that in this case the absence of procedural safeguards and access to the court amounted to a breach of **Article 5(1)** and **(4)**. In *Austin v Commissioner of Police of the Metropolis* (2007), the Court of Appeal held that the police practice of 'kettling' demonstrators did not amount to false imprisonment. The fact that Neil is quite happy to remain in the greenhouse is not relevant to liability, although it would be relevant to any issue of damages, should this arise. Two defences are relevant to Martin's actions here – namely, the provisions of the **Police and Criminal Evidence Act 1984** and the common law defences.

Under **s 24** of the Act, a constable may arrest without warrant anyone who is in the act of committing an arrestable offence or anyone who he has reasonable grounds for suspecting of committing such an offence or where an offence has been committed. A defence does exist in limited circumstances under the **PACE** that permits a citizen a limited power of arrest. This is a codification of a long-existing common law power of arrest, which was dependent upon the actual (past) or continuing commission of an offence. **Section 24A** of **PACE** limits this power of arrest without warrant for non-police officers to situations in which a person knows or reasonably suspects that an indictable offence has been or is being committed. So, for example, if a citizen effects an arrest in the mistaken belief that an offence has been committed, the arrest will be unlawful (*Walters v WH Smith* (1914) and *R v Self* (1992)). The latter case was a criminal case involving a charge of shoplifting. When the defendant was subsequently acquitted of the shoplifting charge, a conviction for assault when resisting arrest was also quashed. By extension, the same principles would apply to a civil claim for trespass to the person. A further limitation restricts non-police action in arrests to situations in which the person reasonably believes that the intervention is necessary to prevent any of the situations in **s 24A(4)** occurring. These situations include preventing the person injuring themselves or others, damaging property or evading police capture.

However, as Neil is a trespasser, for he has entered Martin's land without invitation and his presence is objected to (*Addie v Dumbreck* (1929)), Martin may use a reasonable degree of force to control his movement (*Harrison v Rutland* (1893); *Alderson v Booth* (1969)).

As regards Martin's retention of Neil's jacket, this is a conversion of Neil's goods, as Martin is performing a positive wrongful act or dealing with the goods in a manner that is inconsistent with the rights of the owner (*Maynegrain v Campafina Bank* (1984)).[6] Neil

---

6   The tort of trespass to goods, e.g. merely touching someone else's property, may become conversion of goods when wrongfully taking over rights of ownership, e.g. trying to sell them, so it is necessary to distinguish them.

can therefore sue Martin in conversion and, by s 3(2) of the **Torts (Interference with Goods) Act 1977**, the remedies available are an order to deliver the goods to Neil, with the alternative of paying damages. The defence of distress damage feasant makes it lawful for an occupier of land to seize any chattels that are unlawfully on his land and have done damage therein, and to detain them until payment of compensation for the damage. The problem for Martin is that Neil's jacket has not caused actual damage and thus his jacket cannot be lawfully detained (*R v Howson* (1966)).

A number of other causes of action are disclosed by the facts of the problem. When Martin says 'Stop there, you thief, I am phoning the police', this is a defamatory statement. Although it is slander, as it imputes a crime punishable by imprisonment, it is actionable without proof of special damage (*Hellwig v Mitchell* (1910)). It refers to Neil, but the question arises as to whether it has been published to a third party. If any person heard Martin's statement, Neil can sue Martin in defamation, but if no one other than Martin or Neil heard the statement, there is no publication. When Martin alleged to the police that Neil was a thief, publication would be covered by qualified privilege, as Martin is under a moral duty to make the statement and the police are under a legal duty to receive it (*Watt v Longsden* (1930)).

The Court of Appeal, in *Kearns v General Council of the Bar* (2002), held that the duty interest test was not always useful, and that it would be more helpful to distinguish between cases in which the communicating parties were in an existing and established relationship, and cases in which no such relationship had been established and the communication was between strangers. The Court held that privilege would attach much more readily in the established relationship situations. It is submitted, however, that *Kearns* was not intended to do away with qualified privilege in the well-established situations of a member of the public giving information regarding an alleged offence to a police officer.[7]

Martin could also[8] sue Neil in nuisance, as there has been an unreasonable interference with Martin's use or enjoyment of his land and, although this was an isolated event, it was due to a wrongful state of affairs – that is, the dog not being on a lead or not being properly controlled (*Pitcher v Martin* (1937)).

Martin could also sue Neil in negligence and under the **Animals Act 1971**. Under s 2(2) of the Act, it would have to be shown that:

(a) the damage is of a kind that the animal, unless restrained, was likely to cause or which, if caused by the animal, was likely to be severe;

----

7   For more on defamation, see Chapter 13.
8   Although Martin may have a number of possible actions in relation to the damage to his garden, he will only be compensated by a single amount of damages, equal to his loss, if he is successful.

(b) the likelihood of the damage or of its being severe was due to characteristics of the animal that are not normally found in animals of the same species, or are not normally found except at particular times or in particular circumstances;

(c) those characteristics were known to that keeper.

As we are told that Neil owns the dog, then by s 6(3), he is the keeper. The damage to plants will come under s 2(2)(a) and a tendency to eat plants is a characteristic not usually found in dogs; Neil is presumably aware of this characteristic, satisfying both s 2(2)(b) and 2(2)(c). Thus, all of the requirements of s 2(2) have been met. There is no need to show any negligence on Neil's part (*Curtis v Betts* (1990); *Mirvahedy v Henley* (2002)).[9]

QUESTION 35

Oliver is employed as a salesman. He is calling on Peter's shop to sell them some office stationery, when he sees a gold watch on the floor. He picks it up and hands it to Peter, who takes his name and address. Some three months later, Oliver is passing Peter's shop, when he sees the watch in the window for sale. Oliver goes in and takes the watch from the window, but Peter grabs the watch from Oliver and there is a scuffle in which Oliver is injured.

▶ Advise Oliver. Would your advice differ if Oliver had found the watch behind the counter of Peter's shop?

How to Answer this Question

This is a relatively straightforward question of title to lost goods and also involves an element of trespass to the person.

The following points need to be discussed:

❖ Oliver's right to the watch as against Peter's;
❖ the rules regarding supervening possession;
❖ necessary intention present in non-public part of shop;
❖ the effect of Oliver being a trespasser.

---

9   For more on the **Animals Act**, see Chapter 12.

Applying the Law

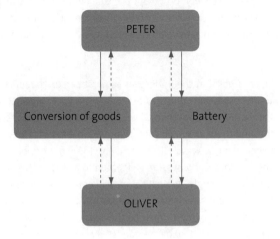

KEY:
Watch in front of shop ⟶
Watch behind counter ----▸

ANSWER

Oliver will wish to sue Peter for conversion of the watch and for trespass to the person.

Conversion has been defined as being 'committed wherever one person performs a positive wrongful act of dealing with goods in a manner inconsistent with the rights of the owner' (*Maynegrain v Campafina Bank* (1984), *per* Lord Templeman).[10] The tort is limited to tangible goods and does not apply to 'choses in action', as determined in *OBG Ltd v Allen* (2005). The tort is one of strict liability, in that, provided that the defendant intends to deal with the goods in a manner that is inconsistent with the rights of the owner (or someone with a superior right to the goods), the fact that the defendant is ignorant of these rights is no defence. So, for example, the innocent purchaser from a thief of stolen goods commits a conversion against the owner (*Moorgate Mercantile v Twitchings* (1977)). Hence, it follows that Peter has committed a conversion of the watch in offering it for sale.[11]

To sue in conversion, Oliver must show that he had the right to possession (*Marquess of Bute v Barclays Bank* (1955)). The owner of the watch, of course, remains the owner but, as

---

10   In dealing with a common law tort, it is helpful to be able to quote a definition from a leading case or text.

11   This demonstrates the application of the law to the facts given.

he has not claimed his property, the normal rule is that the finder – that is, Oliver in our case – has a right to it against everyone except the true owner, if he has reduced the goods into his possession. Thus, in *Armory v Delamirie* (1721), the finder of a jewel was held to be able to recover it from a jeweller to whom it had been handed and who refused to return it.

All of this, however, assumes that the finder was the first person to reduce the goods into his possession and the possession counts as title (*The Winkfield* (1902)). However, we must decide whether someone other than Oliver had obtained earlier possession of the goods when Oliver found them, in which case, that person and not Oliver has the right to the goods. This can occur in two ways. Firstly, if an employee finds goods in the course of his employment, the employee's possession is deemed to be that of his employer and the employee gains no possessory right against his employer (*Parker v British Airways Board* (1982)). The important element here is that the goods must be found in the course of employment – that is, the employment must be the cause of the finding of the goods and not merely the occasion of the finding of the goods (*Byrne v Hoare* (1965)). We are told that Oliver is a salesman and that he calls on Peter's shop to sell some stationery. Oliver was undoubtedly going about his employer's business when he found the watch, but it seems that Oliver's employment was the occasion of his finding the watch, rather than the cause, and so it is submitted that Oliver's employer does not have a right of possession to the watch.[12]

Secondly, if goods are found on land not occupied by the finder, in certain situations, the occupier's occupation will confer upon him a possession of the lost goods, which is earlier in time than the finder and this previous possession can exist even though the occupier was unaware of the presence of the lost goods on his land. Such earlier possession will arise where the goods are buried on the land or attached to the land in such a manner as to suggest that the occupier is exerting exclusive control over the relevant area (*South Staffordshire Water Co v Sharman* (1896) and *Waverley BC v Fletcher* (1995)). Where the goods are found only lying on the premises and the public have access to the premises, the finder generally has a superior right to the occupier (*Bridges v Hawkesworth* (1851); *Hannah v Peel* (1945)), unless the occupier has 'manifested an intention to exercise control over the building and things which may be in or on it' (*Parker v British Airways Board* (1982), *per* Donaldson MR). In *Bridges*, the finder of some cash in a shop was held to be entitled to it as against the shopowner and the more modern case of *Parker* shows that the required intention is not easy to establish. In *Parker*, the finder of a bracelet in an airport lounge was held to be entitled to it as against the occupiers of the lounge. Thus, the weight of authority would allow Oliver a superior right to the watch as against Peter. By s 3 of the **Torts (Interference with Goods) Act 1977**, Oliver may

....

12 Although it is relatively easy to show that Peter is liable in conversion, it is more complex to demonstrate Oliver's right to the watch.

obtain a court order to the watch or damages or delivery with the alternative of damages.

As Oliver is entitled to the watch, he is entitled to recover it from Peter using reasonable force if necessary to protect his property. As Peter has directly and intentionally applied hostile touching to Oliver's person, Oliver can sue Peter in battery (*Wilson v Pringle* (1987)) and in assault, if he was first put in reasonable fear of immediate physical contact.

If the watch was found behind the counter,[13] Peter will find it easier to establish the intention described in *Parker*, as it would be easier to show that Peter intended to exercise control of the area behind the counter and any things in it. In addition, if Oliver was trespassing when he went behind the counter, as it was not part of the premises to which he was invited (*The Carlgarth* (1927)), then, as a trespasser, he would acquire no rights as against the occupier (*Parker*).

It seems likely that Peter did demonstrate the required intention in respect of the area behind the counter. Thus, he has a right to the goods as against Oliver and, when Oliver removed the watch from the window, Oliver was committing a conversion of the goods. Peter was entitled, therefore, to use reasonable force to protect his property, and he would be able to sue Oliver in battery and possibly assault as regards the ensuing struggle.

----

13 When a question asks 'will your advice differ if . . .?', it almost always will, so do not overlook this part of the answer, as it gives you the opportunity to display further relevant knowledge.

Animals

INTRODUCTION

Questions involving animals may arise in examinations in a number of ways. A question of which the main ingredient is nuisance or *Rylands v Fletcher* (1868) or negligence may involve animals, but in this chapter we are concerned with questions in which the topic being tested is mainly the **Animals Act 1971** and related common law issues.

Checklist ✔

To attempt a question on animals, students must be familiar with the following areas:

(a) the common law situation;

(b) the definition of a dangerous species;

(c) liability for damage caused by dangerous and non-dangerous species, and the decision of the House of Lords in *Mirvahedy v Henley* (2003);

(d) defences;

(e) the definition of a keeper of an animal;

(f) straying livestock.

QUESTION 36

Henry owns a large dog that has a tendency to attack people in uniform. Henry keeps the dog tied up in his garden with a substantial chain. Unfortunately, there is a latent defect in one link of the chain and, when Pat the postman goes to the front door of the house to deliver some letters, the dog attempts to attack Pat. The chain breaks and the dog bites Pat. Pat is taken to hospital and given an anti-tetanus injection, to which he suffers a rare and unforeseeable allergic reaction, and his leg has to be amputated. Richard, a policeman, calls to investigate the situation, and the dog jumps over the garden fence and bites Richard. While Richard is doubled up in pain on the pavement, Steven, whom Richard arrested for a drug offence a little while ago, sees Richard on the floor and kicks him in the head.

▶ Advise Henry.

How to Answer this Question

This question ranges over a number of aspects of liability for animals, both under the **Animals Act 1971** and under other causes of action.

The following points need to be discussed:

- ❖ Henry's liability under **s 2(2)** to Pat;
- ❖ the defences available to Henry in respect of Pat;
- ❖ Henry's liability under **s 2(2)** to Richard;
- ❖ the defences available in respect of Richard;
- ❖ Henry's liability for the action of Steven.

Applying the Law

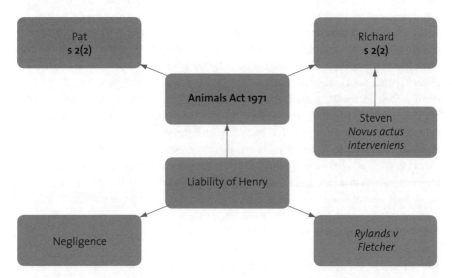

ANSWER

Under the statutory classification of the **Animals Act 1971**, Henry's dog is a non-dangerous species, because it is commonly domesticated in the British Isles (**s 6(2)**). By **s 6(3)**, Henry is the keeper of the dog, as he is the owner. By **s 2(2)**, the keeper of an animal belonging to a non-dangerous species is liable for the damage caused by the animal if:

(a) the damage is of a kind that the animal, unless restrained, was likely to cause or that, if caused by the animal, was likely to be severe;

(b)   the likelihood of the damage or of its being severe was due to characteristics of the animal that are not normally found in animals of the same species, or are not normally found except at particular times or in particular circumstances;

(c)   those characteristics were known to that keeper.[1]

Considering now Henry's liability to Pat, s 2(2)(a) is satisfied, because the bite from a large dog is likely to be severe. The tendency to attack persons in uniform is not a characteristic of dogs (see, for example, *Kite v Napp* (1982)), so s 2(2)(b) is satisfied. **Section 2(2)(c)** is also satisfied because this characteristic would be known to Henry (see *Cummings v Grainger* (1977) and *Mirvahedy v Henley* (2003) for liability under s 2(2) generally). Thus, Henry is liable for the damage caused to Pat, subject only to the defences within the **1971 Act**.

These defences include *volenti* (s 5(2)), contributory negligence (s 10) or that the damage was wholly due to the fault of the person suffering it (s 5(1)). **Section 5(3)** also provides a defence against trespassers, but this would not apply to Pat (see s 2(6) of the **Occupiers' Liability Act 1957**). It should be noted that neither the act of a stranger nor an act of God provide a defence to s 2(2), as they are not mentioned in the Act. Thus, the fact that the dog broke free from the chain due to a latent defect in the chain is not a defence, as liability under s 2(2) does not require negligence (*Curtis v Betts* (1990); *Mirvahedy v Henley* (2003)). Henry is liable for the bite suffered by Pat and he is also liable for the medical consequences of the anti-tetanus injection, because liability under the Act is strict and subject only to the defences contained within the Act. There is thus no necessity for the damage suffered to be reasonably foreseeable; it merely has to be a direct consequence of the action of the animal, so that *Re Polemis* (1921) is the appropriate test of recovery of damage. In any event, even if the foreseeability was required, as Henry must take his victim as he finds him (*Dulieu v White* (1901)) – that is, with an allergy to tetanus injections – or if the need for such an injection is foreseeable, Henry will be liable for its consequences (*Robinson v Post Office* (1974)). Hence, Henry will be liable for both the bite and the loss of Pat's leg.

Turning now to Richard, following our discussion above, Henry will be liable to Richard for the bite and none of the statutory defences are valid. (Note that Richard is not a trespasser in this case, because he has not entered Henry's property.) The question arises as to whether Henry is liable for the kick perpetrated by Steven. **Section 2(2)** states that the keeper is liable for damage caused and, as we have seen, there is no requirement of foreseeability, merely directness. However, Henry could argue that the kick by Steven is a *novus actus interveniens* that breaks the chain of causation – that is, the injury from the kick was not caused by his dog and therefore that harm does not come within s 2(2). In *Re Polemis*, where directness was considered, Scrutton LJ stated that indirect damage meant damage caused by the 'operator of independent causes having no connection with the . . .

----

1   When setting out the main relevant provisions of the **Animals Act 1971**, be sure to cite the sections/ subsections accurately and apply them to the question set.

act, except that they could not avoid its results'. Where it is alleged that the act of a third party, over whom the defendant has no control, has broken the chain of causation, then it must be shown that the act was something unwarrantable, a new cause that disturbs the sequence of events. It must be something that can be described as either unreasonable or extraneous or extrinsic (*per* Lord Wright in *The Oropesa* (1943)). Thus, the defendant will remain liable if the act of the third party is not truly independent of the defendant's act. In *Knightley v Johns* (1982), the Court of Appeal held that negligent conduct was far more likely to break the chain of causation than non-negligent conduct, so it would follow that a deliberate act is even more likely to break the chain and be found to be truly independent of the defendant's original act.[2]

In the circumstances, the act of Steven is unreasonable, extraneous, extrinsic and deliberate, and would breach the chain of causation, so that Henry would not be liable for those consequences.

Henry could not be sued by Pat in negligence, as there has been no breach of duty on his part, as we are told that the chain was substantial, but had a latent defect. Henry could be sued in negligence by Richard as, once the dog broke free, Henry would have been negligent in not securing the dog if he was aware of the broken dog chain.

Richard could possibly sue Henry under *Rylands v Fletcher* (1868), although whether liability exists for the escape of an animal is debatable (*Read v Lyons* (1947)). However, the rule in *Rylands* has been held to be applicable in the case of an escape of caravan dwellers (*AG v Cooke* (1933)), so arguably it could cover the escape of animals. But even if *Rylands* did apply to the escape of an animal, it is at best debatable whether it can cover personal injuries: see the *obiter* statements in *Transco v Stockport Metropolitan Borough Council* (2004).[3]

QUESTION 37

Jenny, who lectures in zoology, has a pet South African monkey called Nigel. Nigel has been hand-reared since he was born and is quite tame. One day, Nigel opened a window catch, climbed out of Jenny's house and went through an open window into the house of Jenny's neighbour, Angela. Angela's mother, Maria, was visiting at the time and, as Maria has a phobia about monkeys because she was bitten by one as a child, she panicked and ran through the glass back door, cutting herself extensively. She went to hospital by ambulance and, while she was at the hospital, a thief entered by the broken back door and stole some of Angela's property.

▶ Advise Angela and Maria.

2 Including short quotes from the cases cited, or attributing arguments to specified judges, will add to the quality of the answer.
3 It is important to consider other possible actions, as the question is not restricted to the **Animals Act**.

How to Answer this Question

The question is a little different from the standard animals question, in that it involves a dangerous species, together with a consideration of the damage for which its keeper is liable.

The following points need to be discussed:

- ❖ the definition of a dangerous species;
- ❖ liability for damage caused – extent and limitations;
- ❖ other causes of action.

Applying the Law

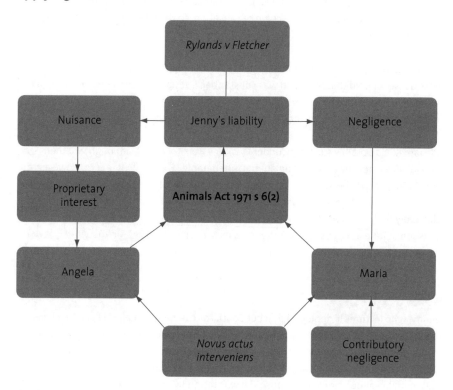

This diagram highlights Jenny's liability to Angela and Maria.

ANSWER

We first have to decide whether Nigel belongs to a dangerous or non-dangerous species. By s 6(2) of the **Animals Act 1971**, a dangerous species is a species:

(a) that is not commonly domesticated in the British Isles;

(b) the fully grown animals of which normally have such characteristics that they are likely, unless restrained, to cause severe damage or that any damage that they may cause is likely to be severe.

It should be noted that, by s 6(2), it is the species that must be dangerous and not the particular animal in question. Thus, the fact that Nigel is tame does not take him out of the category of dangerous species. In addition, s 6(2) requires that the animal be of a type that is not commonly domesticated in the British Isles – the fact that Nigel might belong to a species that is commonly domesticated in South Africa again will not take Nigel out of his classification. Thus, s 6(2)(a) is satisfied. Section 6(2)(b) is satisfied, as the bite from a fully grown monkey is likely to be severe. Thus, both heads of s 6(2) are satisfied and Nigel belongs to a dangerous species. By s 2(1), the keeper is liable for any damage caused, except where the Act provides a defence. There is no restriction on the damage caused by Nigel or the damage that Nigel is likely to cause, or whether or not that damage is severe. It is also clear from the wording of the Act that there is no requirement that the damage be foreseeable; it is enough that it is caused by the animal. Jenny is the keeper of the animal under s 6(3), as we are told that Jenny owns Nigel. The fact that Nigel is stated to be tame is of no consequence either, as in *Behrens v Bertram Mills Circus Ltd* (1957).[4]

From s 2(1), it follows that Jenny is liable for the harm caused by Nigel. The only defences available to Jenny are those contained within the Act – namely, *volenti* (s 5(2)), contributory negligence (s 10), the defence with regard to trespassers and guard dogs (s 5(3) and (1)), and where the damage is wholly due to the fault of the person suffering it. Clearly, s 5(2) and (3) are not relevant to Jenny, but could she claim that the injury suffered by Maria was wholly Maria's fault in running through the glass door? As s 2(1) makes the keeper liable for the damage caused (subject to the statutory defences), s 5(1) covers the situation in which the victim causes the damage wholly by himself. We should thus ask whether Maria's act of running through the door was a *novus actus interveniens* that broke the chain of causation – that is, that the appearance of Nigel merely provided the opportunity for Maria to be the author of her own misfortune. The problem for Jenny in running this defence is the well-established rule that a tortfeasor takes his victim as he finds him (*Dulieu v White* (1901)) and, in this case, the victim has a phobia about monkeys. No question of foreseeability arises under s 2(1) (although even if it did, it would be disposed of by the above rule: see *Robinson v Post Office* (1974); *Bradford v Robinson Rentals* (1967)).[5]

---

4   Consideration of whether Nigel is a dangerous animal under the **Animals Act 1971** requires careful use and application of the statute.

5   Defences should always be considered, both those specific to the tort and the general defences, on which see more in Chapter 15.

The act of the claimant may break the chain of causation where his act is so careless that his injury cannot be attributed to the fault of the defendant. Comparing *McKew v Holland and Hannen and Cubitts* (1969) with *Wieland v Cyril Lord Carpets* (1969), it seems clear that to constitute a *novus actus interveniens* on the part of the claimant, the act must be unreasonable. As Jenny must take Maria as she finds her – that is, with a phobia about monkeys – Maria's acts are not likely to be found so unreasonable as to constitute a *novus actus interveniens*. Again, it is settled law that if a person, in the agony of the moment, causes himself harm, the act causing the harm will not necessarily break the chain of causation: *Jones v Boyce* (1816). Hence, it is submitted that Maria's action will not constitute a *novus actus interveniens*, but that contributory negligence under s 10 would be a more appropriate defence (if any).

As regards the theft of property, the damage has been caused by a third party, so the question arises as to whether or not the act of the thief caused the damage rather than Nigel – that is, was the theft a *novus actus interveniens*? Where it is alleged that the act of a third party, over whom the defendant has no control, has broken the chain of causation, it must be shown that the act was something unwarrantable, a new cause that disturbs the sequence of events. It must be something that can be described as either unreasonable or extraneous or extrinsic (*per* Lord Wright in *The Oropesa* (1943)). Thus, the defendant will remain liable if the act of the third party is not truly independent of the defendant's act. In *Knightley v Johns* (1982), the Court of Appeal held that negligent conduct was far more likely to break the chain of causation than non-negligent conduct, so it would follow that a deliberate act is even more likely to break the chain and be found to be truly independent of the defendant's original act. The problem facing Jenny is that we are told that the thief entered by the broken back door, which suggests that the act of the thief may not be truly independent of Jenny's original act, in that the thief may not have entered the premises had the back door not been broken. If the court were to make such a finding, Jenny would be liable for the loss resulting from the theft. It is not likely that Jenny would succeed in claiming that the true cause of the theft was a *novus actus interveniens* by Maria in failing to secure the back door before going to hospital. Maria's actions seem reasonable in the 'agony of the moment' caused by Jenny's original tort and would not break the chain of causation (*Jones v Boyce* (1816)). Although in *Stansbie v Troman* (1948), it was held that the act of a thief did not break the chain of causation, this was explained by Lord Goff in *Smith v Littlewoods Organisation* (1987) as being due to the contractual relationship between the parties in question.

Jenny could also be liable to Maria in negligence.[6] There would be no difficulty in establishing a duty of care and breach of that duty, and the problem of causation (that is, did Maria herself cause her injuries?) has already been considered above. Similarly, with Angela, it would be straightforward enough to show the existence of a duty of care and breach of that duty (and again, we have considered the problem of causation above).

---

6   As the question was not restricted to the Act, other possible forms of liability should be considered.

Jenny might also be liable under the rule in *Rylands v Fletcher* (1868) for the escape of Nigel if the rule applies to animals. This was doubted in *Read v Lyons* (1947), but the rule has been held to cover the escape of caravan dwellers (*AG v Cooke* (1933)), so by analogy it could cover the escape of an animal. However, even if *Rylands* does cover the escape of an animal, it is at best debatable whether it can cover personal injuries: see the *obiter* statements in *Transco v Stockport Metropolitan Borough Council* (2004).

Jenny could also be liable to Angela in nuisance. Although the escape of Nigel was an isolated event, in *Bolton v Stone* (1951) it was stated that although a nuisance could not arise from an isolated happening, it could arise from a state of affairs, albeit temporary. Thus, in *Midwood v Manchester Corp* (1905), a gas explosion was held to be a nuisance because, although it was an isolated event, it was due to a pre-existing state of affairs – namely, the build-up of gas. Hence, Angela could argue that the escape of Nigel was due to a wrongful state of affairs on Jenny's property – namely, that Nigel was not kept within Jenny's property. Whether Maria could sue in nuisance is a difficult point – it has been held traditionally that, as the tort of nuisance protects interests in land, the claimant must have an interest in the land affected to sue (*Malone v Laskey* (1907)). Despite the relaxation of this requirement by the Court of Appeal in *Khorasandjian v Bush* (1993) and *Hunter v Canary Wharf Ltd* (1996), the House of Lords reinstated this requirement when it decided *Hunter* (1997). Thus, Maria lacks the necessary interest in land to sue in nuisance and, in addition, in *Hunter* (1997), the House of Lords held that personal injuries could not be recovered in an action in nuisance. Thus, Maria has no right in nuisance.

Aim Higher

Getting to grips with the concept of what a dangerous animal is will ensure that you approach this sort of question with more confidence. This is a key element of the liability pertaining to animals and is often a feature of questions on the subject.

Common Pitfalls

It is not unusual for candidates to forget that there is a statutory scheme that deals with liability for animals and so often students get themselves tied up in knots trying to apply *Rylands*, or negligence principles.

Defamation and Privacy

13

Please note that in May 2012 a Defamation Bill was introduced into Parliament. If passed, this statute will make significant changes to the law represented in questions 34, 35, 36 and 37, to include: a requirement that the defamatory statement causes serious harm; new statutory defences; and a move away from jury trial. Students should therefore check the current status of this legislation, as in its final form it is likely to have considerable impact on this area of law.

INTRODUCTION

Questions on defamation appear regularly in examination papers. Defamation is a major topic and encompasses a considerable volume of law. In practice, examiners tend to concentrate on several specific topics – notably, the defences of fair (now 'honest') comment and qualified privilege, although students will also have to have a good grasp of the elements of liability and of the provisions of the **Defamation Act 1996**. Also in this chapter are questions on the publication of personal information that, although not defamatory, might be damaging or upsetting to the claimant. While there is no absolute tort of privacy in English law, common law is developing to ensure that people's rights are protected.

Checklist ✔

Students must be familiar with the following areas:

(a) the distinction between libel and slander;

(b) defamatory statements and innuendoes;

(c) reference to claimant;

(d) publication;

(e) defences, with especial references to honest comment and qualified privilege;

(f) the tort of breach of confidence;

(g) the impact of the **Human Rights Act 1998** on the development of the common law.

QUESTION 38

Dimitri, an extremely wealthy and eccentric football supporter, decided to invest millions of pounds in a successful non-league team, Worthless FC. His stated intention was to win eventual promotion to European competition. *The Daily Post*, a national tabloid, ran a story in which it stated that the new breed of overseas football entrepreneurs were 'virtually to a man involved in large-scale fraud and money laundering, and were ripping the soul from English football'. An Internet football chatroom, 'Shinned', contained many criticisms of Dimitri: one message by a poster called 'Yuriy' stated that 'he had connections with the secret police and had stolen most of his fortune'; another poster, 'WFC', considered that his only intention for Worthless FC was to 'launder his dirty roubles' and that Dimitri was the 'subject of a criminal investigation in Russia'. When Dimitri discovered this, he asked the website owner to remove these untrue comments and to identify the posters. A month later, neither had been done. Subsequently, *The Daily Post* ran a sports editorial column that called for better regulation of football club ownership, which was necessary to prevent corruption. The column did not name Dimitri, but included a link to the 'Shinned' website for a so-called 'fans-eye view'.

▶ None of the allegations made about Dimitri are true. Advise Dimitri as to any remedies he might pursue in tort.

How to Answer this Question

This is a standard type of defamation question, which also requires some appreciation of the reach of the tort into 'cyberspace' and considers the defences of privilege and honest comment.

The following points will require discussion:

- ❖ whether Yuri's statements are defamatory;
- ❖ whether Shinned is liable as a publisher;
- ❖ whether the 'true' identity of the defamer can be discovered;
- ❖ whether any defences might be claimed.

Applying the Law

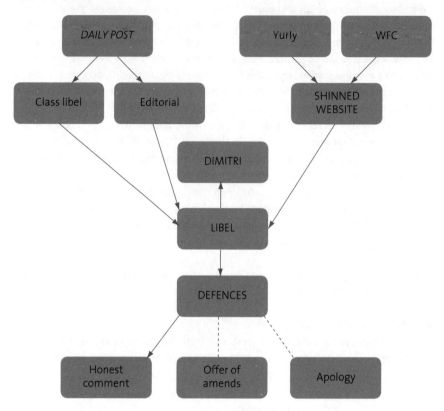

This diagram shows the possible liability to Dmitri for libel.

ANSWER

Dimitri will want to use the tort of defamation to seek redress for the damage to his reputation. Defamation is constituted in the publication of a false statement that injures the reputation of the person to whom it refers. The tort is subdivided into slander, which is understood as being temporary, such as the spoken word, and libel, where the statement is made in a more permanent form, such as in writing, broadcast media (**Defamation Act 1952**) or theatre performances (**Theatres Act 1968**). Dimitri would be advised that the statements made, if proved to be defamatory, would be libellous, as all have been written either electronically or in print. The distinction is important because libel is actionable *per se*, meaning that Dimitri does not have to prove any 'special' damage. He merely needs to demonstrate that the statements were defamatory. For Dimitri to succeed in a defamation action, he needs to prove three things: firstly, that the statement complained of was defamatory; secondly, that the statement made actually referred to him; finally, that the statement was published to a third party.[1]

Firstly, it is necessary to understand what is meant by a defamatory statement. There is no precise definition and so the traditional view is that something is defamatory 'if it would tend to lower the plaintiff in the estimation of right-thinking members of society' (*Sim v Stretch* (1936)), or it would cause people to 'shun or avoid the plaintiff or regard the plaintiff with hatred, contempt or ridicule' (*Youssoupoff v MGM* (1934)). The basis of this approach is the effect that the statement *could* have on a 'right-thinking member of society' (*Byrne v Deane* (1937)), rather than definitively proving that this was in fact the case.[2]

Dealing with the statements made in turn, we can assess whether any are capable of holding a defamatory meaning and thus satisfying the first hurdle that Dimitri needs to overcome to sustain an action. Firstly, *The Daily Post*'s article referring to large-scale fraud and money laundering would appear on its face to be defamatory within the definition above. The messages posted on the Internet website would also fall within this category; although it is doubtful whether the statement that Dimitri was being investigated by the Russian authorities would be capable of defamatory meaning, because it is not the same as stating that a person is actually guilty of a criminal offence (see *Lewis v Daily Telegraph* (1964)).

It is clear that the website statements identify Dimitri by name, so it would be simple for him to prove that the statements refer to him. What is not so clear is the status of *The Daily Post*'s article in which it was claimed that overseas football entrepreneurs in general were fraudulent. The issue of identification of a member of a group or class of people was considered in the case of *Knupffer v London Express Newspapers* (1944) . In that case, the House of Lords were asked to determine whether a statement that a group of ex-patriot Russians had fascist leanings was defamatory. Worldwide, the group had over 2,000 members, and there were over 20 of the group living in London. The House of Lords – rejecting the plaintiff's case – held that in order for an individual member of a class to succeed in an action for defamation, they would normally need to be identified definitively by the words themselves. Where the class was particularly small, each member of the class would be able to have a remedy, if the words could be said to apply to each member of that class. In Dimitri's case, it would need to be determined whether the class of overseas entrepreneurs was so small as to indicate that the words referred to each one of them. The words are certainly unequivocal; but as we are not certain as to the size of the class, it is something that would have to be determined by a jury

....

1   The introductory paragraph identifies and introduces the relevant law which will be applied to the problem's facts.

2   In these introductory paragraphs, the basic principles of the relevant law are set out; why this is libel rather than slander and the advantage of the latter being actionable *per se*.

(remembering that defamation actions are an anomaly in the civil law as there is the possibility of a jury trial, in which the judge determines questions of law and the jury questions of fact, as well as having some input into the final award of damages).[3] Finally, *The Daily Post*'s editorial column raises the concept of linked publications. Here, Dimitri would be seeking to establish that the editorial, which did not name him, could be defamatory of him because of the fact that it linked to defamatory comments that directly referred to him and was suggestive of the fact that he was one of the corrupt overseas owners in need of stronger regulation. It is likely that he would be able to succeed in this enterprise (see *Hayward v Thompson* (1981)).

Having established that the words are comparable of defamatory meaning and that they may or may not refer to Dimitri, it remains to determine whether or not they have been published. Any communication of a defamatory statement to a person other than the claimant is a publication (*Pullman v Hill* (1891)). The **Defamation Act 1996 (s1)** identifies authors, editors and commercial publishers as those with the primary responsibility for publication. The section also provides a defence if publication is made by a person other than the identified parties, without the want of reasonable care and without knowledge that the material was defamatory. The defence will be considered more fully below. While it is clear that all of the statements have been 'published' as such, it remains to determine upon whom liability for their publication should fall. It should be noted that each subsequent republication of a defamatory statement creates a new cause of action against the person who published them.

A problem with the rule on successive publications is that a variety of people may become liable: for example, website owners, Internet service providers (ISPs), distributors or even retail outlets (*Goldsmith v Sperrings* (1977)). In *Tamiz v Google Inc* (2012) , it was held that as a platform provider for bloggers, Google was not a publisher. The common law developed a defence of 'innocent dissemination' (see *Vizetelly v Mudie's Select Library Ltd* (1900)) in circumstances under which there was no knowledge of a libel contained in the material in question, that there was no reason for belief that there was libel contained within it and the publisher was not negligent in failing to know that. The defence has been maintained, but codified in **s1** of the **Defamation Act 1996**, as above. The online environment alone has provided a new means by which defamatory material might be published to a virtually limitless audience. The case of *Godfrey v Demon Internet* (1999) considered the application of **s1** of the **Defamation Act** to Internet service providers. In the case, defamatory material had been published about the claimant on a website hosted by the defendant. Had the defendant responded to the fact that the claimant had advised them that the material had been posted and removed it within a reasonable time, the defence would have applied. They did not and so were unable to prove that they had exercised reasonable care (see also *Bunt v Tilley* (2006)). This also raises an issue in

3   This uncertainty about the facts gives the opportunity to demonstrate understanding about the role a jury may play in a defamation action.

relation to material that is archived by any number of organisations, particularly media outlets. If a claimant succeeds in defamation proceedings, it would be necessary to remove any related material from archives (see *Loutchanksy v Times Newspapers (No 2)* (2002)). We are not certain whether Dimitri did in fact notify the ISP in this scenario, but the website owner's failure to respond would most likely incur liability. The ability for persons to hide behind 'virtual' identities also presents its own problems as identifying the originator of defamatory statements becomes difficult, if not impossible, to trace. As above, the owner of the site might be made liable, but the question has recently arisen as to whether anonymous posters can be identified. In the case of *Sheffield Wednesday Football Club v Hargreaves* (2007) , the High Court ordered the defendant, who operated a website, to reveal the names of certain posters who posted defamatory statements about the club and its directors. Applying this development to Dimitri's situation, it would appear that he would be able to discover the true identity of 'Yuriy' and 'WFC', and join them in any action.

It remains to consider whether there are any defences that might apply.[4] The first to consider would be the defence of justification – in that the material published is in fact true. We are told that it is not and so this defence would not be available to any of the parties to the action. As above, it would be unlikely that the website owner, who would likely be classed as a commercial publisher by **s**1 of the **Defamation Act**, could rely on the innocent dissemination defence as it could not be argued that he had not been negligent, having been told that the material was defamatory.

The Daily Post might seek to argue that the editorial column was covered by the defence of fair comment, now known as honest comment since *Spiller v Joseph* (2010). This defence demands that the defendant establish that the statement made was an honest comment upon true facts which was made in good faith and in the public interest (*British Chiropractic Association v Singh* (2010)). Each of these components needs to be identified. Public interest is defined widely. In *London Artists v Littler* (1969), the court determined that issues of both political life and social interest (to include artistic, business and sporting matters etc) would fall within the definition. The ownership of football clubs, given the prominence of the sport, would undoubtedly therefore be of public interest. *The Daily Post* would not, however, be able to show that the comment was based upon facts (see *Lowe v Associated Newspapers* (2006)). We are told that the material posted on the website is untrue and so the defence would fail.

It would appear then than Dimitri would be able to maintain a successful action in relation to the website comments and the editorial in *The Daily Post*. It is less certain that he would be able to succeed in relation to the 'class' libel of the first article, however. *The Daily Post* might take advantage of **s**1 of the **Libel Act 1843** and issue an apology. While

---

4   Consider the special defences that apply, which are especially important in the tort of defamation.

this is not of itself a defence as such, it can have the effect of reducing a damages award, if it is made at the time that the case is brought. Additionally it could make an offer of amends by a procedure introduced in **ss 2–4** of the **Defamation Act 1996**. *The Daily Post* would be required to make a written offer to Dimitri to publish an apology or correction, and to pay an amount of damages. However, if it were to do this, it would have to be done at a point prior to seeking to rely on any other defence. Should Dimitri accept this offer, then the parties will agree the matter between themselves without the involvement of the court, unless there is significant disagreement about, for example, the level of compensation. Should Dimitri reject the opportunity, *The Daily Post* may withdraw the offer, make a further offer, or let it remain in place. If the final option was followed and, as would be likely, Dimitri won his case, the courts would have the ability to reduce any damages award made to him, taking account of the offer of amends.

It would appear that Dimitri has a high chance of success in his claims against the Internet posters and *The Daily Post* editorial. Were the case to go to court, Dimitri would seek damages and possibly an injunction to prevent any repetition. Defamation cases are notoriously expensive and complex; as a result, the **Defamation Act 1996** provides for a 'fast-track' procedure (**ss 8–9**) whereby, should a defendant have no realistic prospect of pleading a successful defence (**s 8(3)**), the court may give judgment to the claimant and grant him 'summary relief'. This would involve a judge only making the determination as of damages, with a limiting figure of £10,000. **Section 9** of the Act also provides that the court may award an injunction to restrain further publication. This might be particularly useful for Dimitri in respect of the website content.[5]

QUESTION 39

The Westfield Chamber of Commerce decides to set up a fund to allow a promising young businessman to spend some months in Europe studying European business methods. A committee consisting of Diana, Edward and Fenella is set up to consider applications. An application is received from George, and Diana circulates a memo to Edward and Fenella, saying: 'I understand that George is on the point of insolvency. He does not seem to be a suitable candidate.' Edward also circulates a memo, stating: 'George is incompetent and not fit to represent Westfield in Europe.' Edward types this himself, but leaves a copy on the photocopying machine where it is seen by Henry. Edward's company recently tendered for some business with George's company, but failed to obtain the contract.

▶ Advise George.

How to Answer this Question

Again, a standard defamation question, requiring mostly a discussion of the defence of qualified privilege and fair, now honest, comment.

....

5   Brief consideration of the special problems in bringing a defamation case to court and the procedure involved provides a suitable conclusion to this problem.

The following points need to be discussed:

- ❖ whether Diana's statement is defamatory;
- ❖ whether Diana can claim qualified privilege or honest comment;
- ❖ the effect of possible malice on Edward's defences;
- ❖ the possible evasion of qualified privilege defence by using negligent misstatement as a cause of action.

Applying the Law

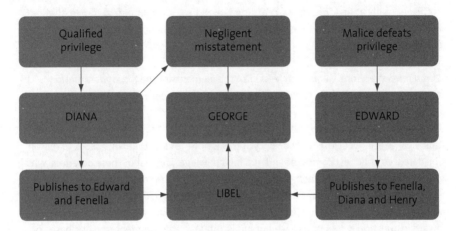

This diagram shows Diana's and Edward's potential liability to George.

ANSWER

The statements by Diana and Edward are in permanent form, so any defamation that has occurred will take the form of libel and will be actionable without proof of any special damage.

In order to succeed in an action for defamation, George will have to prove that the relevant statement was defamatory, that it referred to him and was published to a third party.

The usual test for a statement being defamatory is that it tends to lower the claimant in the estimation of right-thinking members of society generally (*Sim v Stretch* (1936)) or exposes him to hatred, contempt or ridicule (*Parmiter v Coupland* (1840)). Diana's statement appears, at first sight, to meet this criterion: in *Read v Hudson* (1700), it was held to be defamatory to impute insolvency to a trader, even though there was no suggestion of discreditable conduct. Also, if the statement contains the false innuendo that George is not competent in his business or profession, that will clearly be defamatory (*Capital and Counties Bank v Henty* (1882)). The fact that George's friends or business colleagues might regard insolvency as something that might happen to even the most talented businessman is not relevant to the issue of whether the statement is defamatory: the statement must be judged by the standard of right-thinking members of society generally, not only the claimant's friends (*Byrne v Deane* (1937)).

Edward's statement is clearly defamatory, reflecting adversely on George's competence. Both Diana's and Edward's statements refer to George by name, and Diana has published the name to third parties – namely, Edward and Fenella. Edward has published the name both to Diana and Fenella and also to Henry, as negligent publication to a third party is sufficient publication (*Theaker v Richardson* (1962)). This is assuming, of course, that Henry understands the defamatory nature of the statement and its reference to George (*Sadgrove v Hole* (1901)).

Prima facie, therefore, George can establish the elements of the tort of defamation against Diana and Edward. Next we shall consider any defences available.[6]

Diana may be able to avail herself of the defence of justification, that is, truth, provided that George is in fact close to insolvency. If this is not the case, Diana may seek to rely on the defences of honest comment and qualified privilege. The first of these defences, which until the case of *Spiller v Joseph* (2010) was known as 'fair' comment, applies where the statement is honest comment based on true facts made in good faith on a matter of public interest. The courts define public interest widely (*London Artists v Littler* (1969)) and the award in question would be a matter of public interest. The comment must be based on true facts (*British Chiropractic Association v Singh* (2010)) that are stated in the comment and following the decision in *Spiller v Joseph* (2010), the facts supporting the honest comment should be explicitly or implicitly indicated, at least in general terms. The problem for Diana is that the comment that George is not a suitable candidate is based on an alleged fact (that he is close to insolvency), but we do not know whether that fact is true.

By honest comment, we mean that Diana must have honestly believed the opinion (*Slim v Daily Telegraph* (1968); *British Chiropractic Association v Singh* (2010)) and not that a reasonable person would agree with the opinion (*Silkin v Beaverbrook Newspapers* (1958)). Although Diana's comment may be honest in this respect, the defence can be rebutted by showing that the defendant acted out of malice (*Thomas v Bradbury Agnew* (1906)). The burden of proving malice will lie on the claimant (*Telnikoff v Matusevich* (1991)). However, the defendant will still have to show that the opinions were honestly expressed and based on accurate facts (*Branson v Bower* (2001)).

Although Diana may well be able to establish that the comment was honest, as there seems to be no evidence of malice, she still has to overcome the hurdle of basing the comment on true facts.

....

6   Examination of defences is vital in defamation questions and will take up much of the answer.

It seems that Diana's best defence would be to rely on qualified privilege – namely, that she was under a duty to make the statement to Edward and Fenella, and they were under a corresponding duty to receive it (*Watt v Longsden* (1930)). The requisite duty would exist in this case and Diana could rely on this defence unless she was acting maliciously. By 'malice', it is meant that the defendant had no honest belief in the truth of her statement (*Horrocks v Lowe* (1975)) and there is no reason to impute malice to Diana.

In *Kearns v General Council of the Bar* (2003) , the Court of Appeal stated that the common interest situation test was not always useful, and that it would be more helpful to distinguish between cases in which the communicating parties were in an existing and established relationship, and cases in which no such relationship had been established and the communications were between strangers. Privilege would attach much more readily in the established relationship situations. If we apply this test, it seems that Diana, Edward and Fenella are in an established relationship, and could not be described as strangers, hence qualified privilege should arise whatever test is used.

It would be possible for George to circumvent Diana's defence of qualified privilege by suing Diana in the tort of negligent misstatement.[7] This route was allowed by the House of Lords in *Spring v Guardian Assurance* (1994), despite the argument that it effectively allowed the defence of qualified privilege to be sidestepped. As a duty of care was imposed in similar circumstances in *Spring*, George would only have to prove breach – that is, that Diana had not taken reasonable care to verify the statement – as causation and foreseeability of damage would appear to pose no problems.

Edward could rely on the defence of justification if his statement were true. As regards honest comment, Edward's problem is that his statement seems to be one of fact, rather than opinion, and there is no substratum of fact as in *Kemsley v Foot* (1952). Edward could of course argue that his statement should be interpreted as 'George is incompetent and therefore not fit to represent Westfield in Europe', and thus is comment based on fact. He would then have to show that the statement 'George is incompetent' is a true fact, which would be difficult to prove. If it were a comment, it would have to be honest in the sense discussed above, but George might well be able to show malice on Edward's part, which would destroy the defence.

If Edward were to seek to rely on qualified privilege, then, although he would be able, like Diana, to show the required reciprocal duty or existing relationship regarding Diana and Fenella, this defence too can be destroyed by showing that Edward was actuated by malice. In any event, Edward could not rely on qualified privilege as regards the publishing to Henry, as Edward is under no duty to make the statement to Henry and Henry is under no duty to receive it (*Watt*).

....

7   It is advisable to be alert to the possibility of other relevant actions, as here with negligent misstatement, even when the question is primarily concerned with another area, as here, defamation.

It would seem, then, that George has a good case against Edward, but that Diana may be able to rely on qualified privilege as a defence to defamation, although she still may have a problem as regards negligent misstatement.

In view of the strength of George's case against Edward, he should be advised that if it is decided that Edward's defence has no realistic prospect of success, George could avail himself of the 'fast-track' procedure provided by ss 8 and 9 of the **Defamation Act 1996**. Under this procedure, damages are assessed by a judge and not a jury, and are limited to £10,000. In addition, George may be able to obtain a declaration that the statement was false and defamatory, a published apology and an injunction to restrict further publication (s 9 of the **Defamation Act 1996**).

George should also be advised that a decision as to whether to institute proceedings in defamation should be made reasonably quickly, as the limitation period for defamation actions is now one year (s 5 of the **Defamation Act 1996**). (This period may be extended under s 32A of the **Limitation Act 1980** (as amended) but the court will require a satisfactory explanation for the delay (*Steedman v British Broadcasting Corp* (2001)).)[8]

QUESTION 40

Ian is a sports commentator for Eastland Television. He decides to make a programme on Eastleith Rovers, a local amateur football team that has reached a regional cup final. In the programme, there is a shot of the team in a public house with the comment from Ian: 'This is how the team prepares on Friday night for its cup final match on Saturday.' In fact, the scene was shot on a Saturday night after a previous game. This film also shows John, the centre forward, eating a hamburger with the comment from Ian: 'As John is single, he has to do his own cooking so he eats out a lot.' John is in fact married to Jane, who is most upset at this comment.

Eastleith Rovers lose their cup final and Ian, in his post-match summary, states: 'They played appallingly badly, even by the standards of an amateur team.' The *Eastland Gazette* reviews the programme and match, repeats Ian's comments regarding the team playing badly and wonders whether this was due to John's poor diet.

▶ **Advise John, Jane and Eastleith Rovers of any action they might have in defamation.**

How to Answer this Question

This is a wide-ranging question that covers the areas of innuendo, references to the claimant and republication.

---

8   It is appropriate to note that the limitation period for defamation is shorter than for other tort actions.

The following points need to be discussed:

- ❖ commentary and slander – the **Defamation Act 1952**;
- ❖ Jane's ability to sue, despite not being expressly referred to;
- ❖ Eastleith Rovers and class defamation;
- ❖ the liability of Eastland Television for repetition of a defamatory statement.

Applying the Law

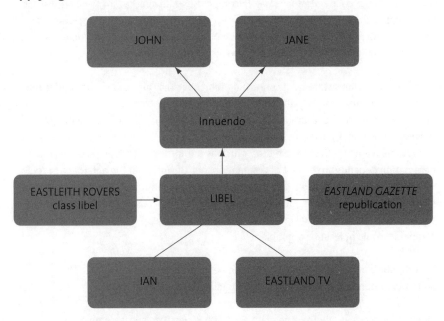

This diagram demonstrates Ian's, Eastland TV's and Eastland Gazette's potential liability in libel.

ANSWER

The statements made by Ian in the television programme are deemed to be publication in a permanent form by **s1** of the **Defamation Act 1952**. They may thus constitute libel and be actionable without proof of special damage.

For any of the potential claimants to sue in defamation, they must show that the statement complained of was defamatory, that it referred to them and that it was published to a third party.

Considering first John, the statement that he is single is not *prima facie* defamatory. However, when coupled with the true innuendo that John is married to Jane, the statement that he is single might lead people who know that he lives with Jane to assume that they are not in fact married (*Cassidy v Daily Mirror* (1929)). Thus, the statement is defamatory, as it would tend to lower John in the estimation of right-thinking members of society generally (*Sim v Stretch* (1936)) or to expose him to hatred, contempt or ridicule (*Parmiter v Coupland* (1840)). The fact that John's friends might not think any the less of him for living with a woman to whom he is not married is not relevant, as the standard is that of right-thinking members of society (*Byrne v Deane* (1937)). It could be argued by Ian that the standards of right-thinking members of society alter with time, so that, for example, it is no longer defamatory to call a person a German, as in *Slazengers v Gibbs* (1916), or a Czech, as in *Linklater v Daily Telegraph* (1964). Given this, Ian could argue that to say that an adult male lives with a woman is no longer defamatory. As, however, it is still defamatory to make this allegation of a woman (**s 1** of the **Slander of Women Act 1891**), it seems most illogical that it would not also be defamatory of a man.

Turning to Jane, Ian's statement concerning John obviously also carries the suggestion that Jane is living with John without being married to him: *Cassidy v Daily Mirror*. This is defamatory and the fact that Jane is not referred to by Ian is no bar to her suing (*Morgan v Odhams Press* (1971)). The fact that Ian is innocent in this matter (for example, because he was mistaken or was even told that John was unmarried) is of itself no defence, as defamation depends on the fact of defamation, not the intent of the defamer (*Hulton v Jones* (1910)). Jane could also argue that the film of John eating out, plus the commentary suggesting that she does not do any cooking for John, could also be defamatory, using the test in *Byrne*, although given contemporary views on people's domestic arrangements this point would at least be arguable.[9]

In both John's and Jane's cases, there would be no problem in showing that the statement referred to them and had been published to a third party.

The next question is whether the team, Eastleith Rovers, can sue in defamation. The statement that the team prepares for a cup final by drinking the night before and the statement concerning how badly they played are both *prima facie* defamatory, and these statements were published to third parties. However, the statements concerning the team are an example of class or group defamation. In *Knupffer v London Express Newspapers* (1944), it was held by the House of Lords that in class defamation, a member of the class could not sue, unless the words pointed particularly to the claimant or that the class was so small that the words must necessarily refer to each member of it. It is submitted that a football team is such a small class that the individual member can sue.[10]

---

9 The two previous paragraphs demonstrate the importance of being aware that what is defamatory will change with society's views, and so no definitive conclusion can be reached. However, it is important to raise and discuss the issue, to show that the concept is understood.

10 It is possible to make a submission based on the likely outcome (here, that a team is sufficiently small so that each can sue) without being definite where there is no direct authority. Contrast this with the uncertainty in Question 38 where a less definite answer could be given because there was no information about how many people were in the class.

Having established Ian's (and Eastland Television's) liability for these statements, we need to consider whether Ian can raise any successful defences.[11] In respect of John and Jane, no common law defences seem available. However, both Ian and the television company could make use of the offer to make amends defence contained within **ss 2–4** of the **Defamation Act 1996**. By **s 2(4)**, such an offer must be to make and publish a suitable correction and apology, and to pay compensation. By **s 3** of the **1996 Act**, if such an offer is accepted, any defamation is ended and, if the parties cannot agree on compensation, this amount may be decided by the court.

If such an offer is not accepted by the claimant, the making of the offer is a valid defence. However, the defence is not available if the defendant knew that the statement could refer to the claimant, and was both false and defamatory. The burden of proving this lies on the claimant. In *Milne v Express Newspapers Ltd* (2003), it was held that the amends defence would only fail where the defendant had actual knowledge of the facts, and that actual knowledge would have provided reasonable grounds to believe that the words were false and defamatory. On the facts given, it seems that Ian and the television company could avail themselves of this defence.

Considering the statement made about the team, there seems to be no defence to the allegations regarding drinking, particularly given the lack of responsible journalism demonstrated by Ian's embellishment of the facts (see *Galloway v Telegraph Newspapers Ltd* (2006)). As regards the allegation that they played appallingly badly, the defences available are justification – that is, truth – and honest comment, which until the case of *Spiller v Joseph* (2010) was known as 'fair' comment. To establish the defence of honest comment, it will have to be shown that the statement was honest comment based on true facts made in good faith on a matter of public interest. The courts interpret public interest widely (*London Artists v Littler* (1969)), and a televised football match would certainly come under this heading. The comment must be one of opinion and not of fact, which is the case here. The comment must also be based on true facts (*British Chiropractic Association v Singh* (2010)), and 'must explicitly or implicitly indicate, at least in general terms, the facts on which it is based' (*Spiller v Joseph* (2010)). In a case such as the present, the comment is an opinion based on the fact in Ian's commentary – Ian does not have to set these all out again in detail before he gives his opinion (*McQuire v Western Morning News* (1903)). 'Honest comment' means that Ian must have honestly believed the opinion expressed (*Slim v Daily Telegraph* (1968); *British Chiropractic Association v Singh* (2010)) and not that a reasonable person would agree with the opinion (*Silkin v Beaverbrook Newspapers* (1958)). Although Ian's comment may be honest in this respect, the defence can be rebutted by showing that the defendant acted out of malice (*Thomas v Bradbury Agnew* (1906)). The burden of proving malice will be on the claimant (*Telnikoff v Matusevich* (1991)). However, the defendant will still have to show that the facts on which

---

11 Defences are especially important in a defamation action, and sufficient emphasis should be made of them.

the comment was based were true and the comment was objectively fair, in that anyone, however prejudiced or obstinate, could honestly have held the views expressed. Hence, overall it would seem that a defence of honest comment would be likely to succeed in the post-match comments. The review in the *Eastland Gazette* constitutes a republication of the comments regarding the team and, by implication, republishes the statement regarding John and Jane. The question is whether any liability for this republication attaches to Eastland Television or whether liability is solely that of the *Eastland Gazette*.[12] In *McManus v Beckham* (2002), the Court of Appeal held that in republishing situations, the question was whether it was just that the defendant should be held liable for the damage. The Court held that the test to apply was essentially one of reasonable foreseeability, but as this test might be too easily satisfied, that the court should ask whether the defendant actually either knew what he or she said was likely to be reported and repeated or whether a reasonable person in the position of the defendant would have known this.[13]

Applying this test, the television company could also be liable for the subsequent repetition of the story of its allegations in the *Eastland Gazette*.

QUESTION 41

Critically assess the relationship between the law of defamation and the area of freedom of expression in light of developments such as 'super-injunctions' and libel tourism.

How to Answer this Question

This essay requires a discussion of the basics of an action in defamation and the available defences, but within a context that takes account of some controversial contemporary issues which may be popular with examiners.

The following points need to be considered:

- ❖ the context within which free speech may be problematic;
- ❖ the basic tests for establishing liability;
- ❖ appropriate defences (here to include justification, the privileges, honest comment);
- ❖ developments in the law and commentary.

12 Where, as here, names are used which are similar (East*land* Gazette and Television, East*leith* Rovers), be sure to leave time to check at the end of the answer that you have not made careless mistakes which could lose marks. An examiner can only mark what is written, not what is intended.

13 Do not overlook the minor, or subsidiary, facts in a problem (here, of republication by the *Gazette*). Always read the question carefully, plan your answer in advance and check back to the plan at the end to ensure you have included everything.

Answer Structure

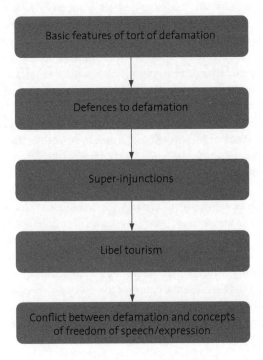

ANSWER

Defamation is premised on protecting a person's reputation against untrue statements published in either permanent form (libel) or non-permanent form (slander) (see, for example, *McManus v Beckham* (2002)). A successful claimant is awarded damages, and may seek an injunction to restrain publication of material. Recent interest has centred on the balance between an individual's right to protect their reputation, and the effect that has on the wider freedom of expression, a right protected by virtue of **Article 10** of the **European Convention on Human Rights (ECHR)**. The perception is that it has shifted too far towards the claimant. Commentators have argued that defamation has a so-called 'chilling' effect because threatened legal action can prevent free expression/public debate. The fact that damages awards are generally very high (see *Loutchansky v Times Newspapers* (2001)) and legal aid is not provided for defamation actions can mean that publication is restrained. The decision in *Morris & Steele v UK* (2005) has cast doubt on the legal aid position, however, and the decision in *Joyce v Sengupta* (1993), where legal aid was made available in the alternative action of malicious falsehood, may diminish this initial obstacle somewhat.[14]

14 The first part of the answer sets out the requirements of the tort of defamation and how it relates to the concept of freedom of expression, which clarifies exactly what will be discussed in the body of the answer.

A primary concern is that the threat of action prevents criticism or investigative reporting of public figures, or corporations (see Baroness Hale in *Jameel v Wall St Journal Europe* (2007)). This is especially pertinent in an era of international communication facilitated by the Internet, and where a person may claim defamation in a legal system outside of the country in which they normally reside, to take advantage of more favourable libel laws. This phenomenon, termed libel-tourism,[15] has made defendants liable in England where an action would fail elsewhere. The recognition that English law imposes a lesser burden on a claimant is recognised worldwide and has drawn criticism from the American courts and the UN Human Rights Committee, which highlighted that critical media reporting was potentially affected, to the embarrassment of the UK government (see *House of Commons, Culture Media and Sport Committee Report on Press Standards, Privacy and Libel* (2010)).[16]

The claimant may be an individual or a company, as in the case of *McDonald's Corporation v Steel and another* (1997), and may not necessarily be domiciled in the UK. Previous cases, such as *Goldsmith v Bhoyrul* (1997) and *Derbyshire County Council v Times Newspapers* (1993) have established that a political party, and a publically elected body such as a local authority, respectively, cannot sue as there would be a restriction on the freedom of speech. This is because the nature of the political system requires opinion, debate and challenge to be effective. A successful action requires a claimant to satisfy three basic tests: that the statement was defamatory, that is, capable of a defamatory meaning; that it could be said to refer to the claimant; and that the material was 'published'.

The test for a defamatory meaning is found in the judgment of Lord Atkin in *Sim v Stretch* (1936) that the statement must tend to lower the claimant in the estimation of right-thinking members of society generally, which leads to them being shunned, avoided or subject to ridicule. It is understood that mere insults or abuse are not defamatory, although in the case of *Berkoff v Burchill* (1996) the claimant successfully argued that the defendant's labelling of him as 'hideously ugly' was defamatory, the Court of Appeal holding that reputation should be interpreted broadly and be applied to situations of contempt, scorn or ridicule even if it did not question professional competence. A principal issue affecting freedom of expression is that all that is required is for a person to demonstrate the statement made people think less of them. They do not face the burden of proving it to be untrue.

It is then necessary to determine who is a right-thinking member of society. In *Byrne v Dean* (1937) it was held that right-thinking people would not think that an allegation that

---

15   It is important to explain phrases on which the question depends (as here with 'libel tourism'), in order to adequately answer the question. 'Super-injunction' is discussed below.

16   Reference to contemporary government publications will add to the quality of the answer.

someone had reported a crime to the police could be defamatory. The right-thinking person is required to assess the full context (*Charleston v News Group Newspapers Ltd* 1995), and also to consider both the ordinary and extended meanings of the words (*Lewis v Daily Telegraph* (1964); *Tolley v Fry* (1931); *Cassidy v Daily Mirror* (1929)).

A claimant must then prove that the words referred to them, which means solely that it could be understood as referring to them. There is no need to name them precisely, or at all (*Morgan v Oldhams Press* (1971); *Hulton v Jones* (1910); *Newstead v London Express Newspapers* (1940)). The final requirement is that the material be published. All this requires is that the statement is communicated to a third party (i.e., not merely the claimant themselves). Each repetition of the statement is a republication, unless done innocently (*Vizetelly v Mudie's Select Library* (1900)); and the basic test is whether someone in the position of the defendant would have reasonably anticipated that the publication would be repeated (*Slipper v BBC* (1991)). This may be significant in terms of material that is available online or archived as shown in the case of *Loutchansky v Times Newspapers (No 2)* (2002) (confirmed by the European Court of Human Rights (ECtHR) in *Times Newspapers Ltd v UK* (2009)). There is a potential risk of the 'airbrushing' of some material from history unless the archive holder is prepared to indicate that the material has been subject to a defamation hearing and should not be treated as the truth. The ECtHR did not however consider that it was disproportionate in terms of **Article 10** to require a qualifying statement.

From the above it can be observed that it is not overly difficult for a claimant to prove that they have been defamed and that there is a potentially wide reach in terms of the tort itself and the impact it may have. There are a variety of defences, statutory and non-statutory, by which a defendant may attempt to escape liability.[17]

In the context of free speech, the first defence to consider is that of justification: in essence, that the statement published was true. The burden of proof is on the defendant to prove the truth of the statement (as above, the claimant does not need to *prove the untruth* of the words; that is presumed). The statement must be true in substance and fact, although if there are a number of allegations and not all of them are proved, **s5** of the **Defamation Act 1952** enables the defence to succeed nevertheless, if those not proved do not materially injure the claimant's reputation by comparison to those that are proved.

Two extremely important defences however are the privileges: absolute and qualified. Certain situations enable the maker of a statement, no matter how ridiculous or untrue, to escape liability. Parliamentary proceedings (*Church of Scientology of California v Johnson-Smith* (1972)) and judicial proceedings are the most obvious examples, and the

17 Defences are crucial to defamation actions and should be given sufficient emphasis.

defence permits and even encourages the airing of opinions that would otherwise be restricted by an action in defamation.

Qualified privilege applies to statements made without malice (*Horrocks v Lowe* (1975)) and applies to a variety of reports set out in **Schedule 1** of the **Defamation Act 1996**. An important defence for freedom of speech, it extends to the fair and accurate reporting of judicial and Parliamentary proceedings, subject to certain restrictions. The ability to restrict the right to report has recently been subject to a degree of controversy over the use of what have been termed 'super-injunctions', which restrict publication about the thing that is in issue (which may or may not be a defamation issue) *and* reporting of the fact that the injunction exists at all and between which parties. In issue was an interpretation of the application of the **Parliamentary Papers Act 1840** and the extent it permitted reporting of Parliamentary business. The issue came to media and public attention in October 2009, when a reporting restriction was placed on the *Guardian* newspaper's reporting of questions raised in Parliament about a pollution incident involving an oil company named Trafigura. The Trafigura incident prompted debate in the House of Commons and the eventual lifting of the restriction by the company's lawyers. The issue was also considered by the *House of Commons, Culture Media and Sport Committee Report on Press Standards, Privacy and Libel* (2010) and they have proposed that 'important elements of freedom of speech should be put beyond doubt through the enactment of a modern statute'. A further example, although in the context of a privacy case, can be seen in the case of *LNS v Persons Unknown* (2010) where, upon lifting reporting restrictions, Tugendhat J stated that democracy needs 'the freedom to criticise – within the limits of the law – the conduct of other members of society as being socially harmful or wrong'.[18]

Qualified privilege also applies to so-called 'responsible journalism', a common law concept developed through the important case of *Reynolds v Times Newspapers* (1999), applied in *Galloway* (2006) and elaborated further in *Loutchansky* (2001), *Jameel* (2007) and *Flood v Times Newspapers* (2012). In this last case the Supreme Court held that it was not appropriate to lay down a general principle as to the approach to be adopted by an appellate court to an issue of *Reynolds* privilege, although in this case it was held to apply. The operation of the 'responsible' journalism aspect of the defence was cautiously approved by the Commons Committee, although recommendations for improvement were made.

The final important defence in the context of freedom of expression is that of fair comment, described by Lord Judge CJ (*British Chiropractic Association v Singh* (2010)) as a 'bulwark of free speech'. To succeed, the defence has to be the comment or expression of

---

18 A direct quote from a named judge will add quality to an answer, as will reference, as here, to named government reports where relevant.

opinion, based upon (true) facts, made in good faith and without malice (*London Artists v Littler* (1969); *Slim v Daily Telegraph* (1968)). The opinion must be 'real' (*Lowe v Associated Newspapers* (2006)), otherwise, showing that the person did not really hold that opinion is suggestive of malice. The defence is hugely important in the context of offering comment or critique, and the *Singh* case, concerning a science reporter's critique of 'bogus' claims made for the benefits of chiropractic treatment was ultimately held to be a case of an opinion offered without malice on the basis of some true facts.

Subsequently, the Supreme Court had an opportunity to consider the defence in *Spiller v Joseph* (2010), the facts of which were described as 'a storm in a tea cup'. However, Lord Joseph took the opportunity to rename the defence 'honest comment' as more reflective of its role. More importantly, the case decided that the comment need now only 'explicitly or implicitly indicate, at least in general terms, the facts upon which it is based' and thus the onus would be on a defendant to show that he subjectively believed that his comment was justified by the facts on which he based it. Coupled with the fact that the *Singh* case widened the understanding of what was comment rather than an assertion of fact, it can be seen that there have been considerable developments in this important area. However, the Supreme Court in *Spiller* called for the whole area to be considered by the Law Commission or an expert committee, and a Private Member's Bill to reform the law on defamation was introduced, but subsequently withdrawn, on the promise of government action. As can be determined from the above, the situation is evolving and the recognition that the current law is in need of some reform is on the political agenda. Balancing the freedom of expression against unwarranted press intrusion is at the heart of the proposals, and much of this has been under discussion as part of the far ranging Leveson enquiry on Culture, Practice and Ethics of the Press set up in 2011 in the wake of the phone-hacking scandal. As a result of this, there almost certainly will be new legislation and/or increased controls in the future, and a new Defamation Bill, to introduce a single publication rule and reduce libel tourism among other things, was introduced in May 2012. SEE NOTE AT BEGINNING OF THIS CHAPTER.[19]

Aim Higher ★

Ensuring that you are comfortable with debates going on within the subject areas will always help to contextualise your work. Draw on real examples such as official reports and/or the work of other respected commentators to illuminate your answer.

---

19 Essay questions are often set on topics which are controversial and/or newsworthy, so any up to date contextual material that can be introduced will add to the quality of the answer. Even when the events have occurred after the end of the relevant lecture programme, inclusion of them in the answer will show that the context is thoroughly appreciated.

QUESTION 42

Consider the extent to which tort law is able to offer protection for a person's right to privacy.

How to Answer this Question

This essay requires the candidate to consider the development of the law in relation to the protection of 'privacy', particularly given the interest in the area as a result of the **Human Rights Act 1998** and recent developments in the common law. There are currently some unresolved issues that make this an interesting subject for study and examination.

The following points require discussion:

- ❖   how privacy is protected in tort law;
- ❖   the influence of the **Human Rights Act 1998**;
- ❖   breach of confidence;
- ❖   the emergence of the concept of misuse of personal information;
- ❖   recent case law and unresolved areas.

Answer Structure

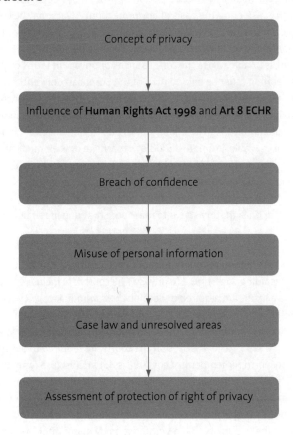

Concept of privacy

Influence of **Human Rights Act 1998** and **Art 8 ECHR**

Breach of confidence

Misuse of personal information

Case law and unresolved areas

Assessment of protection of right of privacy

ANSWER

Technically speaking, privacy is not explicitly recognised as a tort in its own right as shown in the very different cases of *Wainwright v Home Office* (2004) and *Kaye v Robertson* (1991), and recently confirmed in *Browne v Associated Newspapers* (2007). The courts have protected aspects of what might be called a person's right to privacy, however, although this has necessitated some creative application and development of some otherwise existing principles. Developments in the common law have extended protection to unjustifiable invasions of a person's privacy in limited circumstances, and the impact of the **Human Rights Act 1998** has both speeded up the evolution of the available protection and made it more inclusive.[20]

20 Careful explanation is needed here of the background to the development of the law relating to privacy, as it needs to be demonstrated that it is understood that this is still not a clearly defined area of law, which is evolving quickly.

Before considering the means by which a person's privacy may be realised though the law of torts, it is worth considering the basis of any protection. Privacy may be contrasted with, for example, reputation, for which there is extensive legal protection through the tort of defamation. However, if what is published is true, a person, despite the distress it might cause them, is unable to use the tort. To speak of privacy in terms of a right to be protected, consideration must be paid to **Art 8** of the **European Convention on Human Rights (ECHR)** as it is incorporated into English law by the **Human Rights Act 1998**. Privacy is a '**Convention** right' by virtue of the **1998 Act** as **Art 8** requires protection of, *inter alia*, a person's 'private and family life'. The unauthorised publication of certain material about a person, such as, for example, intimate details of a marriage or their medical history, might well be seen to contravene that right. Indeed, in the important case of *Von Hannover v Germany* (2004) concerning the publication of photographs of Princess Caroline of Monaco, the European Court of Human Rights held that **Art 8** imposes a positive obligation upon signatory states to make sure that due protection is given to privacy rights.

Section 6 of the **1998 Act** requires public authorities to positively protect **Convention** rights, obviously including **Art 8** rights to privacy. The courts are included as public authorities and as a result are required to develop the common law in a way that is consistent with the **Convention** rights, and by reference to the jurisprudence of the European Court of Human Rights (**s 2**). This does not mean, however, as was suggested by the claimants in *Douglas v Hello!* (2001), that the courts are required to develop a new tort of privacy. It is also worth remembering that **Art 8** is not an absolute right and that it should also be viewed as an area in which a balance is to be drawn between the **Art 8** right to privacy and the right to freedom of expression in **Art 10** of the **Convention**. **Section 12** of the **1998 Act** specifically requires that regard is to be paid to **Art 10** in any case where there is the possibility that a granted remedy might interfere with the right to freedom of expression. Of interest in that regard is **Art 10(2)**, which provides qualifications on the right, including in circumstances under which it is necessary for the protection of, *inter alia*, reputations of others and disclosure of information received in confidence. That would mean that any case brought on the basis of **Art 8**, or the tort of breach of confidence, would automatically involve consideration of **Art 10**.

Instead of developing a free-standing tort of privacy, which according to Lord Hoffmann in *Wainwright* would be better undertaken by Parliament, the courts have attempted to protect privacy interests by reference to the law relating to breaches of confidence. A development of an equitable principle, breach of confidence seeks to protect an individual against the wrongful disclosure of confidential information. Lord Woolf in *A v B plc* (2002) noted that **s 6** of the **1998 Act** requires the court not to act incompatibly with a **Convention** right. In the area of 'privacy', it was able to achieve this by absorbing into the long-established action for breach of confidence the rights that **Arts 8** and **10** protect. The basic elements of the tort, prior to recent developments, require that there should be information that would be considered private and that the defendant disclosed the information when that would involve a breach of confidentiality owed to the owner of the information. In the case of *A v B plc* (2002), a case involving a footballer's unsuccessful attempt to restrain publication of details of an extramarital affair, it was stated that a duty of confidentiality would arise when a party subject to a duty knew or ought to know that the other party could reasonably expect his privacy to be protected. Some time previously, in *Argyll v Argyll* (1967), the courts had determined that a breach of confidence was not limited to a commercial context and could include personal information.

Recent case law has provided a greater insight into the area. The leading case of *Campbell v MGN* (2004) has developed the law further from a mere 'breach of confidence' approach to one that seeks to deal with situations in which private information is misused. In that case, Lord Nicholls explicitly stated this position, reflecting that the need for the tort to be premised upon the existence of a pre-existing confidential relationship had been 'shaken off'. He said that the phrase 'a duty of confidence' and the description of the material as confidential did not really work when applied to a person's private life such that 'the more natural description today is that such information is private'. Therefore, in circumstances under which a person received information that they should know is reasonably regarded as confidential (private), a duty not to misuse that information was owed, regardless of any existing relationship. The case itself saw the claimant, an extremely famous 'supermodel', attempt to claim damages from the defendant newspaper group. The action was commenced in relation to articles published about her supposed drug addiction and her attendance at meetings of Narcotics Anonymous (a self-help group for people addicted to drugs). Part of the complaint related to the publication of a photograph of her leaving a building where Narcotics Anonymous meetings were held.[21]

The claim was based on breach of confidence as well as for a breach of her **Convention** right to privacy under the **Human Rights Act 1998**. A complicating factor in the case, and something conceded by the claimant, was the fact that she had previously publicly denied her drug addiction. The House of Lords held, by a 3:2 majority, that the photograph and details of her treatment were a breach of confidence. This was because the information was in excess of what was needed to correct the public perception created by the claimant that she did not have a drug problem. The judgment recognised the fact that any reasonable person would (or should) realise that the details of a person's medical treatment were the kind of information that would attract the obligation of confidence and that, in this situation, such personal information had been misused. In relation to **Art 8**, both Lord Nicholls and Lord Hoffmann were of the view that the concepts involved in the privacy aspects of **Art 8** and the freedom of expression

---

21 Being able to refer to a named judge and selectively quote from and paraphrase his/her arguments will add quality to the answer.

protection in **Art 10** of the **ECHR** should form part of the cause of action for breach of confidence.

The *Campbell* case represents a high point in the evolution of the protection granted for the misuse of private information.[22] The genesis of the developments in the modern context may be traced back to the decision in the first of the series of *Douglas v Hello!* judgments. In that case, the claimants were awarded damages and successfully restrained the defendant's further publication of photographs of their 'show business' wedding, to which they had previously sold exclusive rights to another publication. The exclusive nature of the picture deal was known to the defendant photographer and a breach of confidence was found. However, there is perhaps a difference in the type of personal information in *Campbell* and that in *Douglas* as, in the latter case, the information (photographs) was confidential in the sense that it was made exclusive for a commercial reason. A further incarnation of the case, *Douglas v Hello!* (2006), has unfortunately not made the issue totally clear, as the language of 'private information' used by Lord Nicholls in *Campbell* was not adopted, with the Court of Appeal once more returning to the breach of confidence formulation. Whether that applies solely to commercially useful information is not absolutely certain.

What is certain is that, according to Lord Phillips MR, the courts were required to continue the development of actions for breach of confidence based on **Arts 8** and **10** – in other words, ensuring respect for the **Convention** right of privacy, whilst at the same time remembering the balancing factor of the right to freedom of expression. The approach has since been confirmed by the Court of Appeal in *McKennitt v Ash* (2006) and *Browne v Associated Newspapers* (2007), the latter concerning information disclosed to the press by a former lover of the chairman of a multinational oil company.

What remains is to draw together some of the threads from the above discussion. It is clear that for a breach of confidence to become actionable, there must be some disclosure of private information. What constitutes private information is understood by reference to Lord Nicholl's definition in *Campbell*, and which has subsequently been approved in *McKennitt* and *Browne* (see also *Mosley v News Group Newspapers Ltd* (2008)). It was also suggested in *Campbell* that private information would generally be obvious but, where it was not, a question of whether disclosure of the material would give substantial offence to the person to whom it related arose. By way of example, in *McKennitt*, it was determined that even trivial details about how somebody behaved at home might fall into this category due to 'the sanctity accorded to hearth and home'.[23] There must also be some reasonable expectation on the part of the person to whom it relates that the information should be kept private.

---

22 The importance of this case to the development of a law on privacy justifies looking at the facts and decision in detail.

23 Memorising a short, relevant phrase to quote adds quality and depth to the answer.

A further area of interest and one not yet conclusively determined is what amounts to an *unjustified* disclosure of private information. Baroness Hale in *Campbell* seemed to suggest that there could be a difference in circumstances under which the information related to public figures, as some information could be seen to be in the public interest. There is also the tension to be considered between **Arts 8** and **10** of the **ECHR**, where the latter right of freedom of expression is clearly something in the public interest and, as above, given special consideration at **s 12** of the **Human Rights Act 1998**. This would especially be the case in relation to certain celebrities who might court publicity in certain circumstances, although in no way does this mean that they are not entitled to privacy. This would particularly be the case in circumstances under which, as in *Campbell*, a person had lied about information that it was in the public interest to correct and this approach has been confirmed in *Browne* where the details of the start of the claimant's meeting with his partner had been lied about. In *Theakston v MGN* (2002), it was legitimate to publish a story about a celebrity who had visited a brothel, although it was not permissible to publish pictures of him whilst inside; the former being held to be in the public interest and the latter not. There is a difficult balance here. In *Mosley v News Group Newspapers* (2008), Mr Justice Eady found that the balance excluded the recording of private sexual activity – however unconventional that may be. The claimant was awarded £60,000 in damages for unauthorised publication of his participation in a sado-masochistic 'orgy' with a number of prostitutes with the cost to the defendant exceeding £1 million. The decision was aggressively criticised in the media with comment that the judiciary was creating a law of privacy unaccountably. On subsequent appeal to the European Court of Human Rights, the claimant failed in his bid to establish that the media were required to give prior notification of items involving someone's private affairs, even though the Court accepted that the publication resulted in 'a flagrant and unjustified invasion' of Mosley's private life (*Mosley v UK* (2011)).

The case of *LNS v Persons Unknown* (2010) concerned a footballer's attempted restraint of a story, by the 'super-injunction' method, of an affair with a team-mate's former partner. Mr Justice Tugendhat refused the injunction, noting that the principal reason for suppressing the story, which had become a strong rumour in any case, was the effect it would have on the applicant's sponsorship deals. Given the profile of the claimant, it was difficult to argue that an injunction would be in the public interest. However, an injunction was granted in the case of *ETK v News Group Newspapers* (2011) because of the effect that publication of their father's affair would have on his children.

The whole subject of media intrusion into private lives has been under discussion as part of the far ranging Leveson enquiry on Culture, Practice and Ethics of the Press set up in 2011 in the wake of the phone-hacking scandal. As a result of this, there may be new legislation and/or increased controls in the future, including a new Defamation Bill.

To conclude, it would appear that recent case law has started to establish some clear parameters as to the types of personal information that a person may be entitled to keep from disclosure to the public. The Leveson enquiry has shown that there are serious concerns about the boundaries between freedom of expression and privacy which might lead to increased legal controls. Currently the impact of the ECHR is clearly reflected in the judgments as the courts seek to maintain a balance between the two.[24]

Aim Higher

The best advice in this fast-moving area of law is to stay as current as you can. This area has grown beyond recognition in 10 years and there is more space for evolution. Keep your eye on developments.

Common Pitfalls

If you're writing an essay on this area of law, it is not difficult to get distracted into writing a general 'rights'-based response (such as should we have a right to privacy?) rather than one charting developments in tort law.

QUESTION 43

Nancy, an Olympic athlete, and Ron, a famous singer, employed Kate as a nanny to look after their two young children. Nancy was a high-profile campaigner against drugs in sport and Ron undertook a considerable amount of work for charities that protected children working in unfavourable conditions in the developing world. The couple held an invitation-only charity fund-raising party at their property and sold the exclusive reporting rights to a Sunday newspaper. Kate sold a story about the couple and a set of secretly taken photographs of the party to *Slur* magazine. The story alleged that Ron used his charity work to spend time away from home because the couple's marriage was not solid. It also promised details of intimate conversations with Nancy revealing her bulimia and stating that she used cocaine in her struggle to stay fit for competition. Finally, *Slur* promised 'shocking insight into the personal and emotional frailties' of Ron, based on bullying that he had suffered as a child. The story was to be serialised over three weeks and was previewed in the edition prior to the serialisation under the headline 'Things they wouldn't want you to know', along with the photographs of the party.

▎ Advise Nancy and Ron, assuming that this information is largely true.

---

24 Even in exam conditions, and particularly in an essay question, it helps to leave sufficient time to be able to draw together your argument in a strong conclusion that refers back to and addresses the question set.

How to Answer this Question

The question involves the consideration and application of various legal principles relating to the protection of a person's privacy. As this area of law is still evolving, there are elements of uncertainty that require a discussion of recent case law and the impact of the Human Rights Act 1998.

The following points would require discussion:

- ❖ how privacy is protected in tort law;
- ❖ the influence of the Human Rights Act;
- ❖ breach of confidence and the emergence of the concept of misuse of personal information;
- ❖ whether Nancy and Ron can protect their personal information;
- ❖ recent case law.

Applying the Law

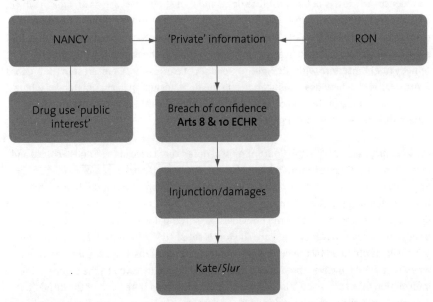

This diagram highlights Kate's and Slur's potential liability.

ANSWER --

On the assumption that the information is not defamatory, as we are told it is largely true, Nancy and Ron might want to sue both Kate and *Slur* for damages in relation to the publication so far,[25] and would also be seeking to prevent *Slur*'s further revelations. While there is no specific tort of privacy at their disposal (*Wainwright v Home Office* (2004); *Kaye v Robertson* (1991); *Browne v Associated Newspapers* (2007)), the courts have developed rights to permit the protection of private information. They have done this by manipulation of the tort of breach of confidence, set against the background of the implementation of Arts 8 and 10 of the **European Convention on Human Rights (ECHR)** in the courts. Privacy, for example, is a '**Convention** right' by virtue of the **Human Rights Act 1998** as Art 8 requires protection of, *inter alia*, a person's 'private and family life'. The unauthorised publication of certain material about a person, such as, for example, intimate details of their family life or their medical history, might well be seen to contravene that right. Since the decision in the leading case of *Campbell v MGN* (2004), it is accepted that **Arts 8** and **10** now form the basis of the cause of action for breach of confidence. **Article 8** is not an absolute right, and so it should be seen as an area in which a balance is to be drawn between the **Art 8** right to privacy and the right to freedom of expression in **Art 10** of the **Convention**. **Section 12** of the **1998 Act** specifically requires that regard is to be paid to **Art 10** in any case in which there is the possibility that granted remedy might interfere with the right to freedom of expression. Of interest in that regard is **Art 10(2)**, which provides qualifications on the right, including in circumstances where it is necessary for the protection of, *inter alia*, reputations of others and disclosure of information received in confidence.[26]

In *McKennitt v Ash* (2006), the Court of Appeal noted that cases in the English courts and in the European Court of Human Rights (*Campbell v MGN* (2004); *Douglas v Hello!* (2006); *Von Hannover v Germany* (2005)) have 'wrestled with the problem of identifying the basis for claiming privacy or confidence in respect of unauthorised or purloined information'. It appears that some principles are settling down now and can form the basis of the advice to Nancy and Ron. The tort is satisfied if information about a person's private life is obtained by the defendant and the defendant discloses the information when that would involve a breach of a duty of confidentiality owed to the owner of the information (*A v B plc* (2002)). In *McKennitt*, it was observed that some of the difficulties with the use of the breach of confidence concept had been overcome by Lord Nicholls in *Campbell* renaming the tort as one of misuse of private information. Indeed, in that case, Lord Hoffmann stated that an action for breach of confidence was also concerned with

----

25 The truth is a complete defence to defamation – justification. Taking a case in either libel or 'privacy' runs the risk of giving greater publicity to the material (as in *Mosley*, see previous question).

26 This branch of law requires demonstration of understanding of both the old common law as it has been adapted to the new situation, and the relevant articles of the **ECHR**.

the protection of 'human autonomy and dignity', and continued that a person had a right to 'control the dissemination of information about one's private life'.[27]

A duty of confidentiality would arise when a party subject to a duty knew or ought to know that the other party could reasonably expect his privacy to be protected. There is no longer any requirement for a pre-existing relationship of confidence between the parties (*Campbell* (2004)), although such a relationship does exist in relation to Kate as a nanny to the family and is not limited to a commercial context (*Argyll v Argyll* (1967)). So far as both Kate and *Slur* are concerned, the duty would arise if they knew or ought to have known that the information they had received was of a private nature. Given the circumstances, it is apparent that they should have been aware of this fact. In determining the meaning of what constitutes 'information of a private nature', Lord Nicholls stated in *Campbell* that 'the touchstone of private life is whether in respect of the disclosed acts the person in question had a reasonable expectation of privacy'. In *McKennitt*, further elaborating on this concept, it was determined that intimate relationship details, intimate conversations between the claimant and defendant in that case, which were understood to be private and which would never be held in public, revelations about the state of a person's health and even trivial details about how somebody behaved at home might fall into the definition (see also *Mosley v News Group Newspapers Ltd* (2008)).

Given the intensely personal nature of some of the revelations, such as Nancy's bulimia, the apparently fragile state of the couple's relationship and Ron's character flaws, it is submitted that Nancy and Ron would face little problem in convincing the court that the information was fully within the category of private information.[28] The fact that the couple are famous should not have a bearing on their entitlement to some privacy, as was noted by Lindsay J in *Douglas v Hello!* (2001) when he observed that even a public figure was entitled to a private life, although he might expect and accept that his circumstances would be scrutinised more carefully by the media. This would be more likely in a situation in which a person courted publicity, but again, did not mean that there was no entitlement to a private life.

So far as the photographs are concerned, the case of *Douglas v Hello!* (2001) , which held that unauthorised photographs of a wedding were private information, is helpful. In that case, the claimants were awarded damages and sought to restrain the defendant's further publication of photographs of their wedding, to which they had previously sold exclusive rights to another publication. The exclusive nature of the picture deal was known to the defendant photographer and a breach of confidence was found. It would be difficult for either Kate or *Slur* to avoid liability for the publication of the photographs

---

27 Use of direct quotes, as in this paragraph, add quality to an answer.

28 This is illustrative of the vital process of applying the stated law to the facts given.

on this authority, as there was an invited guest list and an exclusive publication deal in place.

Nancy may face a problem in relation to the revelation that she used cocaine in order to help her to remain fit for competition. Because of the balance that must be struck between a person's right to a private life under **Art 8** of the **ECHR** and the equally important freedom of expression protected by virtue of **Art 10**, there is a tension that arises, as both cannot be protected in respect of the same information. In this circumstance, particularly where the 'flip-side' of the fact that celebrities should expect some level of greater scrutiny of their lives is concerned, it may be felt that there is a genuine public interest in the revelation (*Theakston v MGN* (2002); *A v B* (2002)). As a result, *Slur* might well be permitted to publish the details. *Slur* could also take comfort from the decision in *Campbell*. In that case, the claimant, a world-famous 'supermodel', had limited success against the defendant newspaper that had published pictures of her leaving a meeting of Narcotics Anonymous, as well as details of her treatment. The House of Lords held that although the photograph and treatment details were an invasion of her privacy, details of her previously denied drug addiction were permitted to be published as a means of setting the record straight. This approach was recently confirmed in the Court of Appeal's decision in *Browne v Associated Newspapers* (2007), in which the details of the circumstances surrounding the way in which the claimant had met his former partner had been lied about. Although the courts have not explicitly set out the conditions under which a claim of public interest would be able to defeat an action for the misuse of personal information, the fact that Nancy had been a high-profile campaigner against drugs in sport might well be fatal to any attempt that she may make to restrain publication of that aspect of the publication of the serialisation.[29]

Beyond the potential for publication of the information in relation to Nancy's drug use, it would appear that Nancy and Ron would be able to claim damages against Kate and *Slur* in relation to the publication of the unauthorised photographs, and would be able to restrain publication of the additional details through applying for an injunction.

---

29 As this is a relatively new and fast developing field of law, considerable detail about the cases will be necessary.

Remedies and Human Rights

INTRODUCTION

The most important remedy in tort is damages and questions involving damages for personal injury or death are often set by examiners. Such questions may take the form of a general essay or a problem question, in which details are given of the claimant's salary and family responsibilities. In the latter type of question, candidates are not expected to produce detailed calculations of damages, but rather to indicate and discuss the particular heads of damage that are recoverable and how they would be calculated.

Checklist ✔

Students must be familiar with the following areas:

(a) types of damages – nominal, contemptuous, general, special damages, special damage (that is, actual loss, which must be proved if the tort is not actionable *per se*), aggravated and exemplary;

(b) damages for personal injury – pecuniary and non-pecuniary loss;

(c) damages for death;

(d) **ss 2, 11** and **33** of the **Limitation Act 1980**;

(e) the application of the **Human Rights Act 1998**.

QUESTION 44

James is crossing the road when he is injured due to the negligent driving of Ken. As a result of this accident, James, who is married with two young children, will be confined to a wheelchair for the rest of his life.

▶ Explain how a court would assess what damages James should receive from Ken. If James were to die one year after the accident and before the trial, how would the damages then be assessed?

How to Answer this Question

Although this is written in the form of a problem, it is in fact a directed essay on the calculation of damages for personal injury and death. It requires a consideration of the various heads of damage under which James could recover, but not actual estimates of the amount recoverable.

The following points need to be discussed:

- ❖ the object of damages;
- ❖ damages for the claimant – the various heads of pecuniary loss and deductions;
- ❖ the various heads of non-pecuniary loss;
- ❖ damages for death.

Applying the Law

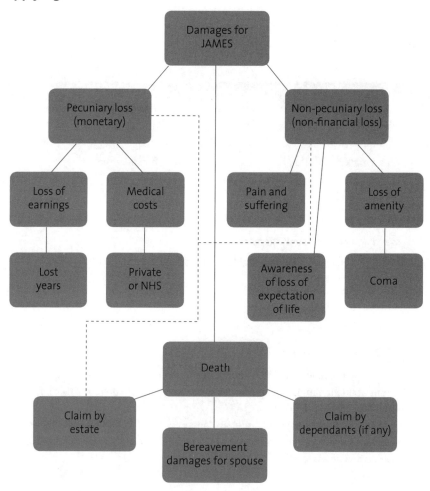

ANSWER

The object of awarding damages in tort is to put the claimant, as far as money can do so, in the position he or she would have been had the tort not happened. Thus, as a general rule, if, as a result of the accident, James has lost money or will have to spend money that he otherwise would not have had to spend, he can recover in respect of these sums.[1]

If we apply this general principle to the pecuniary loss that James has suffered, we can see that the first thing James has lost is wages, as he is now confined to a wheelchair (assuming for the present that James ceases to be paid any salary by his employer from the date of the accident). James will have lost a certain amount of wages up to the date of trial and this is calculated using his net wages as a basis, as James has only lost his take-home pay, not his gross pay. For further loss, the problem is more difficult, due to uncertainties of future income, life expectancy etc. The court will calculate James's net annual loss and multiply that by a figure based on the number of years the loss is likely to last (the multiplier). The multiplier is not simply the duration of the disability, but a lower figure with a maximum value of around 25 (see *Wells v Wells* (1998)) to take account of the fact that James has received the money as a lump sum, rather than over a period of years. The multiplier is also designed to take account of the 'general vicissitudes of life'. It should also be noted that any award will be final and, should James's condition worsen, he will not normally be able to go back to court to claim any added sums (*Fitter v Veal* (1701)). Thus, it is essential to wait until James's medical condition stabilises before any trial. **Section 32A** of the **Senior Courts Act 1981** does allow a provisional award to be made with the right to additional compensation (once only) should the condition worsen, but s 32A has been given a somewhat restrictive interpretation by the High Court in *Willson v Ministry of Defence* (1991).

An obvious problem for James is the effect of future inflation if he receives a lump sum. No especial protection is given in respect of this (*Lim Poh Choo v Camden Health Authority* (1980)), but recently courts have begun to approve 'structured settlements', in which part of the sum payable to the claimant is invested by the defendants in an annuity that can provide an index-linked annual sum for the rest of the claimant's life (*Kelley v Dawes* (1990); s 2(1) of the **Damages Act 1996**, as amended by the **Courts Act 2003**). The court now has a duty to consider whether periodical payments are appropriate.

It may be that, as a result of the accident, James has a reduced expectation of life. If so, James can recover the earnings that he would have received during the years he has lost due to his reduced expectation of life (*Pickett v British Rail Engineering* (1980)), although, following the general principle of damages in tort, James's living expenses must be deducted (*Harris v Empress Motors* (1983)).

James will also be compensated for any loss of pension rights that accompanies his loss of salary.

---

1   It is not necessary to establish the liability of Ken, because the question states that he is negligent.

James can claim in respect of any future expenses to which he will be put as a result of the accident. Thus, James can recover for nursing care and this may be obtained privately even if it is available under the NHS (s 2(4) of the **Law Reform (Personal Injuries) Act 1948**). He may also recover the reasonable value of gratuitous services rendered to him by way of voluntary care by a member of his family (*Hunt v Severs* (1994)), or free hospice care (*Drake & Starkey v Foster Wheeler Ltd* (2010)).

James can also claim for any changes necessary to his accommodation: for example, the provision of wheelchair ramps, additional costs of lighting or heating and future costs of a gardener, tradesmen, etc, if James did these jobs himself and now cannot do so (see, for example, *Willson*).

It may well be the case that James receives compensation from a person other than the tortfeasor[2] and deduction from the previous amounts may have to be made to prevent double recovery.

The **Social Security (Recovery of Benefits) Act 1997** provides that no deduction for social security benefits is to be made against awards for pain and suffering, and that specified benefits only may be deducted from awards for loss of earnings, cost of care and loss of mobility.

For other benefits, the general rule is that a benefit received by the claimant is only deducted where it truly reduces the loss suffered (*Parry v Cleaver* (1970)). Hence, sick pay or wages paid during the period following the accident are deducted, but not any insurance sums that James receives (*Bradburn v Great Western Railway* (1874)) or charitable donations, ill health awards or higher pension benefits (*Smoker v London Fire and Civil Defence Authority* (1991)).

James will, of course, also suffer non-pecuniary loss. Firstly, there will be the pain and suffering that James has endured and will suffer in the future. Also, if, as a result of the accident, James has suffered a loss of expectation of life and is aware of this, then by s 1(1)(b) of the **Administration of Justice Act 1982**, the court is required to take this into account when assessing damages. Next, James will be compensated for any loss of amenity – that is, his capacity to engage in pre-accident activities – and this award may be made even if he is in a coma (*West v Shepherd* (1964); *Lim Poh Choo*). James will also be compensated for the injury itself and, to obtain some consistency in this respect, a listing of awards is made in Kemp and Kemp, *The Quantum of Damages*. James should be advised that the Court of Appeal held in *Heil v Rankin* (2000) that awards for non-pecuniary loss were too low and that, for the most severe injuries, the awards should be increased by about one-third.

---

2   The tortfeasor is Ken, but in fact his insurance company will be paying, as it is obligatory to have third-party motor insurance (or the Motor Insurers' Bureau will pay if the driver is uninsured).

Finally, James will be awarded interest on his damages in respect of losses up to the date of trial under s 35A of the **Senior Courts Act 1981**.[3]

If James dies before the trial as a result of the accident, two causes of action arise. Firstly, under s1 of the **Law Reform (Miscellaneous Provisions) Act 1934**, all causes of action vesting in the deceased survive for the benefit of his estate. The damages that the estate can claim are assessed in a similar way to those in a personal injuries claim, except that a claim for lost earnings in the lost years can only be brought by a living claimant (s 4(2) of the **Administration of Justice Act 1982**). Secondly, an action may be brought under the **Fatal Accidents Act 1976** by James's dependants,[4] such as James's two young children and, possibly, if she was dependent on his income, his wife. She can make a claim for a fixed sum of £11,800 as non-pecuniary damages for bereavement for loss of a spouse (s1(A)) (the only other recipient of this would be parents for the loss of an unmarried child under the age of 18, so would not apply here. His children have no claim for grief etc). Under s1 of the **1976 Act**, actual and future pecuniary loss of the dependants can be claimed, and funeral expenses (if not paid by the estate). This is calculated by assessing the dependency on the deceased, which is normally found by taking the deceased's net earnings, deducting a sum for his personal and living expenses, and multiplying this sum by the duration of the dependency (which is calculated on a similar basis to the multiplier in personal injury cases). In assessing dependency and duration, any chance of a widow remarrying is to be ignored (s3(3) of the **Fatal Accidents Act 1976**), but not the chance that the parties might have divorced (*Martin v Owen* (1992)). Also, by s4 of the **1976 Act**, any benefits accruing as the result of the death are to be disregarded. Thus, for example, any widow's pension paid by James's employers to his widow is to be disregarded (*Pidduck v Eastern Scottish Omnibus* (1990)).

QUESTION 45

It is a general rule of law that damages are awarded to compensate the claimant, rather than to punish the defendant. Are there any situations in which a claimant could make a profit out of the damages awarded to him?[5]

How to Answer this Question

This question calls for a discussion of the following aspects of the law of damages:

❖ the purpose of damages;
❖ general and special damages;

---

3 Note that the majority of claims will be settled out of court before trial, but with damages assessed on the principles stated here.
4 Always apply the law to the facts given: even if they are limited, as here, it can be highlighted that James's young children are likely to be dependent on him and thus have a claim under the **Fatal Accidents Act**, although his wife may not have been a 'dependant'.
5 This question will take considerable thought and planning to extract relevant information from your knowledge of remedies (see diagram), unless of course you have been taught this as a specific topic. Time spent planning an essay will not be wasted.

❖ aggravated damages;
❖ exemplary damages;
❖ non-deduction of insurance sums;
❖ possible double compensation under the Fatal Accidents Act 1976;
❖ damages in defamation.

Answer Structure

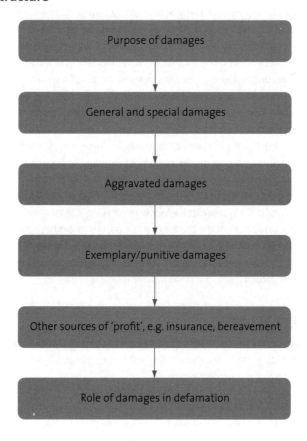

Purpose of damages

General and special damages

Aggravated damages

Exemplary/punitive damages

Other sources of 'profit', e.g. insurance, bereavement

Role of damages in defamation

ANSWER

The general principle governing an award of damages in tort is to put the claimant in the position in which he would have been had the tort not occurred, as far as this can be done by an award of money. In some cases, for example damages for negligent misrepresentation, the loss may be purely financial and it may be possible to calculate this loss precisely. However, in many situations, this will not be possible. For example, in personal injury cases the loss of wages suffered by the claimant can be calculated exactly, but such a calculation is impossible as regards a broken thigh that caused an absence from work. Similarly, precise calculations of damages in (say) nuisance or trespass will generally not be possible. A claimant must expressly plead any special damage that he has suffered, for example, medical expenses or loss of wages, and will in addition be awarded general damages that are not quantified in the statement of claim, but are assessed by the court. These general damages attempt to compensate the claimant for the non-financial consequences that have flowed from the tort and represent an estimate by the court, in money terms, of the claimant's loss. By definition, therefore, these general plus special damages, together with any interest awarded, should match the loss suffered by the claimant.

However, in certain circumstances, the court may make an award of aggravated damages. These damages are still regarded as compensatory damages, in that they are awarded to compensate the claimant for loss that he has suffered, rather than to punish the defendant. Aggravated damages may be awarded where the defendant's conduct caused injury to the feelings or pride of the claimant: see, for example, *Harsford v Bird* (2006), a claim in trespass in which the Privy Council, refusing an award of aggravated damages, stated that there would be a requirement of 'high-handed, insulting or oppressive conduct' before such a claim would succeed. In *Archer v Brown* (1985), it was stated that sums awarded in respect of aggravated damages should be moderate (see also *W v Meah* (1986)). An example of circumstances that might justify an award of aggravated damages can be seen in *Marks v Chief Constable of Greater Manchester* (1992). In *Marks*, the Court of Appeal held that a chief constable's conduct in persisting in a denial of liability in a civil action, despite comments that had been made by a recorder in criminal proceedings against the claimant as to conflicting police evidence, was capable of aggravating the claimant's damages should she be successful in her civil case and might be grounds for an award of additional damages. It should be noted that, in *Kralj v McGrath* (1986), it was held that medical negligence cases were not appropriate for an award of aggravated damages, but that, rather, the general damages should be increased to take into account the fact that the actions of the defendant had delayed the claimant's recovery. This approach ties in with the general principle that the function of damages is to compensate the claimant, rather than to punish the defendant. It can be seen from the discussion on general and special damages, and aggravated damages, that both of these types of damages are compensatory in nature and that a claimant will not make a profit out of them. Although greater sums may be awarded in the case of aggravated damages, these increased sums only reflect the increased loss or suffering to which the defendant has subjected the claimant. Where truly moderate sums are awarded for aggravated damages, this rationale is unexceptionable, but where much larger sums are awarded, it may be difficult to distinguish between aggravated damages and exemplary damages, as Lord Wilberforce pointed out in *Cassell v Broome* (1972). The distinction is important, because the function of exemplary damages is to punish the defendant and it is in such situations that one might suggest that the claimant is making a profit out of the damages awarded.

In *Rookes v Barnard* (1964), the House of Lords described those circumstances in which exemplary, or punitive, damages could be recovered in tort.[6] Lord Devlin held that such damages could be awarded in three situations only: where authorised by statute, for example s 13(2) of the **Reserve and Auxiliary Forces (Protection of Civil Interests) Act 1951**; in the case of oppressive, arbitrary or unconstitutional acts by a government servant; or where the defendant has calculated that he will make a profit out of the tort, even if normal compensatory damages are awarded.

These categories have been strictly adhered to. Thus, in *Cassell*, Lord Reid stated that the oppressive, arbitrary or unconstitutional category did not extend to oppressive action by a company. However, in *Holden v Chief Constable of Lancashire* (1987), it was held that exemplary damages could be awarded for unlawful arrest even if there had been no oppressive behaviour by the arresting officer, since the category contemplated that the action be oppressive, arbitrary *or* unconstitutional and not oppressive, arbitrary *and* unconstitutional. The last category is illustrated by the facts of *Cassell*, where the defendants published a book containing defamatory statements about the plaintiff. The defendants were aware that the plaintiff intended to sue if the book was published with these statements, but they calculated that this was a risk worth running, as they estimated that the profits that they would make on the sales of the book would outweigh such ordinary compensatory damages. It was held that, in such circumstances, an award of exemplary damages was appropriate.

In *Cassell*, it was held that exemplary damages are only available in those categories described in *Rookes*, and this whole area has more recently been considered in *Kuddus v Chief Constable of Leicestershire Constabulary* (2001). In *Kuddus*, the House of Lords held that the award of exemplary damages was not limited to cases in which the cause of action had been recognised before 1964 as justifying such damages; rather, the question was whether the facts fell within the categories described by Lord Devlin in *Rookes*. In *Kuddus*, the House held that exemplary damages could be awarded for the tort of misfeasance in public office. In *Mosley v News Group Newspapers* (2008), exemplary damges were refused,[7] but in *Ramzan v Brookwide Ltd* (2010) they were granted in a case of trespass where a profit had been made.

Thus, it can be seen that the situations in which a claimant can profit from exemplary damages are subject to some limitations. Indeed, the fear that claimants may profit from exemplary damages was stated in *Thompson v Commissioner of Police of the Metropolis* (1997). Here, the Court of Appeal held that limits should be placed on exemplary damages

---

6   Note that exemplary or punitive damages are much more widely used in other common law systems, notably the USA, which partly accounts for the much higher levels of damages paid out in that jurisdiction.

7   See further on this case, Chapter 13.

awarded for unlawful and violent conduct by the police, and set an 'absolute maximum' figure.

Another way in which a claimant may profit from an award of damages is where he or she sues in respect of a consequence of the defendant's conduct for which he or she is already insured. In such situations, the rule is that insurance benefits are ignored for the purpose of assessing damages (*Bradburn v Great Western Railway* (1874)) and a similar rule applies to charitable donations (*Parry v Cleaver* (1970)). Thus, a person whose house or car is destroyed by a runaway lorry may well make a profit on the damages received if the insurance company forgoes its right of subrogation. Applying the rule in *Bradburn*, the House of Lords held in *Hussain v New Taplow Paper Mills* (1988) that where an employer funded his sick pay scheme through an insurance company, payments so received by an employee should be taken into account in assessing the damages payable in respect of loss of earnings. In contrast, the Court of Appeal in *McCamley v Cammell Laird Shipbuilders* (1990) held that insurance benefits received by an employee did not fall to be taken into account, as the payments in that particular case were in the nature of true insurance benefits. The difference between *Hussain* and *McCamley* depends on whether the court decides, on the facts of the case, that the payments in question are truly sick pay, when they will be deducted, or that they are true insurance benefits, when they will be ignored. However, in *Gaca v Pirelli General plc* (2004), the Court of Appeal overruled *McCamley* and held that insurance benefits received by an employee after an accident at work were no longer to be disregarded unless the employee had contributed to the insurance premium. Thus, if contributions have been made by the employee, the employee may profit from the insurance payment. Any *ex gratia* payments made by the tortfeasor would, however, normally be deducted from the damages awarded.

A certain amount of double recovery is allowed in respect of state benefits. By the **Social Security (Recovery of Benefits) Act 1997**, some state benefits may be deducted from awards of damages, while others are ignored for the purposes of deduction. Thus, no deduction is made against awards for pain and suffering, and only certain specified benefits may be deducted from awards for loss of earnings, cost of care and loss of mobility. Hence, to the extent that the **1997 Act** specifies no deduction of state benefits, a double recovery situation exists, allowing the claimant to make a profit. In addition, deductions cease after a five-year period (**s 3** of the **1997 Act**).

Another area where double recovery is allowed by statute is in the award of damages under the **Fatal Accidents Act 1976**. By **s 4** of the **1976 Act**, any benefits that accrue to the dependants as a result of the death of the deceased are to be disregarded. Thus, in *Pidduck v Eastern Scottish Omnibus* (1990), a widow's pension that was paid to a widow following the death of her husband was held to be non-deductible. The **1976 Act** also provides, in **s 3(3)**, that in assessing damages for a fatal accident, the chances of the widow remarrying are to be disregarded. In *Martin v Owen* (1992), it was held that the chance that the parties might have divorced should be taken into account. This conclusion seems rather surprising at first but, when one realises that s4 of the 1976 Act expressly contemplates double recovery, it will be interpreted strictly to restrict any such double recovery to that stated in the Act. So, a widow who remarried after being awarded damages for loss of dependency could make a profit out of those damages, as could a claimant whose medical condition dramatically improved after an award of damages, either through an unforeseeable medical improvement, or because of an advance in medical science made after the award, as the original award will dispose of the case (*Fitter v Veal* (1701)).

It could also be argued that as, by s1(A) of the Fatal Accidents Act 1976, a sum of £11,800 is paid for loss of a spouse or minor child, the sum could represent a disproportionately high figure amounting to double recovery. Alternatively, it has been argued that this figure is insultingly small.

Finally, one might consider the position of successful claimants in defamation actions. Where the defendant is a newspaper, juries do seem to forget the principle that the object of awarding damages in tort is to compensate the claimant and not to punish the defendant, and the very large damages that are sometimes awarded against newspapers especially do seem to contain an element of punishment. While the man in the street may well find this quite acceptable, it does represent legally incorrect principles, and claimants who are awarded sums for damages that are in the six- and seven-figure range are surely making a profit out of their damages. In this respect, it should be noted that, under s8 of the Courts and Legal Services Act 1990, the court has the power to order a new trial or to substitute another award in any case in which the damages awarded by a jury are 'excessive'. In *Rantzen v Mirror Group Newspapers* (1993), the Court of Appeal reduced an award by some 50 per cent and stated that juries could be referred to these substituted awards as establishing norms. In *John v Mirror Group Newspapers Ltd* (1996), it was realised that the *Rantzen* procedure would take time and the Court of Appeal was prepared to allow juries to be told of awards in personal injury cases. The idea of this is not to promote equality of damages, but to enable a jury to compare a serious libel with, for example, a serious head or spine injury. In time, this may have the effect of reducing damages awarded by juries in defamation cases. In the Elton John case, above, his damages were reduced by the Court of Appeal from £350,000 to £75,000.

QUESTION 46

Comment upon the influence of the Human Rights Act 1998 on the development of English tort law.

How to Answer this Question

The Human Rights Act (HRA) is increasingly a feature of modern tort law, and thus is now becoming a feature of some examiners' questions. This question requires a broad view of the impact of the **Human Rights Act** on tort law, while at the same time necessitating a recognition and assessment of areas in which examples can be provided of the impact.

The following points require explanation and discussion:

- ❖ the basic duty of the courts in relation to human rights compatibility;
- ❖ the difference between *vertical* and *horizontal* effects of the HRA;
- ❖ specific examples of human rights interaction with tort liability:
    - ❖ nuisance and human rights;
    - ❖ 'privacy' and human rights.

Answer Structure

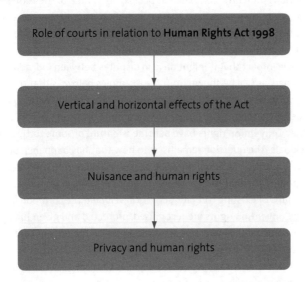

Role of courts in relation to **Human Rights Act 1998**

Vertical and horizontal effects of the Act

Nuisance and human rights

Privacy and human rights

ANSWER

The **Human Rights Act 1998 (HRA)**[8] has undoubtedly had profound effects on the structure and practice of law in the UK since it came into force in 2000. The **HRA** has made the majority of the rights contained in the **European Convention on Human Rights (ECHR)** (so-called 'Convention rights' – s 1) available as remedies in the UK courts and requires public authorities to act compatibly with the **Convention** rights (s 6), subject to limited exceptions. While it is clear that the **HRA** has had a significant impact in relation to public authorities, the implication for private law was, initially, less obvious, especially

---

8   It is sensible to use an abbreviation for an Act that is to be mentioned throughout an answer (particularly in exams in order to save time), but ensure that the name and date are written out in full initially, and the chosen abbreviation put in brackets.

if the challenge was not made against a public authority. However, as the definition of public authorities, according to s 6(3), includes courts and tribunals, it would be unlawful for either to act inconsistently with a **Convention** right. Additionally, s 2 of the HRA provides that a court or tribunal must take account of decisions, *inter alia*, of the European Court of Human Rights when determining any question that has arisen in respect of any **Convention** right.

What then does this mean for the law of tort? Firstly, it is necessary to explain the difference between *vertical* and *horizontal* effects of the HRA. As a piece of law primarily directed at public authorities, the vertical effect between authority and citizen, or decision-maker and affected person, is clear. This can also be seen in the potential for 'stand alone' actions under the combined impacts of ss 7 and 8 of the HRA. Section 7 permits a person to bring proceedings against a public authority that has violated or intends to violate a **Convention** right and s 8 provides for the payment of damages. What is less clear at first glance, however, is the way in which the HRA could have horizontal effect – that is, the impact that it might have in disputes between individuals. Essentially, what has happened, as will be shown from the examples below, is that the basic duty placed on the courts, as public authorities, to ensure compatibility with **Convention** rights, whilst being mindful of the jurisprudence of the European Court of Human Rights, has ensured that **Convention** rights have become a feature of some tortious actions between individuals. The question remains as to how that has happened precisely. It raises the further question as to whether the courts should merely *interpret* the law against a background of what the **Convention** rights demand, or go further and seek to work at the margins of existing tort law, actively *developing* the common law so as to ensure that the **Convention** rights are recognised, protected and given full effect. Perhaps an analogy here could be the incremental development of the duty of care in negligence to novel situations (*Sutherland Shire Council v Heyman* (1985); *Caparo Industries plc v Dickman* (1990)). What seems to be clear, however, is that the HRA does not permit the courts merely to create a new cause of action.

In the years since the HRA has been effective, there are plenty of examples of the interaction of **Convention** rights with tort liability, some of which have led to considerable developments in the common law. Two of the most fertile areas have been in relation to the tort of private nuisance and the evolving tort protecting the dissemination of private information. Although in the case of the latter it is not a strictly accurate label, for shorthand's sake, we shall call it privacy.

The courts have been required to decide a number of cases in private nuisance by reference to questions of breaches of **Convention** rights. The principal **Convention** rights that have been called into question have been **Art 8**, which contains the right to respect for private and family life, and **Art 1** of the **First Protocol** to the ECHR, which entitles a person to peaceful enjoyment of property. As the tort of nuisance is essentially concerned with unreasonable interferences with a person's use or enjoyment of their property, it is plain to see how these **Convention** rights might be affected. Prior to the **HRA** coming into force, the European Court of Human Rights had held that certain interferences with a person's ability to enjoy their property as they wished, and which would more than likely amount to a nuisance in English law, would fall within the protection offered by **Art 8** and **Art 1** of the **First Protocol** (*López Ostra v Spain* (1995); *Guerra v Italy* (1998)). **Article 8** and **Art 1** of the **First Protocol** are not unqualified rights, however. **Article 8(2)** permits interference by a public authority with the right in circumstances where it is necessary in a democratic society, in the interests of national security, public safety or the economic well-being of the country amongst others. A similar qualification attaches to **Art 1** of the **First Protocol**. Examples in English law have included the decision in *Dennis v MOD* (2003), which was concerned with noise nuisance created by low-flying military aircraft. The claimants brought a claim in nuisance as well as under **Art 8**. The court held that there was a nuisance, but refused an injunction because it was held that the claimant's private rights were overridden by the public interest in maintaining a trained air force. In seeking to give effect to **Art 8**, Buckley J stated that the public interest involved was 'greater than the individual private interests of Mr and Mrs Dennis, but it is not proportionate to pursue or give effect to the public interest without compensation'.[9] His judgment on this point was affected by the decision of the European Court in *S v France* (1990), in which it had been held the nuisance caused to the claimant by a nearby power station had interfered with the claimant's **Convention** rights, but the payment of compensation to her ensured that the interference did not go beyond what was necessary in a democratic society.

The House of Lords' decision in *Marcic v Thames Water Utilities* (2004) demonstrates some of the limits applied to the application of the **HRA** in nuisance cases. The claimant suffered persistent and serious flooding of his property. This was caused by the defendant's inadequate sewer network in his area. The defendants had a system in place for the upgrade of sewers throughout its area, but it was based on a system of priorities and the claimant's area was a long way down the list. He sued in nuisance and the Court of Appeal upheld the nuisance claim. The House of Lords overturned the decision, however. This was done on the basis that there was a statutory scheme through which any complaints should be taken and that the scheme also precluded any private law (nuisance) action to complain about any breach of statutory duty. Additionally, the Lords disposed of Mr Marcic's claim under **Art 8** and **Art 1** of the **First Protocol**. The essential question was whether the statutory system that prevented the claimant from bringing an action in nuisance was **Convention**-compliant. They held that it was, because Parliament had considered that there should be a balance based on the cost implications and that the defendant's system of priorities was permitted to reflect that. That finding was based on the earlier decision of the European Court in *Hatton v UK* (2003), which was concerned with night flights from Heathrow Airport. In that case, the European Court of

---

9   Short quotes from the case law will add to the quality of the answer.

Human Rights determined that the national authorities were best placed to make decisions on the policy around night flying as they had 'direct democratic legitimation' and that they had a broad margin of discretion in balancing the various competing factors, of which the economic well-being of the country was one. The impact of the **HRA** would seem to accord a greater consideration of a balancing exercise between private and wider public interests than the tort of nuisance alone may have done.

A further consideration of the relationship between private nuisance and human rights can be seen in the requirement that a successful action in nuisance requires that the claimant has an interest in land (*Hunter v Canary Wharf* (1997)). The compatibility of that requirement with **Convention** rights was called into question, by Neuberger J in *McKenna v British Aluminium* (2002) (see also *Dobson v Thames Water Utilities* (2009)), when he refused to strike out the claims of children with no proprietary interest in their home. He could not overrule the decision of the House of Lords in *Hunter*, but made it clear that there was concern in relation to the limit on a remedy in nuisance to those with an interest in the property affected. In *Dobson v Thames Water No 2* (2011), a declaration of the breach of all the occupants' **Article 8** rights was made by the court, but having awarded damages in nuisance to the legal occupiers of homes affected by smells from the sewage plant, it did not consider it necessary to award damages to children living in them. So the effect of the **HRA** in the tort of nuisance has clearly been felt and there remain areas of uncertainty that the law still needs to resolve.

Tort law directed towards protection for what we may call 'privacy' over the last few years seems to be inextricably linked with human rights considerations and is seemingly more straightforward than the position in relation to private nuisance. At the heart of the issue is the **Art 8** right to respect for private and family life, set against the **Art 10** right to freedom of expression. If a hospital were to publish information about an individual's treatment for a disease, or a government department to wrongly disclose material concerning a person's application for social security payments, there would be a clear right of action against them under the **HRA**. The majority of recent interest has centred on publication of stories or pictures about the famous, in circumstances under which private organisations, not public authorities, are the source of the publication. Of crucial importance in the modern context is the decision of the European Court in *Von Hannover v Germany* (2004) concerning the publication of photographs of Princess Caroline of Monaco. The Court confirmed that **Art 8** imposes a positive obligation upon signatory states to make sure that due protection is given to privacy rights and that means that such rights should be protected as between private parties. This represents a further example of the *horizontal* application of the **Convention** rights. The case readily confirms the approach of the English courts in recent cases as they have more or less accepted that position as a result of the impact of the **HRA**, as will be seen below.

Section 12 of the HRA specifically requires that regard is to be paid to Art 10[10] in any case in which there is the possibility that granted remedy might interfere with the right to freedom of expression. Of interest in that regard is Art 10(2), which provides qualifications on the right, including in circumstances under which it is necessary for the protection of, *inter alia*, reputations of others and disclosure of information received in confidence. That would mean that any case brought on the basis of Art 8 or the tort of breach of confidence would automatically involve consideration of Art 10, and so the law has developed on this basis. Lord Woolf in *A v B plc* (2002) noted that s 6 of the HRA requires the courts not to act incompatibly with a Convention right. In the area of 'privacy', it was able to achieve this by absorbing the rights that Arts 8 and 10 protect into the long-established action for breach of confidence. Later, in the now-leading case of *Campbell v MGN* (2004), Lord Nicholls went so far as to say that the 'values enshrined in Articles 8 and 10 are now part of the cause of action for breach of confidence'.

So how did the courts get to this position? A very good starting point for an explanation of the law is the decision in *McKennitt v Ash* (2006), in which Lord Justice Buxton reviewed the development of the law to date. *McKennitt* considered the meaning of 'private information' for the purposes of the tort of breach of confidence and held that it could actually involve quite mundane details of a person's home life. Previously, in *Campbell*, it was suggested that private information would generally be obvious, but where it was not, a question of whether disclosure of the material would give substantial offence to the person to whom it related arose. Also, there must be some reasonable expectation on the part of the person to whom it relates that the information should be kept private. In *Douglas v Hello!* (2001, 2006), the claimants were awarded damages and successfully restrained the defendant's further publication of photographs of their wedding, which they had previously sold to another publication. The exclusive nature of the picture deal was known to the defendants and a breach of confidence was found.

As Art 10 protects freedom of expression, not all information will be protected, however. In certain circumstances, publication might be in the public interest and may disclose wrongdoing or hypocrisy. Baroness Hale, in *Campbell*, noted that if people were in the public eye, they may naturally attract more attention, although obviously their rights to privacy would not be removed. In that case, the details of the claimant's previously denied drug addiction were permitted to be published as a means of setting the record straight. This approach was confirmed in the Court of Appeal's decision in *Browne v Associated Newspapers* (2007), in which details of the circumstances surrounding the way in which the claimant had met his ex-partner had been lied about. Although the courts have not explicitly set out the conditions under which a claim of public interest would be able to defeat an action for the misuse of personal information, it is clear that it is something to

----

10 Take care to distinguish, and not confuse, the *sections* of the **Human Rights Act 1998** with the *articles* of the **ECHR**.

be determined in the balancing exercise of a claimant's **Art 8** and **Art 10** rights. The debate was drawn into sharp focus by the cases of *Mosley v News Group Newspapers* (2008) and *LNS v Persons Unknown* (2010) which clearly set out the considerations undertaken by the courts.

Therefore it can be seen from a brief analysis of private nuisance and 'privacy', that the **HRA** is clearly having an impact in these, as well as other, areas within the law of tort.[11] To quote Neuberger J in *McKenna*, 'we are in the early days of the **Human Rights Act 1998** and of its application to the common law'. How the continuing development of human rights and common law principles will develop is difficult to predict, although certain parameters seem to have been set by the courts.

Aim Higher

In a human rights context, being able to refer to the jurisprudence of the ECtHR insofar as it relates to tort law will give your answers a more cohesive and reasoned feel in, say, answers relating to privacy, nuisance or trespass to the person cases.

Common Pitfalls

A common assumption is that a recourse to 'human rights' will mean that a claimant is compensated. It won't always be like that. Most of the rights engaged in tort law are qualified rights rather than absolute rights and so will generally need to be balanced.

---

11   Any general essay answer on nuisance or privacy should include reference to the **HRA** at some point, as it is having such an influence on the legal developments in this area, even if it was not mentioned in the question. For more on nuisance and privacy, see Chapters 9 and 13.

General Defences

INTRODUCTION

The general defences to tort are often tested by examiners. This may take the form of a specific question on, say, *volenti*, or may form part of another question. Thus, contributory negligence is regularly tested in questions involving a variety of aspects of the tort of negligence. Where contributory negligence is tested, apart from the seat-belt guidelines in *Froom v Butcher* (1975), candidates would not be required to estimate figures for any reduction in damages.

Checklist ✔

Candidates must be aware of the following defences:

(a) necessity;

(b) statutory authority;

(c) *volenti*;

(d) illegality;

(e) contributory negligence.

QUESTION 47

Norman and Mark went out for a social evening using Mark's car. They called at a public house, where they both consumed a large amount of drink. Mark then drove Norman home and, due to his intoxicated state, crashed the car into a lamp post. Norman, who was not wearing a seat belt, was thrown through the car windscreen and was severely injured. Rita, who witnessed the accident, went to help Norman and cut her hands badly in so doing.

▶ Advise Norman and Rita of any rights that they might have against Mark. Would your advice differ if, rather than going out together, Norman had met Mark in the public house when Norman had had little to drink, but Mark was already intoxicated, and Norman had then accepted a lift from Mark?

How to Answer this Question

The following points need to be discussed:

- ❖ the liability of Mark to Norman;
- ❖ the defences available to Mark:
  - ❖ *volenti* – consideration of case law and statute law;
  - ❖ *ex turpi causa*;
  - ❖ contributory negligence in accepting the lift;
  - ❖ contributory negligence in not wearing a seat belt;
- ❖ the liability of Mark to Rita;
- ❖ the defences available to Mark:
  - ❖ *volenti*;
  - ❖ contributory negligence;
- ❖ the effects of Mark's existing intoxication on any defences available to him.

Applying the Law

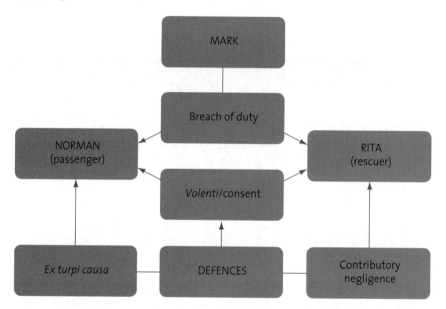

This diagram demonstrates Mark's liability to Norman and Rita.

ANSWER

We must first decide whether Norman could sue Mark and, if so, whether Mark has any defences available to him.

Norman must first show that Mark owes him a duty of care. In those situations in which a duty of care has previously been found to exist, there is no need to apply the modern formulation of the test for the existence of a duty of care preferred by the House of Lords in *Caparo Industries plc v Dickman* (1990) or *Murphy v Brentwood District Council* (1990). We could note here the statement of Potts J at first instance in *B v Islington Health Authority* (1991), in which he stated that, in personal injury cases, the duty of care remains as it was pre-*Caparo* – namely, the foresight of a reasonable man (as in *Donoghue v Stevenson* (1932)), a finding that does not appear to have been disturbed on appeal (1992). In fact, a duty of care has been found to exist in a number of cases involving drivers and their passengers – for example, *Nettleship v Weston* (1971) – but, even without knowledge of such cases, we could deduce the existence of a duty of care as it is reasonably foreseeable that by driving carelessly, a passenger may suffer injury.[1]

Next, Norman must show that Mark was in breach of this duty – that is, that a reasonable person, or rather a reasonably competent driver, in Mark's position would not have acted in this way (*Blyth v Birmingham Waterworks* (1856); *Nettleship v Weston* (1971)). It seems clear that a reasonable driver would not run into a lamp post and so Mark is in breach of his duty. Norman will also have to show that this breach caused his injuries and the 'but for' test in *Cork v Kirby MacLean* (1952) proves the required causal connection. Finally, Norman will have to prove that the damage that he has suffered was not too remote – that is, it must be reasonably foreseeable (*The Wagon Mound (No 1)* (1961)). This should not give rise to any problem, as all that Norman will have to show is that some personal injury was foreseeable. He will not have to show that the extent was foreseeable, nor the exact manner in which the injury was caused (*Smith v Leech Brain* (1962); *Hughes v Lord Advocate* (1963)).[2]

Thus, having decided that Mark has been negligent in his conduct towards Norman, we next need to see if any defences are available to Mark. The first possible defence is that of *volenti* on Norman's part – that is, that Norman voluntarily submitted or consented to the risk of injury. To establish that Norman was *volens*, Mark will have to show that Norman was able to choose freely whether to run the risk or not and that there were no constraints acting on his freedom of choice, such as fear of loss of his employment (*Bowater v Rowley Regis Corp* (1944)). In the instant case, no such restraints were acting on Norman. The next point that we must consider is whether there was any agreement between Mark and Norman, whereby Norman agreed to accept the risk of injury. If there was an express agreement that Mark would not be liable to Norman in respect of his negligence then, subject to the provisions of the **Unfair Contract Terms Act 1977**, that agreement would prevail. There is no evidence on the facts that we are given to suggest such an agreement, so we need to consider whether there was an implied agreement. In

---

1   A standard opening paragraph like this could be useful in many negligence questions.
2   Although the main focus of this question would seem to be on defences, it is important to establish the breach of duty.

cases involving persons who have accepted lifts from persons whom they know to be intoxicated, the courts are usually unwilling to find that the person accepting the lift has impliedly agreed to waive his right to sue the intoxicated driver (*Dann v Hamilton* (1939)). Although an implied agreement was found in *ICI v Shatwell* (1965), that case involved such an obviously dangerous act that it was not difficult for the court to imply an agreement that the two defendants had accepted the risk of any injury following from that most dangerous practice. Given then that there is no agreement, express or implied, between the parties, we next have to consider whether the *volenti* defence could be valid in those circumstances under which there is no agreement between the parties. In *Nettleship*, Lord Denning stated that nothing short of an express or implied agreement would suffice to found a defence of *volenti*. However, this view has not been universally accepted. In *Dann*, the court held that *volenti* could apply to those situations in which the claimant comes to a situation in which a danger has been created by the defendant's negligence (although, on the facts of *Dann*, it was held that *volenti* had not been made out). Also in *Pitts v Hunt* (1990) and *Morris v Murray* (1990), it was held that the defence could apply in appropriate circumstances to passengers who accepted lifts from drivers who were obviously highly intoxicated. Thus, it would seem that, despite *Nettleship*, Mark could raise the defence of *volenti* if he was obviously extremely drunk but, unfortunately for Mark, **s 149(3)** of the **Road Traffic Act 1988** rules out *volenti* in road traffic situations – see *Pitts* and compare *Morris*, which was not a road traffic situation.

Thus, Mark cannot rely on the *volenti* defence, but he may attempt to raise the defence of *ex turpi causa non oritur actio* (which has been expressly held to apply to actions in tort – *Clunis v Camden and Islington Health Authority* (1998)), in that both he and Norman were jointly participating in an illegal activity – namely, driving a motor vehicle whilst under the influence of excess alcohol, contrary to **s 4** of the **Road Traffic Act 1988**. This defence was upheld in *National Coal Board v England* (1954) and *Ashton v Turner* (1981), but there must be a causal connection between the crime and the damage that the claimant has suffered (*National Coal Board*). In *Euro-Diam v Bathurst* (1988), Kerr LJ stated that the defence would apply where it would be an 'affront to the public conscience' to allow the claimant to succeed. This test was also used by Beldam LJ in *Pitts*, but Dillon and Balcombe LJJ preferred to determine whether the claimant's damage was incidental to the unlawful conduct. It is submitted that the defence would fail because there is not the required causal connection between the damage and the crime, as in *National Coal Board* and *Ashton*. In *Tinsley v Milligan* (1993), the House of Lords rejected the 'affront to public conscience' test, preferring the test as to whether the claim is based directly on the illegal conduct, and this test has been used by the Court of Appeal in *Cross v Kirkby* (2000) and *Vellino v Chief Constable of Greater Manchester* (2002). Here, it does seem that Norman's damage is incidental to Mark's illegal activity. Certainly, in a number of cases, passengers have been allowed to recover in similar situations: for example, *Dann*. In support of this conclusion, one might note the Scottish case of *Weir v Wyper* (1992), in which it was held that the *ex turpi causa* defence could not be raised against a passenger who accepted a lift from a driver whom she knew possessed only a provisional driving licence. The *ex turpi causa* defence was also given a restricted application in *Revill v Newberry* (1996).

Although the above two defences, which would provide a complete defence to Mark, are not applicable, Mark may be able to raise the defence of contributory negligence to reduce the damages that he will have to pay Norman (s 1(1) of the **Law Reform (Contributory Negligence) Act 1945**). By s 1(1), where a person suffers damage as the result partly of his own fault and partly of the fault of any other person, his damages will be reduced by such an extent as the court thinks just and equitable, having regard to the first person's share in the responsibility for the damage. To raise this defence, Mark will have to show that Norman was careless for his own safety (*Davies v Swan Motor Co* (1949)). In *Jones v Livox Quarries Ltd* (1952), Lord Denning said that 'a person is guilty of contributory negligence if he ought reasonably to have foreseen that, if he did not act as a reasonable prudent man, he might hurt himself; and in his reckonings he must take into account the possibility of others being careless'.[3] On this basis, Norman has been careless in accepting a lift from a driver whom he knows to be intoxicated (*Dann; Pitts* at first instance; *Owens v Brimmel* (1977)). Thus, any damages that Norman receives will be reduced due to this particular act of contributory negligence. In addition, we are told that Norman was not wearing a seat belt at the time of the crash and, as we are told that he was thrown through the windscreen, it is clear that, if he had been wearing a seat belt, the extent of his injuries would have been reduced. Although Norman's act in not wearing a seat belt did not contribute to the accident, it has contributed to the extent of the damage he has suffered and so his damages will be further reduced (*Froom v Butcher* (1975)).[4]

Hence, Norman should be advised that he can recover damages from Mark, but that these damages will be reduced to take into account his contributory negligence.

Turning now to Rita, she is a rescuer[5] and can sue Mark (*Haynes v Harwood* (1935)). Mark will almost certainly be unsuccessful in attempting to raise the defence of *volenti* against Rita (*Haynes v Harwood* (1935); *Chadwick v British Transport Commission* (1967)). The only situation in which a rescuer will be held to be *volens* is where a rescue is attempted in circumstances in which there is no real danger (*Cutler v United Dairies* (1933)), which is not the case here. Mark may try to run the defence of contributory negligence against Rita in an attempt to reduce any damages payable to her, but the courts are reluctant to find rescuers guilty of contributory negligence. This has been done where the circumstances

....

3 Using a quote from an identified judge will add quality to the answer.
4 Emphasise that contributory negligence, unlike the two preceding defences which are unavailable to Mark, is only a *partial* defence, but could be used to reduce Norman's damages considerably.
5 Look out for those who could be classified as 'rescuers', who may be in a special position, as the courts are not likely to find that they consented to the risk or contributed to the harm caused.

warrant it (*Harrison v British Railways Board* (1981)) but, in judging whether or not the rescuer has been careless for her own safety, the courts take into account the fact that, by the negligence of the defendant, the claimant may have been placed in an emergency and will be sympathetic to a claimant who makes a wrong decision in the agony of the moment (*Jones v Boyce* (1816) and more recently see *Tolley v Carr* (2010)). Thus, on the facts that we are given, it seems unlikely that a finding of contributory negligence would be made against Rita, who could recover in full against Mark.

If Norman had met Mark in the public house when Norman had had little to drink, but Mark was already intoxicated, then *prima facie* it would be easier for the court to find that Norman was *volens* to the risks of being a passenger in Mark's car. In *Dann*, it was said that if the drunkenness of the driver was extreme, the *volenti* defence might apply. However, even if this were to apply to Mark, s 149(3) would still render the defence invalid.[6]

QUESTION 48

Discuss the operation and effectiveness of the so-called 'general defences' in tort.

How to Answer this Question

The question demands that the candidate explains and offers opinion in relation to the operation of the general defences. As well as requiring explanation of how the defences are applied, it also necessitates consideration of their limitations and the difficulties inherent in the use of some of them, as around their margins there are areas of complexity and uncertainty.

A competent answer would certainly contain the following:

- ❖   contributory negligence;
- ❖   *volenti non fit injuria*;
- ❖   illegality;
- ❖   statutory authority;
- ❖   necessity;
- ❖   (limitation).

---

6   Do not forget to consider a 'tailpiece' to a question, which allows further knowledge to be demonstrated.

Answer Structure

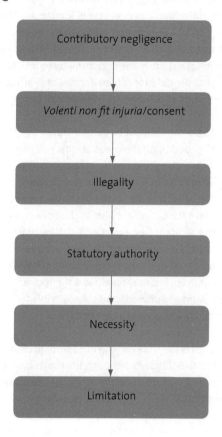

ANSWER --

Although many specialist defences exist in the law of torts, such as, for example, the privilege defences in defamation, there also exists a series of defences with more general application. Common to the majority of defences is the fact that the burden of proving them will generally fall upon the defendant, the person seeking to rely upon them to excuse their conduct. Most of the time, a successfully pleaded defence will exonerate the defendant from liability, although as we shall see this is not true of all of them.

The first to consider is the statutory defence of contributory negligence. However, it must be remembered that this is only a partial defence. The defendant still has to pay compensation, but it will be reduced by the amount the claimant is judged to be responsible for their own harm. Until the Law Reform (Contributory Negligence) Act 1945, the law operated harshly, so that if a claimant made any contribution by their own fault to the damage suffered, a defendant would be exonerated from liability. Clearly, this operated unjustly towards a claimant and the law was changed. The current situation, as set out in s 1(1) of the Act, states that a person's claim for damage that was partially as a result of their own fault shall not be defeated, although the quantum of damages that they receive 'shall be reduced to such an extent as the court thinks just and equitable having regard to the claimant's share in the responsibility for the damage'. Section 4 of the Act expressly states that the defence applies in cases of death or personal injury, but it does not exclude other forms of damage, such as damage to property or economic loss.

In order for the defence to operate, it must be demonstrated that the claimant failed to take care of their own safety and that failure was at least a partial cause of the damage that was suffered.[7] So it is necessary to prove that the claimant was at fault, that the claimant had fallen below the required standard of care (for their own safety) and then to determine the contribution of both of the parties to the damage suffered. Sometimes it will be obvious that the claimant has contributed to their own injury, for example by being a partial cause of the accident (see, for example, *Baker v Willoughby* (1970), in which the claimant was held partially responsible for being struck by a car due to the manner in which he crossed the road). In other situations, the claimant's behaviour may have had no part to play in the accident itself, but may have had a significant impact on the damage caused: for example, the damage suffered to an otherwise blameless person involved in a car accident when they had failed to wear a seat belt (*Froom v Butcher* (1975)).

The standard of care applied is the usual negligence standard of the reasonable person in that situation. It is an objective standard, although the courts have given special consideration to children and their appreciation of the risks that they may be facing. For example, in the case of *Gough v Thorne* (1966), a 13-year-old girl was injured by a car while crossing the road. She had been waved across by the driver of a lorry that was obscuring her view, but, unfortunately for her, a car had overtaken the lorry at that point. It was held that she was not contributorily negligent as she had done all that a child of her age would have done in the circumstances (contrast *Morales v Eccelstone* (1991), in which an 11-year-old playing football in a busy road was held to be 75 per cent contributorily negligent as the risk would have been obvious to a child of that age).

On occasion, a claimant will simply have made an error of judgment and, depending on the situation – say, for example, an emergency – they may not be held to have fallen below the standard of care. See *Tolley v Carr* (2010) where it was held that someone going to the aid of a crash victim on a motorway was not liable for contributory negligence. An interesting contemporary example can be seen in *Brannon v Airtours plc* (1999), in which the defendant holiday company was held to be 50 per cent liable for the injuries suffered

---

7   It is important to remember that contributory negligence is negligence *by the claimant*, not by *another defendant* who can be argued to have 'contributed' to the harm. For more on the issue of this latter point, see the Civil Liability (Contributions) Act 1978.

by the claimant, who had climbed onto a table and was injured by an overhead fan at a social evening organised by the defendant. The defendant was held to have encouraged heavy drinking to create a 'party atmosphere' and, in such circumstances, a person's appreciation of risk and danger would be lowered. The courts have also held that self-harming, rather than mere carelessness, may also lead to a finding of contributory negligence: in *Reeves v Metropolitan Police Commissioner* (2000), a prisoner not suspected of being a suicide risk killed himself while in police custody. The police were held liable for failing to prevent the death, but the suicide amounted to contributory negligence such that the damages amount was reduced by 50 per cent. In making the assessment, the courts will determine what percentage the claimant was at fault (defined in **s 4** of the Act as meaning 'negligence, breach of statutory duty or other act or omission which gives rise to a liability in tort or would, apart from this Act, give rise to the defence of contributory negligence'). In certain situations, this has led to the development of guidelines, such as where a person fails to wear a crash helmet or seat belt (see *Froom v Butcher* (1975)). Rarely, in the past the courts had held that a person was so to blame for their injury that there was a 100 per cent reduction in their award of damages, but in *Pitts v Hunt* (1990) the Court of Appeal held that there could not be 100 per cent contributory negligence as in effect this meant that the defendant was not liable in the first place. Recently, in *Co-operative Group v Pritchard* (2011), the Court of Appeal held that the defence of contributory negligence did not apply to intentional torts such as trespass to the person (assault and battery), so there was no deduction in damages even though it was argued the claimant had partially provoked the assault against her.

The next situation to consider is that in which the defendant has consented to run the risk of being injured, expressed in the Latin maxim *volenti non fit injuria*. Consent is a complete defence, unlike contributory negligence, and raising the defence successfully would mean that the defendant is not liable. Clearly, the defence would apply in a situation in which harm was inflicted intentionally, such as in a boxing ring or at a wrestling match (trespass to the person), but it can also be applied to situations in which harm is caused unintentionally. While, on first glance, the defence seems to be straightforward, it is necessary for the defendant to prove two key criteria: firstly that the claimant had knowledge of the risk involved in terms of the nature of it and also its extent; and secondly, that the claimant *willingly* agreed to run that risk. The courts apply an objective test, which considers the claimant's behaviour in relation to determining the first limb, but mere knowledge of the risk does not mean that a claimant consented to it (*Smith v Baker* (1891)). In *Smith*, an important point was made by the House of Lords, which was considering the extent to which a person consents to being placed in a position of danger at work. When the choice is, effectively, 'do the job and run the risk, or have no job', the employee cannot be said to have consented freely to run that risk (see also *ICI v Shatwell* (1965) for a different result).

In certain situations, it is unlikely that *volenti* would apply, despite the risk that the claimant has undertaken. Rescuers, for example, are generally not subject to the defence

(*Chadwick v BTC* (1967)) and persons who take their own lives while held in custody (*Kirkham v Chief Constable of Greater Manchester* (1990) – a mentally ill patient could not be *volenti* and *Reeves v Chief of Police for the Metropolis* (1999) – the police could not claim *volenti* for an act that they were duty-bound to prevent). The fact, however, that a person is intoxicated, as in the case of *Morris v Murray* (1990), does not necessarily mean that *volenti* will not apply. Sporting injuries have provided another specialist application of the defence, although there is a distinction made between a participant who agrees to run the risk of injury through the normal playing of the sport/game within the rules (*Simms v Leigh Rugby Football Club* (1969); *Condon v Basi* (1985)) or a spectator (*Wooldridge v Sumner* (1963)).

Finally, it is worth noting that statute has placed a limitation on the consent defence. **Section 149** of the **Road Traffic Act 1988** does not permit the defence of consent in a situation in which a passenger sues a driver. This is related to the fact that compulsory third-party insurance is required for all road vehicles and was instrumental in *Pitts v Hunt* (1990), in which a passenger was not held *volenti* when injured by the negligent riding of the drunken motorcycle rider that he had been egging-on to more dangerous riding.

The general defence of illegality is again expressed in a Latin maxim *ex turpi causa non oritur action* meaning that a person cannot base their legal claim upon an illegal act. For this reason, the claimant failed against the defendant motorcycle rider in *Pitts* (above). The basis of the defence is generally referred to public policy, in that it would generally be considered as offensive to permit a claim for a person who was committing a crime. A classic application can be seen in the case of *Ashton v Turner* (1981), in which the parties had been involved in a burglary. The defendant getaway driver crashed the car injuring the claimant, who attempted to sue, unsuccessfully as it turned out, as the court applied the defence. So we can see that there should be a causal link between the criminal and the tortious act (*National Coal Board v England* (1954)). The test to determine whether the defence applies seems to relate directly to the criminal conduct of the person involved (see *Cross v Kirkby* (2000) and *Vellino v Chief Constable of Greater Manchester Police* (2001)). The House of Lords considered the application of the defence in *Gray v Thames Trains Ltd* (2009) and determined it was more in the character of a 'policy' than a principle. The policy itself had a wide and narrow application: a wide view was that a person could not recover for damage which was the consequence of their criminal act; the narrow view would be that a person could not recover for damage consequent upon a sentence imposed for a criminal act. In this case the claimant suffered psychiatric harm resulting from a train crash caused by the defendant's negligence. He was held unable to claim for loss of earnings, loss of liberty and reputation, and feelings of remorse, after having been convicted for manslaughter for stabbing a person to death. Thames admitted liability up to the point of manslaughter but argued that *ex turpi causa* operated to end liability at that point.

Statutory authority permits a course of action that would otherwise be a tort if the course of action is permitted by a statute. The impact is that an affected person may not sue the creator, so long as the conduct falls within that permitted. The defence is most often seen in relation to the tort of nuisance (*Allen v Gulf Oil Refining* (1981), but see also *Barr v Biffa Waste Services Ltd* (2012) where the defence was not successful in relation to odour nuisance from authorised waste disposal), but does have limited application in negligence and seems to apply in situations in which a public body is given an element of discretion in the exercise of statutory powers. They may seek some relief from the defence unless the course of action for which they opt is unreasonable in the *Wednesbury* sense (*X v Bedfordshire County Council* (1995)).

The defence of necessity poses certain problems. The defence, premised on the idea of committing intentional damage on the basis of avoiding a wider or more significant loss in a situation in which there is no real alternative, is difficult to maintain except in more specialist circumstances. As there is the requirement that the damage be intentional, it is not applicable to negligence cases (see *Rigby v Chief Constable of Northamptonshire* (1985) and *Esso Petroleum Co Ltd v Southport Corporation* (1956) for a successful application) and thus the defence is somewhat limited. It has been unsuccessfully claimed in trespass as a defence for squatting *LB of Southwark v Williams* (1971), and while protesting about GM crops (*Monsanto plc v Tilly and Others* (1999)).

Although not strictly a 'defence' in the character of those discussed above, it is also worth noting the operation of the **Limitation Act 1980**. The Act imposes time limits after which an action in tort may not be commenced. Perhaps most importantly for tort cases, s 2 of the Act states that a tort action may not be brought after a period of six years from the occurrence of the cause of action (as to the time that the limitation is operative, see s 14A), although in the case of personal injuries, that period is halved to three years. The rule is not, however, hard and fast as regards personal injuries and the court is entitled by virtue of s 33 to apply its discretion to permit claims that would otherwise be out of time. In *A v Hoare* (2008), the House of Lords allowed appeals from those who had been the victims of sexual abuse many years before to bring their claims within s 33, although previously the courts had not been able to apply the discretion to intentional torts. In cases of defamation, the limitation period is one year.

Thus there are significant considerations to take into account when attempting to plead the general defences. Issues of policy and the courts' discretion are factors that may affect the success or otherwise of the defendants' attempts. It is clear that not all of the defences are as 'general' in their application as they might seem at first glance; they are nonetheless important stages in determining a defendant's liability or otherwise.[8]

....

8   Knowledge of these defences can be used in problem questions where, although not expressly asked for in the question, they would be relevant. This can apply particularly to contributory negligence, which can usefully be argued in many negligence-based answers.

Aim Higher

It really is important to remember the range of defences that are
(theoretically at least) general defences to tort. Learn the defences
pervasively, as you learn the subject to which they apply – you will appreciate
the point a lot more clearly and explain them better as a result.

Common Pitfalls ✗

Frequent problems include not remembering that *contributory negligence*
is only a partial defence, forgetting that a person consents to run the risk
of *an* injury, rather than, necessarily, the one that they actually suffer, and
forgetting that the burden is on the defendant to prove that a defence
applies.

Index